T0330222

Aristotle, Adam Smith and Karl Marx

For Sophia and Alexander

Aristotle, Adam Smith and Karl Marx

On Some Fundamental Issues in 21st Century Political Economy

Spencer J. Pack

Professor of Economics, Connecticut College, USA

Edward Elgar
Cheltenham, UK • Northampton, MA, USA

Published by
Edward Elgar Publishing Limited
The Lypiatts
15 Lansdown Road
Cheltenham
Glos GL50 2JA
UK

Edward Elgar Publishing, Inc.
William Pratt House
9 Dewey Court
Northampton
Massachusetts 01060
USA

A catalogue record for this book
is available from the British Library

Library of Congress Control Number: 2009940656

Mixed Sources
Product group from well-managed
forests and other controlled sources
www.fsc.org Cert no. SA-COC-1565
© 1996 Forest Stewardship Council

ISBN 978 1 84844 763 9

Printed and bound by MPG Books Group, UK

Contents

Acknowledgements

Earlier versions of Chapters 1 and 4 were presented to the Eastern Economic Association Conference, New York, 2005; sections of Chapters 2 and 5 to the History of Economics Society Conference, Grinnell, Iowa, 2006; Chapter 2, Section 2.3 to the Capabilities and Happiness Conference, Milan, 2005; Chapter 10 to the History of Economics Society Conference, Denver, 2009; and an overview of Part I to the World Congress of Social Economics, Albertville, France, 2004. An outline of the entire project was presented to the Amsterdam Research Group in the History and Methodology of Economics, January 2007.

Special thanks go to Mark Blaug who read and commented upon an earlier version of the entire manuscript; Warren Samuels who read and commented upon an earlier version of Parts I, II and III; and John Henry who read and commented upon Parts I, III and IV. My colleagues Ed McKenna and Maria Cruz-Saco, and Jack Bishop of Kingsbury International commented on Chapters 11 and 12; and Jane Clary gave me general support and commented on Part II on Smith.

The Economics Department at Connecticut College has been interested in and strongly supportive of my work for almost three decades now. I thank my colleagues Gerald Visgilio, Don Peppard, Rolf Jensen, Ed McKenna, Maria Cruz-Saco, Candace Howes, Yong-Jin Park and Monika Lopez-Anuarbe. They have always taken a broad view of what is economics, and have let me teach such unconventional economics courses as 'Capitalism as a Moral System', 'Ancient Greek and Jewish Economic Thought' (co-taught with Roger Brooks who extensively and lovingly tutored me in Talmudic economics) and 'International Financial Management'. Special thanks also to all my hard-working, intelligent students who grappled with difficult controversial issues; and the librarians (now information service facilitators) at Connecticut College, particularly Ashley Hanson, James MacDonald and Marian Shilstone.

Connecticut College has been supportive of my work with generous sabbatical leaves throughout the years, as well as travel and research funds. The college is an excellent place to do interdisciplinary teaching and research. I particularly want to thank, for the extensive help I have received over the years, Dirk Held in the Classics Department; Larry Vogel and the late Lester Reiss in the Philosophy Department; and of course the late Jerry Winter in the Sociology Department. Thanks also to other colleagues at the school who have helped me over the years: Kenneth Bleeth, John Coats, Mark Forster, Robert Gay, David Patton, Fred Paxton and Robert Proctor. Also of enormous help to me at critical times throughout my career were the now departed Robert F. Barlow, John Kenneth Galbraith, David Hawkins and Jolane Solomon. I thank Eric Schliesser for his support and insight concerning Smith and philosophical issues; S. Todd Lowry for first encouraging me to study ancient Greek economic thought and for his insight, wisdom and help throughout the years; former teachers Robert Albritton and Pradeep Bandyopadhyay for their extensive help and guidance in studying Marxist economics; and former teachers Stephen Berger and David Osher for first emphasizing the importance of taking a historical approach to the study of social theory. Finally I would like to thank my secretary Nancy Lewandowski; the remarkable Reverend Eddie Kjelshus for his help, support and encouragement throughout the decades; as well as, of course, my wife, Susan Solomon.

Introduction

According to Kenneth Boulding, there are different aspects to economics. For Boulding (1970), economics is simultaneously a social, ecological, behavioral, political, mathematical and moral science. This suggests that there are different ways to do, to study, economics. For me, economics is largely a branch of social theory. Hence, it is necessarily historical. Social theorists today study theorists of the past to help come to grips with and understand present issues and concerns; for similar reasons may contemporary economists study past economic theorists. For Mark Blaug, the 'knock-down' argument for studying the history of economic thought is that no 'idea or theory in economics . . . is ever thoroughly understood except as the end-product of a slice of history, the result of some previous intellectual development' (2001: 156).[1] I agree. Indeed, I consider this present study on a few fundamental, common issues in the work of Aristotle, Adam Smith and Karl Marx to be a study both in the history of economic thought and in contemporary theory. Schumpeter once said, apparently borrowing the phrase from Joan Robinson, that economic theory may be considered to be 'a box of tools' (1954: 15). The history of economic thought itself may be considered a tool in that box. When coming upon a problem or issue, it may (indeed most likely will) be helpful to ask: what would Adam Smith (probably) say? What would Aristotle (probably) say? What would Karl Marx (probably) say?[2]

I realize there is a trend among some in the history of economic thought to argue that the history of economic thought is much too complex, indeed

---

[1]   Hence, for Blaug, 'History of economic thought is not a specialization within economics. It *is* economics – sliced vertically against the horizontal axis of time' (ibid.: 157, emphasis in original).

[2]   Moreover, I think the history of economic thought itself will only overcome its Eurocentric and modernistic bias when it views itself as in part a part of the history of law (see for example Pack, 2001a: 178–80). As Warren Samuels has argued, it is probably severely misleading to even think of government (or polity) and markets (or economy) as separate and self-subsistent. Instead they are jointly produced and are part of a legal–economic nexus (1992, Chapter 4, 'Some Fundamentals of the Economic Role of Government' and Chapter 5, 'The Legal–Economic Nexus': 156–86; 1989). Smith's *Wealth of Nations* itself came out of his course at Glasgow University on Jurisprudence; and that course itself was largely historical (for more detail see below Chapter 7; also Pack, 1991, Chapter 7, 'Lessons from the *Lectures on Jurisprudence*': 119–37).

fantastically complicated, and the work of the past economic theorists too historically and contextually specific, to be able to offer much (if anything) to contemporary theorists or to understanding contemporary issues and concerns.[3] Instead, past theorists will be sorely misread and misunderstood by all but the most well-trained professionals, deeply grounded in the pertinent historical and rhetorical specificities of their subject's particular milieu. I think this approach tends to be excessively cautious, timid, fearful; ineffectual.[4] This approach could help further the apparent professionalism of the sub-discipline history of economic thought; but I think it will also lead to professional irrelevance. Instead, aspiring economists should be encouraged to read people such as Adam Smith, Karl Marx and Aristotle, for largely the same reasons as, for example, aspiring Christians should read the Bible: to see what these works can teach us today, for today's societies, for today's peoples.

Moreover, there is a long, broad and deep tradition; an economics tradition. For example, as will be demonstrated, Smith read and knew his Aristotle, and was in part responding to him. Marx read and knew both Aristotle and Smith and was in part responding to both of them. Thus, there was in a sense a dialogue, or a dialectic in the original sense of the term, between Aristotle, Smith and Marx. Aristotle was the great systematizer of the ancient world. Smith and Marx were two of the great systematizers of the modern world.[5] Although Aristotle, Smith and Marx may all be viewed as great system-builders, this is not a case of paradigms in collision, where they completely miss each other (and 21st century readers) because of their incommensurate differences. Rather, as will be demonstrated, the three systems are intimately related to each other, and to us.

This study concentrates on just six key concepts: exchange value, money, capital; character, government and change.[6] I will discuss other pertinent concepts, for example credit, only insofar as they are directly related to these primary concepts.[7] Aristotle's contributions to these concepts are

---

[3] This, I believe, is in line with the general geist of post-modern thought, which tends to stress the utter complexity of phenomena, and the limits of human reason to really understand what is going on – a problem which I will discuss below in Chapter 13.

[4] See Pack (2001b). This excessive timidity opens the explanatory door too wide to charlatans and various secular and religious quacks eager to supply the demand for soothing explanations of the world.

[5] Although Smith, I believe, perhaps purposely left his system incomplete; see Pack (1997). The other major systematizer of the modern world was, of course, Hegel. I will refer to him as necessary, throughout this work, largely in the footnotes.

[6] I have been personally pondering these concepts for decades, alas!

[7] I realize some readers may be disappointed in this approach, given the current world economic difficulties, which appear to have largely originated in the credit markets for subprime mortgage backed securities. I do comment on the current difficulties in various footnotes throughout the text. Although I do not explicitly deal with or go into depth on

primarily in his *Politics* and *Ethics* (both *Nicomachean* and *Eudemian*). I draw on these texts, as well as various parts from the rest of his corpus as needed. To make this study manageable, for Smith and Marx I concentrate only on their mature economic writings published under their auspices. This means, for Smith I concentrate on his *Wealth of Nations*. For Marx, I concentrate on *Capital, Volume I* and, to a lesser extent, his 1859 *A Contribution to the Critique of Political Economy*.[8] However, I will occasionally also draw on the rest of Smith's *Collected Works* and other of Marx's writings as needed.[9]

Part I deals with Aristotle's seminal position concerning exchange value, money, capital; character, government and change. Chapter 1 discusses Aristotle's analysis of exchange value and the development of money in *The Politics* and his discussion of justice, exchange value, money and commensurability in *The Nicomachean Ethics*. It also discusses what is meant by commensurability in general for Aristotle, and the perceived need for commensurability or a common unit for goods to be exchanged in definite proportions.

Chapter 2 argues that according to Aristotle money can be used to acquire more money. This is money used as capital or, as Aristotle calls it, chrematistics. Chrematistics for Aristotle is unnatural. It wrecks people's character, making them overly greedy and desirous to accumulate more money. It causes people's passions to dominate their reason. I explain what Aristotle means by the natural and the unnatural, and discuss the formation of character in general in Aristotle for humans and other living things.

Chapter 3 argues that change for Aristotle is basically circular. The world is permanent, and there is no concept of unidirectional natural and/

---

the concept credit, it will be seen that issues surrounding character development related to capital, as well as the role of government, are extremely pertinent to the current economic difficulties; and these issues will indeed be explored in detail below.

[8] Actually, strictly speaking, even the first volume of *Capital* was given final shape by Engels after Marx's death. See Heinrich (2009: 88–9); however, Engels' editorial input in this volume was rather minimal, particularly compared to the other volumes of *Capital*.

[9] For Aristotle, I used the two volume *Complete Works of Aristotle*, revised Oxford Translation edited by Jonathan Barnes. References are to the numerals printed in the outer margins of that text which are keyed to the translation of Bekker's standard edition of the Greek text of Aristotle of 1831. I give the title of Aristotle's work and refer to the page number and the column letter only of the Bekker edition. For Smith, I used the six volume *Glasgow Edition of the Works and Correspondence of Adam Smith*. For *The Wealth of Nations* I generally followed the now standard citation practice of giving the book, chapter, section, and so on, and paragraph number added in the margin of the Glasgow edition. For the rest of Smith's works I generally just give the title and the page number in the Glasgow edition. For Marx, I used various editions of his writings, including the 1976 translation of Volume I of *Capital* by Ben Fowkes. Unless otherwise specified, all references to *Capital* are to the first volume.

or social historical evolution as with the moderns. The government for Aristotle should promote the potentialities and capacities of its citizens. Aristotle's theory is literally a theory of the welfare state. Also, the state will be best and most stable when it has a strong middle class and promotes that class. The state will have a natural tendency to become corrupt (or unnatural) and rule in the interests of the governing rather than the governed.

Part II presents Smith's debate with Aristotle over various chrematistic/economic issues. Chapter 4 argues that Smith knew his Aristotle intimately well. Smith basically begins *The Wealth of Nations* with Aristotle, and the Aristotelian difference between exchange and use value. I argue that although Smith is ambiguous as to what causes value,[10] he is adamant that human labor is the real, ultimate, accurate measure of value. From an Aristotelian perspective, if labor is the real measurer of value, then in some sense value must be labor itself.

Chapter 5 argues that, for Smith, the use of money (or value) to produce (or acquire) more money, which Smith calls capital, is quite natural. Here Smith argues against Aristotle. In so doing, Smith changes the meaning of natural from the best, to the normal or ordinary. Smith may be viewed as in an argument with Aristotle, insisting that capitalism or commercial society is natural and good.

Chapter 6 shows that Smith in some ways follows Aristotle on the importance of a person's character, and how character is formed in society through education, habit, experiences, and so on. However, Smith decisively departs from Aristotle in not thinking that a person's character will be corrupted in a chrematistic or commercial society which largely depends upon the use of money used to acquire more money. Indeed, Smith generally likes and admires the characters formed in commercial society. Nonetheless, there are also major flaws in the character types produced in commercial society, including the capitalists, their managers, the landlords, and the workers. Moreover, workers will have a tendency to be attracted to disagreeable and potentially dangerous, enthusiastic religious sects – a problem in Smith's day and again in ours.

Chapter 7 argues that Smith was not a dogmatic proponent of laissez-faire, nor a libertarian; yet, neither was he a full-fledged theorist of the social welfare state as was Aristotle. For Smith, government arose at a definite time in history, largely to defend the interests of the propertied rich against the poor. To some extent, Smith distrusted government since it tended to be ruled by and for the rich and powerful. Also, for Smith,

---

[10] Or what value is; or, in explicitly Aristotelian terms, what is the material cause of value.

history was not circular as with Aristotle and the ancients. Rather, as with most secular moderns, history was one of evolution, and human history was largely the result of the unintended results of human actions. This change in the conception of history may have resulted in part from the realization that animal species are not eternal. Species may die out and become extinct; this also suggests that new ones may arise.

Part III argues that Marx's critique of modern, classical political economy was to some extent also a new modern return to Aristotle. Chapter 8 argues that Marx in a sense combines Aristotle and Smith on what is value, what enables commodities to be exchanged in determinant proportions, and what makes them commensurable. Following Smith, labor time is the real, true, accurate measure of value. Following Aristotle, this means that labor time is therefore also the substance of value. This substance of value, or value itself, can only manifest itself in exchange value, in the actual exchange of commodities for each other.

In analyzing commodities, Marx also stresses Aristotle's formal cause. Following Aristotle (and Smith), for Marx the commodity form of value will necessarily in time generate money, or what Marx calls the money form of value. Since exchanges of commodities are not necessarily spot exchanges, credit itself will arise out of the mere exchange of commodities, where the buyer of a commodity becomes a borrower, the seller a lender. Thus, the mere circulation of commodities may potentially generate credit crises.[11]

Chapter 9 argues that for Marx, capital is the use of both money and commodities to acquire more money. Since money and commodities are value, or embodied labor, then capital is self-expanding value: the use of labor power to create more value or surplus value. Since for Marx only the commodity labor power can create surplus value, then capital is the creation of surplus value through the exploitation of labor power, of living workers. It is the appropriation of labor, or surplus labor, from these workers.

Returning to themes introduced by Aristotle, this use of money to acquire more money wrecks the character of the capitalists. It makes them want to passionately acquire and accumulate more and more wealth or surplus value. Moreover, capitalists are also forced to do so by competition. The competitive, capitalist system also degrades the moral character of the workers through low pay, overwork and tyrannical working conditions subject to the dictates of capital.

Chapter 10 argues that as with Smith, Marx has what may be termed

---

[11] Credit itself is not extensively developed by Marx until the posthumously published Volume III of *Capital*.

functional as well as instrumental theories of the state. Marx also has a theory of the state as alienated power; however, as with Smith, Marx has no fully developed mature work on the state. Also, as with Smith, Marx is in the modern world, with an evolutionary view of history (and the state). However, Marx also gives a largely Aristotelian interpretation of the rise and fall of the capitalist mode of production, stressing all four of Aristotle's causes: the material, formal, final and efficient causes. This is what makes Marx's *Capital* so complex. Also, Marx views his work as in some sense scientific. He is waging battles on two distinct fronts: against what he considers bourgeois political economy (which he is explicitly critiquing); but also against religion, particularly the religions of the poor and the working class.

Part IV sums up the previous three parts, comparing and contrasting Aristotle, Smith and Marx on the crucial concepts of exchange value, money, capital; character, government and change. It also carries forth the analysis of these concepts into the 21st century. It shows how these concepts are still, of course, of crucial importance and concern. Also, it demonstrates that their theories are currently extremely topical, and they shed crucial light on such contemporary issues as, for example, the continuing development of world money; saving; managerial capitalism; corrupt governments; and various movements for social change.

PART I

Aristotle's seminal position

1. Aristotle on exchange value and money

1.1 ARISTOTLE'S ANALYSIS OF EXCHANGE VALUE AND THE DEVELOPMENT OF MONEY IN *THE POLITICS*

In Book I, Chapter I of Aristotle's *Politics*, Aristotle holds that 'every community is established with a view to some good; for everyone always acts in order to obtain that which they think is good' (12521a). Here, as most everywhere in Aristotle, the emphasis is on the end, the goal, the reason why people do things. Aristotle further claims that 'In the first place there must be a union of those who cannot exist without each other; namely, of male and female, that the race may continue' (ibid.). Therefore, 'the family is the association established by nature for the supply of men's everyday wants' (1252b). Note here the necessary importance of economic concerns for Aristotle at the very beginning of *The Politics*. Men and women join together to form a family for at least partly economic reasons: to help supply their wants, since 'the individual, when isolated, is not self-sufficing' (1253a). Aristotle then goes into a brief discussion of home economics, or household (or estate) management. He holds that 'seeing then that the state is made up of households, before speaking of the state we must speak of the management of the household' (1253b).[1] Included in this discussion of household management is a seminal, forever-after controversial discussion concerning 'another element of a household, the so-called art of getting wealth' (ibid.).

Aristotle believes 'the amount of property which is needed for a good life is not unlimited' and says that riches may be 'defined as a number of instruments to be used in a household or in a state' (1254b). Elsewhere, in the *Rhetoric* Aristotle explains his position that 'Wealth as a whole

---

[1] Aristotle's study of households distinct from the study of states, since states are made up of households, is in line with his general methodological approach of studying parts in their relation to the whole; see his methodological comments at the beginning of *Parts of Animals*. As Baeck points out, this is also a criticism of the theories of Xenophon and Plato, as well as the practice of Alexander, for conflating the differences between the rule of a household, a city-state and an empire (1994: 77).

consists in using things rather than in owning them; it is really the activity
– that is, the use – of property that constitutes wealth' (1361a). In the
Politics Aristotle then briefly discusses shepherding, hunting, fishing and
farming; all of these activities are 'a natural art of acquisition which is
practiced by managers of households and by statesmen' (1256b). Natural
here means good;[2] these are arts of acquisition approved of by Aristotle.
Unfortunately, 'there is another variety of the art of acquisition which is
commonly and rightly called an art of wealth-getting' (ibid.) which gives
the erroneous impression that 'riches and property have no limit' (1257a).
This will be the art or use of money to acquire more money. Aristotle will
call this form of acquisition unnatural, and will disapprove of it.[3]

Following Aristotle: 'Let us begin our discussion of the question with
the following considerations. Of everything which we possess there are two
uses: both belong to the thing as such, but not in the same manner, for one
is the proper, and the other the improper use of it' (ibid.). Again, one use
Aristotle approves; one he does not. 'For example, a shoe is used for wear,
and is used for exchange . . . He who gives a shoe in exchange for money or
food to him who wants one, does indeed use the shoe as a shoe, but this is
not its proper use, for a shoe is not made to be an object of barter' (ibid.).
Thus, a shoe may be said to have a use value, to be used as a shoe; and to
have an exchange value, in that it may be exchanged for another good or
for money.[4] At this point Aristotle does not appear to be assuming commodity production; that is, the shoe is not produced with the goal of being
exchanged. For Aristotle, 'the same may be said of all possessions, for the
art of exchange extends to all of them, and it arises at first from what is
natural, from the circumstance that some have too little, others too much'
(ibid.). So, presumably the person with the shoes happens to have too
many shoes to use in his own family. The person with the other good has
too much of that good, and they exchange them for each other.

Aristotle then holds that 'retail trade is not a natural part of the art of
getting wealth; had it been so, men would have ceased to exchange when
they had enough' (ibid.). At one time, members of a single, particular
family held things in common, and they did not practice exchange with
each other. Later, when the families divided up 'into parts, the parts

---

2   Natural for Aristotle should never be interpreted as the merely normal. Aristotle's particular use of the word natural will be discussed in detail in the following chapter.
3   About two thousand years later, Adam Smith will take these various modes of acquisition, historicize them, and they will basically form his four stage theory of socioeconomic
development: the hunting, shepherding, farming, and finally commercial stages of society.
See, for example, Meek (1976, 1977 Part One, 'Smith') and below, Chapter 7.
4   In the *Eudemian Ethics* Aristotle talks of being able to sell or even eat a human eye, in
addition to using it to see (1245a).

shared in many things, and different parts in different things, which they had to give in exchange for what they wanted, a kind of barter which is still practiced among barbarous nations who exchange with one another the necessaries of life and nothing more; giving and receiving wine, for example, in exchange for corn, and the like' (ibid.). Thus, at this level of socioeconomic organization, there is simple barter of food for drink, and so on. For Aristotle, this is also good: 'This sort of barter is not part of the wealth-getting art and is not contrary to nature, but is needed for the satisfaction of men's natural wants' (ibid.)

Out of this barter or exchange of different goods, money came into being. 'When the inhabitants of one country became more dependent on those of another, and they imported what they needed, and exported what they had too much of, money necessarily came into use' (ibid.). Thus, according to Aristotle money arose from the exchange between countries, that is, from international trade, as opposed to trade within a country (or within a household). For Aristotle, 'the various necessaries of life are not easily carried about, and hence men agreed to employ in their dealing with each other something which was intrinsically useful and easily applicable to the purposes of life, for example, iron, silver and the like' (ibid.). Thus, a certain good that had a use value and could be easily transported, was selected to act as money, as something which could be exchanged for all the other goods. This moneyed-good measured the exchange value of the other goods. For Aristotle, 'Of this the value was at first measured simply by size and weight, but in process of time they put a stamp upon it, to save the trouble of weighing and to mark the value' (ibid.). So, money was at first a good which had to be weighed. In time each unit of the moneyed-good was stamped as being of a certain uniform size and weight, thus having a certain definite exchange value *vis-à-vis* other goods.

When this money was stamped, it became a coin. Coinage, and the ensuing use of coins, led to more exchange and the art of using money to profit and hence acquire more coins. Aristotle: 'When the use of coin had once been discovered, out of the barter of necessary articles arose the other art of wealth-getting, namely retail trade; which was at first probably a simple matter, but became more complicated as soon as men learned by experience which and by what exchanges the greatest profit might be made' (1257b). It is coins that 'the art of getting wealth is generally thought to be chiefly concerned with . . . and to be the art which produces riches and wealth, having to consider how they may be accumulated. Indeed, riches is assumed by many to be only a quantity of coin, because the arts of getting wealth and retail trade are concerned with coin' (ibid.). Wealth becomes erroneously confused with, or identified with, coins. People think they may accumulate wealth by accumulating coins – money! Of course, just as

Midas in the fable would starve to death if all he touched did indeed turn
to coins, so in truth coins are not the real source of wealth: 'hence men seek
after a better notion of riches and of the art of getting wealth, and they are
right' (ibid.).

Therefore, while natural riches and the natural art of wealth-getting are
part of the management of a household, retail trade, the art of acquiring
wealth by exchange, is not.[5] 'There is no bound to the riches' which arise
from the art of retail trade, so 'all getters of wealth increase their hoard
without limit' (ibid.). Their goal, their end, is simply to accumulate more
coins.[6] In contradistinction, 'the art of wealth-getting which consists in
household management, on the other hand, has a limit; the unlimited
acquisition of wealth is not its business' (ibid.). Let us now temporarily leave *The Politics* and turn to Aristotle's discussion of justice in the
exchange of goods in Chapter 5 of his *Nicomachean Ethics*.

1.2   JUSTICE, EXCHANGE VALUE, MONEY AND COMMENSURABILITY IN *THE NICOMACHEAN ETHICS*

Book V of Aristotle's *Nicomachean Ethics* discusses justice, including
reciprocal justice, which has been interpreted as justice in the exchange of
goods.[7] Aristotle says that we should 'ascertain the different ways in which
a man may be said to be unjust. Both the lawless man and the grasping
and unequal man are thought to be unjust' (1129a). That is, someone
who wants too much, in the exchange of goods or other things, is unjust.
Indeed, says Aristotle, 'since the unjust man is grasping, he must be concerned with goods' (1129b). Moreover, justice in general, is 'thought to be
another's good, because it is related to others; for it does what is advanta-
geous to another, either a ruler or a partner' (1130a). Therefore, justice for
Aristotle is primarily related to other people.

---

[5]   Lowry (1965) points out that in general for the classical Greeks true wealth was both
natural and static; for the most part, true wealth did not grow.

[6]   See Lowry (1974) who argues that retail trade was not subject to a 'natural limit'
because it was conducted by foreign 'metics', people who were not subject to the constraints
of the close-knit city (the polis); also Pack (1985a) and Perrotta (2003).

[7]   Indeed, as the great historian of European medieval economic thought (and hence
of Aristotle's thought) Odd Langholm pointed out, most all 'value theory can be read as
a history of comments on *Ethics*, V.5, on justice in exchange' (1998: vii–viii). For a useful
introduction to medieval economic thought, and its relationship to Aristotle, see Wood
(2002). For a complex analysis on the relationship between medieval and classical economic
thought, arguing that Smith was in a sense the last scholastic (and hence the first of the classical economists), see Lapidus (1986).

Justice, or rather injustice, is particularly associated with making a gain, with wanting too much (1130a–b). A particular type of justice concerns voluntary transactions such as 'sale, purchase, usury, pledging, lending, depositing, letting' (1131a). Now, according to Aristotle, 'the unjust man is unequal and the unjust act unequal' (ibid.); therefore, the equal will be just. 'And since the equal is intermediate, the just will be an intermediate' (ibid.). Also, if the just is intermediate, 'it must be between certain things (which are respectively greater and less)' (ibid.). Therefore, justice in the exchange of goods will involve a relationship between four terms: two people and two goods. Thus, 'the man who acts unjustly has too much, and the man who is unjustly treated too little, of what is good' (1131b).

According to Aristotle, the names:

> loss and gain, have come from voluntary exchange; for to have more than one's own is called gaining, and to have less than one's original share is called losing, e.g. in buying and selling and in all other matters in which the law has left people free to make their own terms; but when they get neither more nor less but just what belongs to themselves, they say that they have their own and that they neither lose nor gain. (1132b)

Aristotle is here dealing with what ought to be the proper exchange ratios between pairs of goods, or, in an economy which has money, with what ought to be the proper price of goods, that is, some kind of just price theory. Aristotle elaborates, 'Let A be a builder, B a shoemaker, C a house, D a shoe. The builder, then, must get from the shoemaker the latter's work, and must himself give him in return his own' (1133a). So, this is an exchange, indeed a spot exchange, where two people are *simultaneously* exchanging their products.[8] Moreover, here, as opposed to the passages previously considered in *The Politics*, Aristotle is definitely assuming a certain social division of labor. A is not just a person, or the head of a household who simply happens to have an excess of houses. Rather he

---

8   This is a crucial assumption casually adopted by Aristotle; it is also a vastly underappreciated point. For if the exchange does not occur simultaneously, on the spot, then a credit arrangement will take place. Credit, interest rates, bills of exchange, discount rates, and so on would then come directly from the exchange relationship itself, rather than a peculiar (and for Aristotle most unnatural) use of money to make more money, that is, money lending. Given the enormous influence of Aristotle's monetary theory in the history of economic thought, for example Schumpeter: 'It is the basis of the bulk of all analytic work in the field of money' (1954: 63), this is indeed an assumption of seminal importance. On the complexity of actual exchange relationships in ancient Greece see von Reden (2003). It is remarkable and merits further investigation that the French anthropologist Marcel Mauss (1990 [1950]) and others following him emphasize that the exchange of gifts is really a credit relationship. Yet, Aristotle and the modern economic tradition tend to always assume that the buying and selling of goods is not – how misleading.

is a 'builder': he builds houses with the goal to exchange or sell them. Similarly, B is not just a person, or head of a household who happens to have an excess of shoes. Instead, he is a 'shoemaker'.

Aristotle continues: 'if, then, first there is proportionate equality of goods, and then reciprocal action takes place, the result we mentioned will be effected. If not, the bargain is not equal, and does not hold' (ibid.). Thus, Aristotle is inquiring: in what proportion should they be exchanged? He assumes that the society under question has a division of labor into various crafts or professions, for he also says, 'it is not two doctors that associate for exchange, but a doctor and a farmer, or in general people who are different and unequal; but these must be equated' (ibid.). Here is the Aristotelian problem: the people are different and unequal, and their products are also different. How then can the products be equated; how can they be equalized, how can they be made commensurate with each other? For Aristotle, 'all things that are exchanged must be somehow commensurable' (ibid.).

So, what then makes the goods commensurable? Is it money? At first Aristotle suggests this answer: 'It is for this end that money has been introduced, and it becomes in a sense an intermediate; for it measures all things, and therefore the excess and the defect – how many shoes are equal to a house or to a given amount of food' (ibid.). So, in fact, in society, money does measure the different goods. But why is money able to do this? Note also that Aristotle is back to a concern with the excess and the defect again: that not too much or too little of one good is being exchanged for another, either directly, or with money acting as an intermediary.

The exchange of shoes for a house also implies something about the relationship between the shoemaker and the builder. Says Aristotle, 'The number of shoes exchanged for a house . . . must therefore correspond to the ratio of builder to shoemaker' (ibid.). Unfortunately, and this is key, exactly what that ratio is, and hence the exchange rate between houses and shoes, is not at all clear.[9] Nevertheless, claims Aristotle, if there is not a

---

[9] Schumpeter thus is correct in that Aristotle basically had no theory of distribution (1954: 60). However, for an argument following Soudek (1952) that for Aristotle the exchange of equivalents probably involved the harmonic (as opposed to the arithmetic or geometric) mean see Lowry (1969, 1987, Chapter VII, 'Aristotle and Two-Party Exchange') as well as Gordon's summary (1975: 62–5). See also the various articles collected in Blaug (1991), most of which try to figure out Aristotle's solution to the proper exchange of goods, with disconcertedly conflicting results. More recently, Frank asserts that reciprocal justice is geometrical (2005: 85–94). Meikle forcefully argues that in fact the different traders are equal and the ratio of builder to shoemaker therefore equals one (1995, 'Justice in Exchange: "As Builder to Shoemaker"'). Such different answers! The real problem is this: there is much in Aristotle's writings that is not clear. His encyclopedic, dialectic approach to the world raises many more questions than he is able to successfully answer (Innis, 1972 [1950]: 93). This helps

certain proportion between the two people and the two goods, then 'there will be no exchange and no intercourse. And this proportion will not be effected unless the goods are somehow equal' (ibid.). Thus, for Aristotle, for the goods to be exchanged, they must in some sense be equal.[10] That also means that for Aristotle in some sense they must be commensurate. Thus, 'all goods must therefore be measured by some one thing' (ibid.). At first Aristotle says that 'this unit is in truth need[11] which holds all things together' (ibid.). Hence, at this point it appears that the thing that makes goods commensurable is they are the objects of human need. Aristotle adds that 'if men did not need one another's goods at all, or did not need them equally, there would be either no exchange or not the same exchange' (ibid.). Aristotle then adds though that 'money has become by convention a sort of representative of need; and this is why it has the name "money" – because it exists not by nature but by law and it is in our power to change it and make it useless' (ibid.). So money comes to represent need, need being what at this point appears to make the goods commensurate with each other.

Aristotle continues along this line, on the importance of need in making goods commensurate. 'That need holds things together as a single unit is shown by the fact that when men do not need one another, i.e. when neither needs the other or one does not need the other, they do not exchange' (1133b). Money, representing need, is also wanted because it can act as a store of value, it can purchase things and thus satisfy future needs. 'And for the future exchange – that if we do not need a thing now we shall have it if ever we do need it – money is as it were our surety; for it must be possible for us to get what we want by bringing the money' (ibid.).

---

to account for the openness of his system, as well as the ever-recurring interest in his work. Aristotle generated various multifaceted research programs, some of which are ongoing to this day, including the relationship between exchange value and use value. For recent attempts to develop an explicitly Aristotelian economics see for example Fleetwood (1997); Crespo (2006, 2008); Langholm (1998, Chapter 10); and most extensively, Staveren (2001).

[10] For arguments against Aristotle's position concerning the necessity for goods to be equal in any sort of a mathematical sense, as well as a questioning of the entire historical accuracy of Aristotle's speculations concerning the development of money, see Fayazmanesh (2001, 2003); and that Aristotle's enormous influence has been deleterious to basically the entire subsequent history of Western economic thought concerning money and exchange, Fayazmanesh (2006).

[11] 'Chreia' is translated as demand by Ross, the text used in Aristotle (1984). Here, I use the word need so as not to confuse it with the technical economic word demand. A starving, penniless person has no demand for food because he has no money. However, he does need food. Moreover, people may and do demand things in the economic sense (narcotic drugs, bad food, body piercing, and so on) that they definitely do not need in the Aristotelian sense. See Meikle (1995), Chapter 2, 'Chreia and Demand: Nicomachean Ethics, 5.5'.

Thus, we use money as an intermediary in the exchange of goods and 'money then, acting as a measure, makes goods commensurate and equates them' (ibid.). People associate together through the exchange of their specialized products. Products are capable of being exchanged for each other in a certain ratio because they are in some sense commensurable, and different products can be made to equal each other.

Nonetheless, as noted above, Aristotle is not clear about exactly in what proportion these products should exchange.[12] He is unable to specify or articulate the exact exchange ratio (or perhaps range) in which these goods should trade.[13] Moreover, somewhat surprisingly, Aristotle then explicitly takes back what he previously stated, that what makes the goods commensurable is need. Now we read that 'in truth it is impossible that things differing so much should become commensurate, but with reference to need they may become so sufficiently' (ibid.). Here he is stating that goods are not really commensurate. Moreover, what does he mean by 'sufficiently'? It is not clear.[14] In any case, Aristotle then immediately jumps back to the role of money: 'There must, then, be a unit, and that fixed by agreement (for which reason it is called money): for it is this that makes all things commensurate, since all things are measured by money' (ibid.).

Thus, at this point we have in Aristotle that things are made commensurable by the use of money. However, money itself is not really the source of the commensurability; rather, the source seems to be human need.[15] Yet, really 'in truth it is impossible that things differing so much should become commensurate'. So we clearly have a muddle.[16] It is not clear what determines in what ratio goods will exchange, nor what enables goods to be

---

[12] Ostwald, in a note to his translation of NE 1133b, explains that 'unfortunately, Aristotle gives us no hint about the way in which such equivalences are to be established' (1962: 126, fn. 36).

[13] See fn. 9 above. Lowry feels that 'Aristotle evidently was unable to formulate a conceptual relationship with sufficient clarity in abstract mathematical terms to guarantee its perpetuation through periods of cultural and economic chaos' arguing that 'a careful retranslation and analysis of the manuscripts from which our Aristotelian material is taken' by more mathematically sophisticated scholars is desirable (1987: 209). Meikle mocks this view (1995: 144–5); yet, in general, Meikle sees a clarity in this part of Aristotle's work which has eluded most recent commentators. Indeed, Meikle, a professional philosopher, maintains that the very training of professional economists completely warps our ability to understand Aristotle; see, for example, Meikle (2001).

[14] Witty and urbane as always, Galbraith argues that 'No one can read his [Aristotle's] works without secretly suspecting a certain measure of eloquent incoherence on economics – "secretly" because, the author being Aristotle, no one can wisely suggest such a thing' (1987: 10).

[15] Not 'demand' as chreia has been frequently translated.

[16] In both the 1859 *Critique of Political Economy* (p. 68 fn.) and then again in *Capital* (151–2) Marx interprets Aristotle as being unable to answer the question of what makes

exchanged at all, that is, how they are commensurate.[17] Let us now leave Aristotle's perplexing discussion of reciprocal justice to investigate what he says about commensurability in general.

1.3   ARISTOTLE ON COMMENSURABILITY

Not all things are commensurable. Consider, for example, a particular pen, or wine: which is sharper than the other? Aristotle: 'E.g. a pen, a wine, and the highest notes on a scale are not commensurable: we cannot say whether any one of them is sharper than any other; and why is this? They are incommensurable because they are homonymous' (*Physics*: 248b). In *Topics*, Aristotle's course in how to be an effective dialectical debater, he elaborates on sharpness: 'a sharp note is a swift note . . . whereas a sharp angle is one that is less than a right angle, while a sharp dagger is one cut at a sharp angle' (107a). In *Categories*, Aristotle defines what he means by homonymous: 'When things have only a name in common and the definition of being which corresponds to the name is different, they are called homonymous' (1a). Therefore, one cannot really say or measure whether a wine or a knife is more or less sharp. The word sharp is not being used in the same way: knives and wine are incommensurable in terms of sharpness.

The idea of commensurability, or the lack thereof, is a recurring theme throughout Aristotle's corpus. For example, in the *Eudemian Ethics*, Aristotle claims that a teacher and pupil may quarrel since knowledge and money have no common measure (1243b).[18] Aristotle gives his most extensive discussion of the issue of commensurability in his *Metaphysics*, following his discussion of 'one'. After inquiring what it means to be 'one', Aristotle decides that among other meanings, one is 'to be the first measure of a kind, and above all of quantity; for it is from this that it has

---

goods commensurable. Meikle essentially follows and elaborates upon Marx's interpretation (1995: Chapter 9, 'Nature and Commensurability' 180–200).

[17]   I apologize to the reader for the fogginess of this exposition. Yet, an accurate, clear representation of a fog should look – well – foggy!

[18]   Here as elsewhere in Aristotle's various discussions of exchange, he is not necessarily thinking of a common market-determined price, where there are many buyers and sellers, and where all are charged the same price. Rather, the exchange is relatively isolated between people who are sort of 'friends' (Pangle, 2003), and making a friendly exchange with at least the pretense of no close or 'sharp' bargaining. There is also what we might now call 'price discrimination'. The determination of these exchanges can also be fruitfully viewed as isolated two-party bargaining; see Lowry (1969, 1987, Chapter VII) and Gordon's discussion (1975: 'Household versus Markets', 65–9). For an analysis using modern game theory see Ferreira (2002).

been extended to the other categories' (1052b). Moreover, 'measure is that by which quantity is known; and quantity qua quantity is known either by a "one" or by a number' (ibid.).[19] Aristotle then goes into a discussion about measuring, and he holds that 'the measure and starting-point is something one and indivisible' (ibid.); or at least that is what he seeks. Thus, he thinks that in music the quarter-tone is the smallest unit, and in speech the letter is used as a unit of measurement because it is the smallest. Yet, the measure is not always one in number. Nonetheless, and this is crucial for our investigation:

> The measure is always homogeneous with the thing measured; the measure of spatial magnitudes is a spatial magnitude, and in particular that of length is a length, that of breadth a breadth, that of articulate sounds an articulate sound, that of weight a weight, that of units a unit. (1053a)

Our question then is, when we are measuring exchange values, what is it that measures them? What makes them commensurate? Aristotle's answer is that the thing that measures must in some sense be homogeneous with what is measured. If, for example, one has a labor theory of value, then, by this line of reasoning, labor would be the measure. If you have a commodity theory of value,[20] then a commodity would presumably be the measure; a subjective theory of value would seem to require some sort of unit of subjectivity as a measurer.

Later in the *Metaphysics* Aristotle returns to the idea that the core meaning of one is to be the first of measuring: 'One evidently means a measure. And in every case it is some underlying thing with a distinct nature of its own, e.g. in the scale a quarter-tone, in magnitude a finger or a foot or something of the sort, in rhythms a beat or a syllable; and similarly in weight it is a definite weight' (1087b). Thus, one is used in measuring things; one is also the starting point. Moreover, 'the measure must always be something predicable of all alike, e.g. if the things are horses, the measure is horse, and if they are men, man' (1088a). So again, for Aristotle, there needs to be some common unit. Therefore, 'if they are a man, a horse, and a god, the measure is perhaps living being' (ibid.). Here, the common unit would be, in Aristotle's view, that all these things are alive; thus, 'the number of them will be a number of living beings' (ibid.). On the other hand, 'if the things are man and white and walking, these will scarcely have a number' (ibid.). You cannot count or enumerate these as

---

[19]   Note that 'one' for Aristotle (as for other Greeks) is not a number. One was not generally considered a number in the western world until the Renaissance (Struik, 1987: 60).

[20]   As arguably with Piero Sraffa; see Pack (1985b), and below Chapter 11.

separate things, although perhaps you 'could have a number of classes, or of some equivalent term' (ibid.).[21]

Aristotle makes a similar point in his *Physics* that 'everything is counted by some one thing homogeneous with it, units by a unit, horses by a horse, and similarly times by some definite time' (223b). Finally, he makes the same general point in *On Generation and Corruption*:

> all the comparables must possess an identical something whereby they are measured. If, e.g., one pint of Water yields ten of Air, both are measured by the same unit; and therefore both were from the first an identical something. On the other hand, suppose they are not comparable in their amount in the sense that so much of the one yields so much of the other, but comparable in power of action (a pint of Water, e.g., having a power of cooling equal to that of ten pints of Air); even so, they are comparable in their amount, though not qua amount but qua having power. (333a)

To conclude: for Aristotle there must be some unit of analysis, some commonality to successfully compare things.[22] That is what Aristotle was searching for in section 1.2 above: some common unit of analysis that enables different heterogeneous products to have the ability to be exchanged in certain proportions. Aristotle was not completely satisfied with either of his proposed answers, be it need or money.[23] Neither should we be.

---

[21] In a related vein, that different sciences will start with completely different principles and hence there is a basic incommensurability between them; see *Posterior Analytics*: 88a. Exactly what the science of economics is, and what principles it should start from, is not uncontested in the 21st century; indeed, it is a source of controversy. As Lowry (for example 1987, 1991, 1995) has persuasively argued, from the time of the ancient Greeks until the 18th century, economics in the western tradition was the study of administration, not merely some form of price theory. There are reasons to believe that economics in an arguably post-modern 21st century will return to its pre-modern concerns and principles. See below, Chapter 13.

[22] On the general incommensurability of goods and moral values in Aristotle's work, see Nussbaum (2001, Chapter 10, Section II, 'The Attack on the Commensurability of Values': 294–7). Nussbaum persuasively argues that for Aristotle the ontological incommensurability of goods and moral values contributes to the preciousness of life, as well as to the fragility of the good life, since it is so easy to lose uniquely irreplaceable things, relationships, people and personal attributes!

[23] According to Schumpeter 'it is much more reasonable to assume that Aristotle simply thought of the exchange values of the market, as *expressed* in terms of money, rather than of some mysterious value substance *measured* by those exchange values' (1954: 61, emphasis in original). Here I think Schumpeter is quite wrong. Schumpeter goes on to conclude, 'We have expended such care on this argument because it disposes once for all of metaphysical speculations about objective or absolute value wheresoever and whensoever they might occur' (62). Again, Schumpeter on this particular issue was quite wrong, and history did not work out the way Schumpeter thought it would (consider, for example, the investigations of Piero Sraffa and his followers). Aristotle himself was indeed searching for some value 'thing' that was value, enabling products to be compared and exchanged.

Lastly, note Aristotle's search for commonality suggests that money itself will lead to a flattening of life. That is, to the extent that everything may be exchanged for another, or, in a monetized society, for a price, then everything is in some rather vague sense basically the same. Each thing just becomes more or less in terms of price.[24] Thus, to the extent that everything has a price, then nothing is priceless, and a certain uniqueness, preciousness, is lost. Therefore, to the extent that land, friends and lovers can be bought for a price, with money, then land, friends and lovers cease to be preciously unique. Instead, they become merely interchangeable.[25] The commoditization of land, friends and lovers leads to the loss of their preciousness, their uniqueness. I suspect this is a main reason that even in contemporary society, the sexual services industry has a high degree of disapprobation; indeed, large parts of it are often made illegal.

---

[24]   See, for example, Simmel (1950: 414).

[25]   See Buchan (1997). Note that Aristotle is the philosopher of heterogeneity. For Aristotle there are various largely incommensurate virtues, types of friends, fields of study (or what became in time academic disciplines), personal attributes, and so on. Modern neoclassical economic theory, largely reflecting our monetized society, stresses the homogeneity of life through utility and cost/benefit analysis where it is assumed that everything may be compared, everything is commensurate. For an argument that the monetization of Greek society in the 6th century BCE was a crucial factor in the formation of both early Greek philosophy and tragedy, see Seaford (2004).

2. Aristotle on the relation between capital (chrematistics) and character

2.1 ARISTOTLE'S PRONOUNCEMENTS CONCERNING THE UNNATURAL USE OF MONEY

Recall from the previous chapter that Aristotle held people may develop a tendency to want to accumulate or acquire coins, to accumulate or acquire money. Aristotle reasoned this to be unnatural. Hence, for Aristotle, 'natural riches and the natural art of wealth-getting are a different thing; in their true form they are part of the management of a household; whereas retail trade is the art of producing wealth . . . by exchange' (*Politics*: 1257b).

Unfortunately, 'some persons are led to believe that getting wealth is the object of household management, and the whole idea of their lives is that they ought either to increase their money without limit or at any rate not to lose it' (ibid.). For Aristotle, these people want to live only and not to live well. They are plagued by an excess of desires. They want too much. Hence, they desire an excess of enjoyments, and they strive ceaselessly after the accumulation of money. Aristotle concludes: 'there are two sorts of wealth-getting . . . one is a part of household management, the other is retail trade: the former is necessary and honourable, while that which consists in exchange is justly censured; for it is unnatural and a mode by which men gain from one another' (1258a). Thus, acquiring money through trade for Aristotle is not really creating or producing wealth. Rather, it is basically redistributing wealth from one person to another.

Aristotle goes further than this. He criticizes not only the gains from trade as unnatural, but even worse and even more unnatural are the gains from the lending of money:

> The most hated sort, and with the greatest reason, is usury, which makes a gain out of money itself, and not from the natural object of it. For money was intended to be used in exchange, but not to increase at interest. And this term interest, which means the birth of money from money, is applied to the breeding

> of money because the offspring resembles the parent. That is why of all modes of getting wealth this is the most unnatural. (1258b)

Thus, moneylending is the worst, the most unnatural way to acquire wealth. Also, according to Aristotle, included in the unnatural ways to acquire wealth is service for hire (wage labor). On the other hand, recall that natural, true, proper ways to acquire wealth include hunting, fishing, shepherding, farming; indeed even bee-keeping. Finally, 'there is still a third sort of wealth-getting intermediate . . . which is partly natural, but is also concerned with exchange, viz. the industries that make their profit from the earth, and from things growing from the earth which, although they bear no fruit, are nevertheless profitable; for example, the cutting of timber and all mining' (ibid.). Thus, the harvesting of timber and mining are partly natural, yet also partly unnatural ways to acquire wealth.

So, what are we now to make of these apparently Delphic pronouncements concerning the natural, unnatural and intermediate ways to acquire wealth? Clearly, for Aristotle, money was invented with the goal of facilitating the handy transfer of possessions from excessive to deficient proprietors, and vice versa. However, the use of money becomes corrupted to serve an unnatural end, that end being to acquire more money. Aristotle called this unnatural use of money, chrematistics. As Odd Langholm explains:

> chremastistike. The word is not used consistently either; sometimes it is used broadly to mean acquisition in general, elsewhere it indicates acquisition by trade, and this is the kind which Aristotle condemns. The root of the word is chrema, a thing needed or used; in plural it means goods, property. But chrematistics in its narrow sense is one of the Aristotelian words which have found their ways into modern languages untranslated; it is hard to convey with precision its particular sense of disdain for the slightly unsavoury skills of the commercial classes. (1983: 51)

At the risk of some confusion, we may also call this use of money to acquire more money capital.[1]

---

[1]   Confusion comes about because modern economic theory tends to restrict the word capital to physical capital: 'which includes manufactured goods that are used to produce other goods and services. Examples of physical capital are computers, factory building, machine tools, warehouses, and trucks. The total amount of physical capital available in a country is referred to as the country's capital stock' (Hubbard and O'Brien, 2008: 16). Controversies permeate the entire discourse of modern economic theory on how to properly define and measure capital.

2.2 ARISTOTLE ON THE NATURAL, OR WHAT IS MEANT BY THIS UNNATURAL CHREMATISTIC USE OF MONEY?

According to Aristotle, a contradiction is an opposition of which itself excludes any intermediate (*Posterior Analytics*: 72a). In contradistinction to an Aristotelian contradiction, a contrary has an intermediary with its opposite. For example, for Aristotle, waking and sleeping are contraries: one may be more or less awake, more or less asleep. Health and sickness, beauty and ugliness, strength and weakness, sight and blindness, hearing and deafness are also contraries (*On Sleep*: 453b). Indeed, for Aristotle, all the human perceptions are contraries (*Sense and Sensibilia*: 445b). It is possible, indeed likely, perhaps even inevitable, for contraries to change into another, into their opposite. The healthy can become sick. The hot can become cold. The strong can become weak. Since, as seen in the above section, things can be more or less natural, this means that the natural is not a contradiction. Our everyday use of language, that things tend to be either natural or unnatural, suggests that natural is a contradiction with no intermediary; not so for Aristotle! Instead, natural for Aristotle is a contrary, and there will be a tendency for the natural to turn into its opposite, the unnatural.

To further understand what Aristotle means by the unnatural use of money we need to briefly consider Aristotle's theory of causality. For Aristotle there are not one but four types of causality. There is the form or formal cause; the matter or material cause; the source of the change or movement or efficient cause; and that for the sake of which a thing is done, that is the goal, or end, or telos, or final cause (*Metaphysics*: 983a ff.; *Physics*: 194b ff.). For example, the moving or efficient cause of a house is the builder or the art of building. The final cause is the function or goal the house fulfills. The material cause is the earth and stones of which it is composed, and the house must have a definite form for it to fulfill the function of a house (*Metaphysics*: 996b). According to Aristotle, of these four causes, the final cause is the most important, and the best. Thus, 'we call cause that owing to which a thing comes about; but the purpose of a thing's existence or production is what we specially call its cause' (*Eudemian Ethics*: 1226b). And 'that for the sake of which tends to be what is best' (*Physics*: 195a); thus, 'where there is an end, all the preceding steps are for the sake of that' (*Physics*: 199a). Therefore, to return to money: if the true end or nature of money is to circulate goods, to facilitate the exchange process, then when money gets away from that function or goal, it becomes unnatural. The farther away money goes from its proper function of circulating goods, of transferring goods from excess to deficient owners, then the more unnatural it will become.

For Aristotle, 'excellence is a perfection (for when anything acquires its proper excellence we call it perfect, since it is then really in its *natural* state)' (*Physics*: 246a, emphasis added). Excellence being a perfection, the perfection of a thing is the most natural, or when that thing is in its most natural state. So, for example, when Aristotle says that man 'is natural in a higher degree than the other animals' (*Progression of Animals*: 706a) he means that we are in some sense better than the other animals.[2] Again, when he says that 'man is the most natural of bipeds' (ibid.: 706b) he means that humans are the best walkers on two feet. As Jowett explained, for Aristotle, 'By the end of a thing is said to be its nature; the best and alone self-sufficing development of it' (1885: 7).

Furthermore, Aristotle has a largely circular view of change (as well as history).[3] A thing reaches, fulfills its capacities, its nature. Then things get worse, corrupt, unnatural. Therefore, 'the unnatural is subsequent to the natural, being a derangement of the natural which occurs in the course of its generation' (*On the Heavens*: 286a). That is, things get good, they reach their perfection and in so doing become more natural.[4] Unfortunately, they then go bad, go away from their excellence or perfection, and become more unnatural: 'the incapacities of animals, age, decay, and the like, are all unnatural' (ibid.: 288b). Thus, the unnatural is in one sense quite natural because, for example, all animals do indeed age, decay and the like (see *Generation of Animals*: 770b). However, for Aristotle, using his distinctive terminology, age, decay and corruption are really the contrary to the natural, the good, the best. Hence, they are basically unnatural. Asserts Aristotle:

> E.g., if the body is potentially healthy, and disease is contrary to health, is it potentially both? And is water potentially wine and vinegar? We answer that it is the matter of one in virtue of its positive state and its form, and of the other in virtue of the privation of its positive state and the corruption of it contrary to its *nature*. (*Metaphysics*: 1044b, emphasis added)[5]

To return to money: the use of money to acquire or accumulate more money for Aristotle is a corruption of its positive state and form. It is

---

[2]   This is basically because we have reason and speech and the potential or capacity to do more things than other animals.

[3]   Historical change will be discussed in more detail in the next chapter.

[4]   As Robinson explains, 'Nature is a built-in principle that operates automatically, although Aristotle seems to think its effects are the same as reason would have chosen if it had been given the job of arranging the world' (1995: 80); and 'to understand the nature of a thing is to understand the final cause that is programmed into it and thus governs its behavior' (ibid.: 81).

[5]   Note also that for Aristotle, 'The primary contrariety is that between state and privation' (*Metaphysics*: 1055a).

contrary to the nature or proper function or excellence of money which is to aid in the circulation of goods.[6] For Aristotle, the unnatural can also be viewed to be a corruption and perversion. These should be studied since 'the corruption and perversion of a thing does not tend to anything at random but to the contrary or the intermediate between it and the contrary ... since error leads not to anything at random' (*Eudamean Ethics*: 1227a). Therefore, when the proper or best use of money becomes corrupted or perverse or unnatural, it will most likely do so in a certain way. Consequently, when money is used to acquire more money in the timber or mining industry, or in retail trade, or through lending it out for interest, it becomes more corrupt, more perverse, more unnatural.

2.3 ON THE CHREMATISTIC USE OF MONEY, CONSUMPTION AND CHARACTER

To further ferret out what for Aristotle are the deleterious, unnatural, corrupting, yes perverted consequences of money when it is used to acquire more money, we may look more closely at Aristotle's views on character. Since for Aristotle much of a person's character is determined by the goods and services that person 'consumes' over a lifetime, and since much of modern economics is concerned with theories of 'consumer demand', I will approach this issue of character development through the modern economistic prism of 'consumption'. This approach runs the risk of being unduly anachronistic.[7] Of course, as opposed to modern neoclassical consumer theory, Aristotle clearly did not have a theory of individual consumers going to the marketplace and purchasing various goods to consume utilities, maximizing utility subject to a budget constraint. Nonetheless, according to Aristotle, in order to fulfill their potentials, their capacities

---

[6] As Langholm explains, 'The telos of things is subordinated to the telos of man. A thing is used wrongly if it leads the user astray. For Aristotle to strive after wealth for its own sake is to mistake means for end' (1984: 65).

[7] There is a longstanding, generally acrimonious debate on how to properly interpret the ancient Greek economy and to what extent people such as Plato, Xenophon or Aristotle should be considered 'economists' at all. Arguing for the so-called primitivist or substantivist position, see, for example, Polanyi (1968 [1957]); and Finley (1970, 1977 [1963], 1999 [1973]). On the so-called modernist or economic formalist side, see for example the work of Nobel Prize winner Hicks (1969, 1989) and Cohen (1992). For an update on this at times tedious debate, see the articles in Scheidel and von Reden (2002). For an earlier review of the literature see Lowry (1979). For my position on the problematic relationship of Aristotle with modern economic theory see Pack (2008a).

This current study largely sidesteps these debates because clearly people such as Adam Smith and Karl Marx knew their Aristotle and were in part responding to him. I am dealing with a clearly defined dialectical (or dialogical) tradition.

as humans, people did need to consume things and to rely on each other's 'services'. They did this either in some kind of a market using money; or, more often, outside of the market through various social networks and organizations. These social networks and organizations ranged in size and complexity from the family or household unit up to (and including) the city-state. Thus, in a sense Aristotle had a theory of consumer behavior on how people do and ought to act and 'consume', and this is intimately related to people's characters. Also, Aristotle always tried to take a comparative approach to his subject matter.[8] Since Aristotle viewed humans as a particular type of living being, in particular as a rational animal, it will be enlightening to first consider Aristotle's views on plant and animal consumption. Afterwards I will deal with the more complex human consumption.

2.3.1   On Plant and Animal Consumption

Aristotle takes a comparative, biological approach to the study of human beings.[9] He divides living things amongst plants, animals and humans. Plants essentially live, acquire nourishment and reproduce. They have what may be termed a plant soul.

For Aristotle, knowledge of any kind is to be 'honored and prized'. Nevertheless, some knowledge is more 'honorable and precious' than others.[10] Such is the knowledge of the soul because of its high 'dignity' and 'wonderfulness' (*On the Soul*: 402a). What has soul has life. Plants have soul, life, or movement in the rather limited sense of nutrition, decay and growth. For Aristotle this plant or nutritive soul is the 'most primitive' form of soul (ibid.: 415a) because of plants' limited capacity, power, or ability to do things when compared to other forms of living things (animals and humans). Aristotle defines things largely by 'their function and power' (*Politics*: 1254a). In Aristotle's view:

> Nature proceeds little by little from things lifeless to animal life in such a way that it is impossible to determine the exact line of demarcation . . . Thus after

---

    [8] For example, as background for his work in the *Politics* Aristotle and his students collected 158 'constitutions' of the various Greek city-states.
    [9] See for example Nussbaum (2001), 'Rational Animals and the Explanation of Action': 264–89.
    [10] Hegel stated that 'there is no empirical point of view or phenomenon, either in the natural or the spiritual world, that Aristotle has considered beneath his notice' (1995: 180). This is probably a bit hyperbolic. Aristotle really was not too interested in studying such things as the work done by slaves; or concerning himself with the psychology or even the physiology of women (Nussbaum, 2001: xx, 371). Nevertheless, overall, the range of his interests is indeed quite impressive; even intimidating.

lifeless things comes the plant . . . whilst [it] is devoid of life as compared with an animal, it is endowed with life as compared with other corporeal entities. Indeed, as we just remarked, there is observed in plants a continuous scale of *ascent* towards the animal. (*History of Animals*: 588b, emphasis added)

Thus, for Aristotle, things in Nature are relatively continuous and hierarchical.[11] In terms of capacity and the power/ability to do things, animals are better than plants, which are better than lifeless things. (Although, for Aristotle, in some ways the entire world should be viewed as a living being.)[12] The ascent in terms of capabilities from plants to animals (and then to humans) may very well have influenced Darwin's world-view. (Note that prescient word ascent. Of course, for Aristotle humans ascend from animals; for Darwin humans descend from animals.)[13] Nonetheless, this ascent for Aristotle must not be seen in historical time, since for Aristotle, all species are eternal.[14]

Thus, for Aristotle, plants basically consume nutrients from the soil below and the light from the sun above. They do not have locomotion, they do not move about, they do not perceive, they do not think and they do not reason; not that much going on there. Above plants in terms of capacity and power are animals and the animal soul. Animals share with plants the capacity/power/ability to live, consume nourishment and reproduce. Additionally, animals have sense, especially the sense of touch (*On the Soul*: 413b). For Aristotle, this sense of touch is the key difference: 'plants live without having sensation, and it is by sensation that we distinguish animal from what is not animal' (*On Youth, Old Age, Life and Death, and Respiration*: 467b). Moreover, animals will generally move

---

[11] See Lloyd (1996, Chapter 3, 'Fuzzy Natures': 67–82). As Lloyd points out in an earlier work, 'Aristotle's conception of the highest life for man reflects his idea of man's place in the scale of living creatures. Plants, animals, man and even gods are, as we have seen, arranged in a single continuous scale according to the faculties of soul they possess, plants possessing simply the nutritive and reproductive faculty' (1968: 239).

[12] See, for example, Lloyd (1996: 171); Aristotle (*On the Heavens*: 292a, 293b).

[13] 'Charles Darwin said more than he perhaps intended when he remarked, in a letter thanking William Ogle for a copy of his translation of the *Parts of Animals*, that his gods, Cuvier and Linnaeus, were "mere schoolboys" to old Aristotle' (Lennox, 2001: 123–4).

[14] See Lennox, Chapter 6, 'Are Aristotelian Species Eternal?' (2001: 131–59). And here is what is arguably the key difference between the ancients and the moderns. I suspect that the empirical realization that species are not eternal, that they do die out forever, therefore that natural history cannot be circular, is one of the principal catalysts for the modern view of history as evolution (or progress). See for example Hegel, who, in his thorough discussion of Aristotle's philosophical system, interjects that 'Without going back to the fabulous monstrosities of the ancients, we likewise know of a number of animal tribes which have died out, just because they could not preserve the race. Thus we also require to use the expression development (an unthinking evolution) in our present-day natural philosophy' (1995: 158). For more on this point, see below, Chapter 7.

towards their food and away from their enemies; that is, they generally have locomotion. According to Aristotle, animals live in a familiar (to modern economists) Benthamite world with natural, animalistic desires, passionately pursuing pleasure and avoiding pain.[15] Aristotle: 'Where there is sensation, there is also pleasure and pain, and where these, necessarily also desire' (*On the Soul*: 413b); also, 'whatever has a sense has the capacity for pleasure and pain' (ibid.: 414b). Note then, that pleasure, pain and desire are at a rather low level of capacity, power and existence. These are attributes which the human animal shares with most all other animals. There is nothing specifically human about having desires and rather mindlessly pursuing pleasure and avoiding pain.[16] At this base animalistic level, there is 'no evidence as yet about thought or the power of reflexion' (ibid.: 413b), which for Aristotle are the specifically human capacities, or capacities of the remarkable human soul.

Animals, then, have at least one sense (that of touch), and appetites. Appetites for Aristotle include desires, passions and wishes (*On the Soul*: 414b). Animals sense objects and 'when the object is *pleasant* or *painful*, the soul makes a sort of affirmation or negation, and *pursues* or *avoids* the object' (ibid.: 431a, emphasis added); 'it pronounces the object to be *pleasant* or *painful*, in this case it *avoids* or *pursues*' (ibid.: 431b, emphasis added). According to Aristotle, 'what is *painful* we *avoid*, what is *pleasing* we *pursue*' (*Movement of Animals*: 701b, emphasis added); and 'whatever is in conformity with nature is pleasant, and all animals pursue pleasure in keeping with their nature' (*History of Animals*: 509a).

When applied to humans, this Benthamite approach should accurately be seen as a simplification, or rather, a dumbing down, of Aristotle's general theory of 'consumer behavior'; more applicable to animal

---

[15]   'Aristotle says that whatever has sensation experiences pleasure and pain, and whatever experiences pleasure and pain, also experiences appetite, appetite being simply desire for what is pleasant' (Lloyd, 1968: 189). The modern mainstream economic theory of consumer behavior replaces Aristotle's 'appetites' with 'tastes' which are typically exogenously given. This substitution of tastes for appetites is basically trivial.

[16]   Veblen acerbically captured this animalistic, mindless aspect to the mainstream economic theory of consumer behavior: 'The hedonistic conception of man is that of a lightning calculator of pleasures and pains, who oscillates like a homogeneous globule of desire of happiness under the impulse of stimuli that shift him about the area, but leave him intact. He has neither antecedent nor consequent. He is an isolated, definitive human datum, in stable equilibrium except for the buffets of the impinging forces that displace him in one direction or another. Self-imposed in elemental space, he spins symmetrically about his own spiritual axis until the parallelogram of forces bears down upon him, whereupon he follows the line of the resultant. When the force of the impact is spent, he comes to rest, a self-contained globule of desire as before. Spiritually, the hedonistic man is not a prime mover. He is not the seat of a process of living, except in the sense that he is subject to a series of permutations enforced upon him by circumstances external and alien to him' ('Why is Economics Not an Evolutionary Science?' in Veblen, 1948: 232–3.)

consumers than to human consumers. Animals basically use their senses to enable them to eat, to go to their food, to avoid their enemies and to reproduce themselves. 'All animals are sensible to the pleasure derivable from food, they all feel a desire for it. For the object of desire is the pleasant' (*Parts of Animals*: 661a). Thus, animals have an appetite for, and they consume, food. They also (as with plants) reproduce themselves: 'the most natural act is the production of another like itself, an animal producing an animal, a plant a plant, in order that, as far as its nature allows, it may partake in the eternal and divine. This is the goal towards which all things strive, that for the sake of which they do whatsoever their nature renders possible' (*On the Soul*: 415a). So all living things strive to exist and to reproduce themselves. Aristotle: 'Now it is true that the business of most animals is, you may say, nothing else than to produce young, as the business of a plant is to produce seed and fruit' (*Generation of Animals*: 717a). Eating and fornicating: that is what it is all about for most animals. 'The life of animals, then, may be divided into two parts, procreation and feeding; for on these two acts all their interest and life concentrate' (*History of Animals*: 588b). Actually, animals also spend a lot of time sleeping. Then they are acting more as plants than as animals (*On Sleep*: 455b). Thus, in terms of consumption, for the most part animals merely consume their food (their needed, necessary nutrients, that which is required to physically exist and to preserve their life) and 'sexual services' from their mates. However, the human animal has the potential, the power, the capacity, to do much more, much better, than merely sleep (as with the plants), and eat and copulate (as with the animals). Humans can pursue their own specific, higher sorts of excellences or virtues.

2.3.2   On Human Consumption

Humans, as with plants, live, acquire nourishment and reproduce. As with most animals, they have sense and physical motion; but in addition, we have reason. For Aristotle, 'Animals lead for the most part a life of nature, although in lesser particulars some are influenced by habit as well. Man has reason, in addition, and man only' (*Politics*: 1332b). Reason is what differentiates humans from the brutes.[17] Thus 'of all animals man alone is capable of deliberation' and, according to Aristotle, 'no other creature except man can recall the past at will' (*History of Animals*: 488b). Above humans are the gods, and it is reason which the human animal possibly shares with these gods. That is, 'man and possibly another like man or

---

[17]   That Aristotle assumes that there is an intelligible world, and that the human mind can grasp reality and become identical with the forms of reality, see Spellman (1995).

superior to man also [have] the power of thinking and thought' (*On the Soul*: 414b). Humans' ability to think and reason is also reflected in our material, physical body:

> Animals, however, that not only live but perceive, present a greater multiformity of parts, and this diversity is greater in some animals than in others, being most varied in those to whose share has fallen not mere life but life of high degree. Now such an animal is man . . . man alone partakes of the divine, or at any rate partakes of it in a fuller measure than the rest. (*Parts of Animals*: 656a)

Our ability to walk erect is also indicative that humans share reason with the gods:

> For of all animals man alone stands erect, in accordance with his god-like nature and substance. For it is the function of the god-like to think and to be wise; and no easy task were this under the burden of a heavy body, pressing down from above and obstructing by its weight the motions of the intellect and of the general sense. (*Parts of Animals*: 672b)[18]

In Aristotle's hierarchical typology,[19] humans are better than animals, and animals are better than plants. Gods, naturally, are the best of all. The basis of this ordinal ranking is essentially the capacity or power to do things: the more capacity a thing has to do things, the better, the more excellent, it is.[20]

Thus, there are for Aristotle three types of souls: plant, animal and human (ignoring gods or any other beings superior to humans). Corresponding to these three types of souls, humans have three types of needs. We have internal needs of the body (as with plants); external bodily needs (as with animals); and needs of the distinctly human soul or of reason. We humans must consume things (including so-called services) to meet these needs.

Humans form families or households partly to help supply their internal bodily needs. These needs are essentially appetites: the sexual appetites

---

[18] 'The end is for man to be able to fulfill his divine nature, that is, thinking; but in order for that to be possible, the body must not weigh on the soul' (Ferrarin, 2001: 283).

[19] 'The Aristotelian world is nothing if it is not hierarchic' (Lawson-Tancred, 1986: 68).

[20] 'Aristotle starts from the principle which runs through most of earlier Greek thought – that the soul, whatever else it is, is the principle of life, i.e. that which makes living things alive, and is responsible, in some sense, for the different living functions. Thus his approach to his subject-matter is that of one concerned with general forms of life, i.e. the general capacities and potentialities which living things possess . . . In other words, to speak of the soul is to speak of the potentialities which a living thing has for different forms of life' (Hamlyn, 1993: ix–x).

and the appetite for food and drink. For Aristotle 'the family is the association established by nature for the supply of men's everyday wants' (*Politics*: 1252b). Households band together to form a village to help supply external bodily needs. Thus, according to Aristotle, 'when several families are united, and the association aims at something more than the supply of daily needs, the first society to be formed is the village' (ibid.).[21] Several villages then combine to form the state.[22] The state will eventually be able to satisfy people's distinctly human needs, the needs of the human soul or of reason, thus enabling people to lead a good human life: 'When several villages are united in a single complete community, large enough to be nearly or quite self-sufficing, the state comes into existence, originating in the bare needs of life and continuing in existence for the sake of a good life' (*Politics*: 1252b).

Internal and external bodily needs are limited. Therefore, the goods which supply these needs are subject to diminishing, indeed, eventually negative marginal utility (Lowry, 1987: 218–23). According to Aristotle, 'it is for the sake of the soul that goods external and goods of the body are desirable at all, and all wise men ought to choose them for the sake of the soul' (*Politics*: 1323b).[23] That is, for Aristotle, external and internal goods of the body are mere means to an end: they should be consumed for the sake of the distinctly human soul. Thus, as with any other instrument of production, external goods and goods of the body may be said to be subject to diminishing marginal productivity (in this case, the production of human happiness): 'external goods have a limit, like any other instrument . . . where there is too much of them they must either do harm, or at any rate be of no use, to the possessors' (ibid.). In contradistinction, 'every good of the soul, the greater it is, is also of greater use, if the epithet useful as well as noble is appropriate' (ibid.)

Thus, for Aristotle, 'soul is better than body' (*Generation of Animals*: 731b). The human *body*, being inferior, then should largely exist to serve the needs of the human *soul*: 'As every instrument and every bodily member is for the sake of something, viz. some action, so the whole body must evidently be for the sake of some complex action . . . the body too must somehow or other be made for the soul' (*Parts of Animals*: 645b). Consumption then of goods and services for the body

---

[21] As Saunders points out in his translation and commentary on the first two books of *Politics*, 'Aristotle's villages are mysterious things; his account is brief, allusive and ambiguous' (1995: 66).

[22] Again Saunders: 'In the account of the formation of the state from several villages . . . there is an irritating lack of hard information (ibid.: 67).

[23] Here Aristotle is referring to the specifically human (not plant or animal) soul. External goods are goods external to both the body and the human soul.

should also be subservient to the needs of the soul. That is, we humans should consume goods and services for the body only insofar as the consumption of these goods and services contributes to our soul. Our human soul, that is our reason, should rule the needs of our body. For Aristotle, 'A living creature consists in the first place of soul and body, and of these two, the one by nature the ruler and the other the subject' (*Politics*: 1253a).

Thus, goods (or services) which satisfy the needs of the human soul, or reason, are not subject to decreasing or negative marginal utility. Indeed, in the aggregate, they may be said to have increasing marginal utility. For Aristotle, 'happiness, whether consisting in pleasure or excellence, or both, is more often found with those who are most highly cultivated in their mind and in their character, and have only a moderate share of external goods, than among those who possess external goods to a useless extent but are deficient in higher qualities' (ibid.: 1323b).[24] Thus, humans need a certain amount of external goods so they can develop their minds, their character, their reason. According to Aristotle, 'the best life, both for individuals and states, is the life of excellence, when excellence has external goods enough for the performance of good actions' (*Politics*: 1323b). Aristotle defines excellence in the *Eudemian Ethics* as 'the best state or condition or faculty of all things that have a use and work' (1218b–1219a). Excellence for humans means to be the best that you can be, to reach your potentials, to realize your capabilities (*Politics*: 1333a). Aristotle says in the *Politics* that 'We maintain, and have said in the *Ethics*, if the arguments there adduced are of any value, that happiness is the realization and perfect exercise of excellence' (1332a); and in the *Nicomachean Ethics* he holds that 'he is happy who is active in conformity with complete excellence and is sufficiently equipped with external goods' (1101a). The excellences towards which people should particularly strive for are of reason and are in the mind since 'in men reason and mind are the end towards which nature strives' (*Politics*: 1334b). And by nature, Aristotle here means, of course, the best, the highest, most noble achievements attainable by humans.[25]

The goods or services which satisfy the needs of the distinctly human soul are basically provided by educators, friends[26] and the political/cultural

---

[24] So for Aristotle, after a certain level of physical wealth, increases in the wealth of a nation will not increase that nation's 'happiness'. On the relationship between wealth and happiness in the history of economic thought see Bruni (2004a, 2004b).
[25] See Lloyd (1996, Chapter 9, 'The Idea of Nature in the *Politics*': 184–204); Jowett (1885: 7).
[26] See for example Pangle (2003); but also Uyl and Griswold (1996).

milieu of the city-state.[27] Thus, on the one hand, Aristotle holds that indeed 'the good life requires a supply of external goods' (*Politics*: 1332a). On the other hand, people, as consumers, need to minimize and control their desires and demands for internal and external goods of the body, so that they can have the time and means to pursue the goods of the soul. To do this well, they will also need a certain amount of leisure (*Politics*: 1334a).[28]

2.3.3 Consumption, Chrematistics, Choice and Character

People do make mistakes in their consumer choices. In particular, 'in bad or corrupted natures the body will often appear to rule over the soul' (*Politics*: 1254b). So, for the mature, adult human, it is good, best and natural (in the Aristotelian sense of the natural as the good and best end or goal for a substance or being) for the soul to use its reason to rule over and guide the body in what to do and what to consume. Yet, of course, this does not always happen. The lower animals (as well as children) basically obey and follow their passions. Human adults should use their minds and the rational elements in their being to rule over their passions in their choices of how to behave and what to consume. For Aristotle, 'the soul of man is divided into two parts, one of which has a rational principle in itself, and the other, not having a rational principle in itself, is able to obey such a principle' (*Politics*: 1333a). Thus, Aristotle divides the human soul into two parts. The rational part of the soul is based on reason; the irrational parts are based on appetites. Reason, being the higher, better part of the soul, should rule since 'the inferior always exists for the sake of the superior, and the superior is that which has a rational principle' (ibid.) Here, once again, Aristotle is thinking and organizing in a hierarchical schema. Humans have reason. Reason is what distinguishes people from lower animals. So people should use their reason to make the right choices to realize or actualize their distinctly human potentials, powers and capacities. This will enable people to flourish as a human being since it is 'always to everyone the most desirable which is the highest attainable by him' (ibid.)

Reason develops in humans as they grow older. Humans basically go through the three hierarchical souls in time.[29] When they are unborn in their mother's womb, they live the life of a plant (*Generation of Animals*:

---

[27] See for example Frank (2005), especially Chapter 5, 'The Polity of Friendship', 138–80.

[28] See also Pieper's (1998) emphasis on the crucial importance of leisure for culture and the development of human excellence.

[29] See, for example, Cohen (1996: 168–70). Cohen's point occurs in the midst of a long, complex argument that for Aristotle a substance may sometimes lack some of its essential attributes (as in the case of a human fetus or a newborn baby).

753b). As a child, they are like animals, as they are largely ruled by their appetites and their passions. Reason develops as they grow older.

> For this reason, the care of the body ought to precede that of the soul, and the training of the appetitive part should follow: nonetheless our care of it must be for the sake of the reason, and our care of the body for the sake of the soul. (*Politics*: 1334b)

So, care of the human body precedes that of the human soul, for without a body, the soul cannot exist in the world. Moreover, we need to train our appetites (or 'tastes'), and not follow them blindly as most animals do, and as most neoclassical models of 'economic man' assume. Thus, humans need leisure and education and control of our base appetites so that we can develop our minds, 'for the deficiencies of nature are what art and education seek to fill up' (*Politics*: 1336a). Consequently, it is not easy to be a good consumer or to make the right consumption choices; children in particular need to be guided in this crucial domain.[30]

Mistakes in how to live and what to consume are exacerbated by the monetized or commercialized sectors of society. Because money can purchase most anything, people are led to believe that their internal and external bodily needs are infinite. People misled by the power of money to accumulate more money spend their days trying to acquire money and more money to satisfy their internal and external bodily desires, rather than using the money to aid in the development of their uniquely human capabilities and powers.

For Aristotle, 'the life of money-making is one undertaken under compulsion, and wealth is evidently not the good we are seeking; for it is merely useful and for the sake of something else' (*Nicomachaen Ethics*: 1096a). Thus wealth is not an end, it is a means to an end, and 'the instruments of any art are never unlimited, either in number or size, and riches may be defined as a number of instruments to be used in a household or in a state' (*Politics*: 1256b). Therefore riches or wealth should be mere means towards the living of the good life.[31]

However, when the accumulation of money, wealth and riches becomes an end in itself, people become ruled by their desires and passions. People seek to get a hold of money so they can purchase more and more goods for

---

[30]   Aristotle would certainly not approve of the massive commercial advertising directed to the children in contemporary societies.

[31]   As Buchan, an insightful admirer of Aristotle writes: 'We need to dispense with economics and book-keeping or rather restore them to their places in the hierarchy of organized thought (which for us might be, as once for Aristotle, below poetry, good conduct, politics and the management of the household)' (1997: 280).

the body. Unfortunately, this use of money to acquire more money may lead to the corruption of all aspects of society:

> For, as their enjoyment is in excess, they seek an art which produces the excess of enjoyment; and, if they are not able to supply their pleasures by the art of getting wealth, they try other causes, using in turn every faculty in a manner contrary to nature. The quality of courage, for example, is not intended to make wealth, but to inspire confidence; neither is this the aim of the general's or of the physician's art; but the one aims at victory and the other at health. Nevertheless, some men turn every quality or art into a means of getting wealth; this they conceive to be the end, and to the promotion of that end they think all things must contribute. (*Politics*: 1258a)

Thus, for Aristotle, in a society where money is largely used with the goal of acquiring more money, it will be difficult to consume wisely.[32] For some, there will be the passionate urge to overwork and accumulate money (for whom money comes to represent abstract desire).[33] Others will choose to overspend their money on excessive goods for the body. Some may do both. For both types of consumers, passions will overwhelm and rule their intellect and reason.

Aristotle further divides the irrational part of the human soul in two. One corresponds to the vegetable soul, the other to the animal soul. 'Of the irrational element one division seems to be widely distributed, and vegetative in its nature, I mean that which causes nutrition and growth' (*Nicomachean Ethics* (*NE*): 1101a). This part of the human soul does not present a major problem for human consumption and choice. Rather, it is the animal part in us that needs controlling: 'the irrational element also appears to be two-fold. For the vegetative element in no way shares in reason, but the appetitive and in general the desiring element in a sense share in it' (*NE*: 1102b). We humans share pleasure and pain and desires with the animals. In choosing how to live and what to consume, we need to control our pleasures and pains, so that we will have the right, correct pleasures and pains.[34] Choice for Aristotle involves reason and thought, and 'by choosing what is good or bad we are men of a certain character' (*NE*: 1121a).[35] Our choices in what to consume and what to be should be guided by the ideal of human excellence. For Aristotle,

---

[32]   As well as to practice the arts fairly and wisely: think of unscrupulous car salesmen or automobile mechanics, and doctors, too.

[33]   See Buchan (1997).

[34]   An example of a wrong pleasure for Aristotle would be having sexual relations with your neighbor's wife.

[35]   'All human action therefore likewise proceeds from desire . . . But man possessing the power of nous [reason] as well as the power of sense, is able to respond to the desired "intelligently"' (Randall, 1960: 72).

> the excellence of the eye makes both the eye and its work good; for it is by the
> excellence of the eye that we see well. Similarly the excellence of the horse makes
> a horse both good in itself and good at running . . . the excellence of man also
> will be the state which makes a man good and which makes him do his own
> work well. (*NE*: 1106a)

To choose the right things, humans need to have right desires as well as accurate reasoning: 'since moral excellence is a state concerned with choice, and choice is deliberate desire, therefore both the reasoning must be true and the desire right, if the choice is to be good' (*NE*: 1139a).

Thus, 'all goods are either outside or in the soul, and of these those in the soul are more desirable' (*Eudamean Ethics* (*EE*): 1218b). Excellence belongs to the soul, and we are looking for and striving for human excellence, not animal or plant excellence: 'For if we speak of him qua man, he must have the power of reasoning, a governing principle, action; but reason governs not reason, but desire and passions; he must then have these parts' (ibid.: 1219b). So reason needs to govern the desires and the passions,[36] including the desire to accumulate unneeded amounts of wealth, to consume unneeded goods, or to subvert such arts as medicine into a mere tool for accumulating money.

Choice for Aristotle is a 'deliberate desire for something in one's own power' which 'arises out of deliberate opinion' (*EE*: 1226b). Therefore, for Aristotle, 'in the other animals choice does not exist, nor in man at every age or in every condition' (ibid.). For Aristotle, all human excellence implies choice. Aristotle is concerned with choice because choices are voluntary; they are under the control of human reason, and 'excellence and badness have to do with voluntary acts' (*EE*: 1223a). So if economics is, as is frequently held, the theory of choice, then Aristotle is certainly concerned with economics. Yet, his humans are not mindlessly pursuing pleasure and avoiding pain, as with the brutes, and as assumed in the neoclassical theory of consumer behavior. Rather, Aristotle is concerned that people carefully, rationally choose the right things so they can become excellent and fulfill their human capacities as much as possible.

---

[36]   This may be usefully contrasted with Hume (or Freud and much of modern thought) where the emphasis is more on reason being a tool of the passions (Adam Smith too – see his *Theory of Moral Sentiments*). The overemphasis in postmodern thought on the limits to reason is in a traditional way politically conservative, inhibiting people's confidence in the ability of their reason to successfully critique the status quo. Modern conservative theorists such as Burke (1968), Hayek (1944), and de Jouvenal (1962) explicitly used arguments about the limited capacity of human reason to *passionately* argue against radical social and political changes. And yet the overemphasis on the limits to reason probably also facilitates the rise of secular and especially religious mysticism (to fill in the explanatory void). This brings about its own potential for radical changes. With this emphasis on religious, mystical political movements, the post-modern world is recycling back to the pre-modern world.

Thus, choice for Aristotle is based upon reason. Nevertheless, habit also influences a person's actions. Therefore, 'whether we form habits of one kind or of another from our very youth; it makes a very great difference, or rather *all* the difference' (*EE*: 1103b, emphasis in original). Moreover, long-standing habits will produce a person's character. What we do largely determines what we become: 'we learn by doing, e.g. men become builders by building and lyre-players by playing the lyre; so too we become just by doing just acts, temperate by doing temperate acts, brave by doing brave acts' (ibid. 1103a). So people need to choose well. What a person chooses to consume and to do will eventually become habit-forming. This will also influence and determine that person's character. For Aristotle, 'Habits are also pleasant; for as soon as a thing has become habitual, it is virtually natural; habit is a thing not unlike nature; what happens often is akin to what happens always, natural events happening always, habitual events often' (*Rhetoric*: 1370a). What we choose to consume and do becomes habitual. Our choices and habits largely form our character. That character is who and what we become.

To conclude: humans need to have their internal bodily needs met so that they can exist as living creatures. They need to have their external bodily needs met so that they can exist as animals, as mere brutes. But they need to have their rational or soulful needs met so that they can exist and flourish as humans.[37] Their human or soulful needs cannot be met unless their basic animal or external bodily needs are also met; and neither of these can be met if their internal, life-dependent needs are not met. The ability for humans to flourish, to realize their human capacities, is dependent upon their lower plant and animal needs being met. Yet, at the same time, our plant and animal needs should be met primarily so that our specifically human needs, capabilities and powers can also be nourished and developed. Therefore, the human mind, reason, must guide and limit the lower bodily passions and desires. This is not easy to do, particularly in a chrematistic society where money is used to acquire more money, where money becomes an end or goal in itself, instead of a mere means to an end.[38] Humans need to make the right choices, with

---

[37]   Maslow's (1954) hierarchical theory of human needs was clearly influenced by Aristotle's work. For a brief description of Maslow's work, and how it was used (or twisted) by the world of commerce and advertising, see Vyse (2008: 119–22).

[38]   Sang the popular Greek lyric poet Anacreon:
'Cursed be he above all others
Who's enslaved by love of money.
Money takes the place of brothers,
Money takes the place of parents,
Money brings us war and slaughter' (*Odes*: XXIX 8).

correct reasoning and the right desires, so we can become excellent beings and fulfill our capabilities. It is thus crucially important, yet quite difficult, to be a good consumer. Making the right decisions about what to consume and what to be will largely determine our character and who we are.[39]

---

[39] Perhaps somewhat surprisingly, contemporary cognitive neuroscientists seem to largely agree with Aristotle. They claim that what we do will indeed even effect the structure and size of parts of our brain. For example, London cabdrivers have a relatively large posterior hippocampus – the area of the brain where spatial representations are stored. Moreover, the size of the posterior hippocampus will also be a function of the number of years on the cabdrivers' job. See Holt (2005).

3. Aristotle on change and government

3.1 ARISTOTLE ON CHANGE IN GENERAL

The last chapter stressed the importance of the final cause, or the goal, for Aristotle. So, for example, when the goal is using money to acquire more money, rather than using money merely to circulate goods, everything changes for Aristotle. Money goes from being a good to a bad thing; from a natural to an unnatural thing. The goal of using money to acquire more money becomes limitless. The situation is similar for the role of the government or the state: its goal or final cause is of pivotal importance. Although the government or state originally comes into existence partly for economic reasons, its final cause or goal should be to assist in the flourishing of its citizens: to help them realize their capacities, their potentials, their powers. Before considering in detail the goal or function of the state, we should first consider in more detail Aristotle's views on historical change, as well as the importance of the mean, and also what he means by change in general.

Aristotle systematically looks at change from several perspectives and taxonomies. So, for example, he considers whether change is accidental or not:

> Everything which changes does so in one of three ways. It may accidentally, as for instance when we say that something musical walks, that which walks being something in which aptitude for music is an accident. Again, a thing is said without qualification to change because something belonging to it changes, i.e. in statements which refer to part of the thing in question: thus the body is restored to health because the eye or the chest, that is to say a *part* of the whole body, is restored to health. And there is the case of a thing which is in motion neither accidentally nor in respect of something else belonging to it, but in virtue of being *itself* directly in motion. (*Physics*: 224a, italics in original)

Non-accidental changes will occur in contraries, where one thing will move more or less gradually to its opposite, for example, the sleeping state to the waking state. Or they will occur in contradictions, where there is no intermediary, such as going from life to death (see *Physics*: 225b). In considering change, Aristotle makes clear this distinction between contraries and contradictions, claiming that 'Every change involves opposites, and

33

opposites are either contraries or contradictories; since a contradiction admits of nothing in the middle, it is evident that what is between must involve contraries' (*Physics*: 227a).

Aristotle also relates change to various sorts of ontological categories,[1] arguing that 'If the categories are classified as substance, quality, place, acting or being acted on, relation, quantity, there must be three kinds of movement – of quality, of quantity, of place. There is no movement in respect of substance . . . nor in respect of relation . . . nor of agent and patient' (*Metaphysics*: 1068a). For Aristotle, movements are a type of change. Yet, not all changes are movements. He claims there are basically only three types of motion:

> there can be motion only in respect of quality, quantity and place; for with each of these we have a pair of contraries. Motion in respect of quality let us call alteration, a general designation that is used to include both contraries. . . . Motion in respect of quantity . . . is called increase or decrease . . . motion in the direction of complete magnitude is increase, motion in the contrary direction is decrease. Motion in respect of place . . . we may designate it by the general name of locomotion. (*Physics*: 226a)[2]

Yet, in the *Categories* he claims that there are six kinds of change: 'generation, destruction, increase, diminution, alterations, change of place' (15a). Generation and destruction are not movements, although they are changes. They involve contradictions, not contraries.[3] [Thus],

> When the change from contrary to contrary is *in quantity*, it is growth and diminution; when it is *place*, it is locomotion, when it is in property, i.e. *in quality*, it is alteration, but when nothing persists of which the resultant is a property (or an accident in any sense of the term), it is coming-to-be, and the converse change is passing-away. (*Generation and Corruption*: 319b–320a, emphasis in original)

So contradictions for Aristotle involve changes, from being to non-being and vice versa; they are changes but not movements. Movements involve contraries, and there are various types of movements. Yet, one, locomotion, is the primary one, is what we really mean by movement: 'Now of the three kinds of motion that there are – motion in respect of magnitude,

---

[1] Traditionally the first book in Aristotle's corpus (*Categories*: 1a–15b).

[2] Modern economics tends to see only motion or changes in respect to quantity; for example changes in the gross domestic product, the unemployment rate, inflation, and so on.

[3] Note that sometimes Aristotle denotes change in quantity as *one* type of change. Sometimes he denotes it as two types of change: increase *and* decrease. He is not consistent in his terminology.

motion in respect of affection, and motion in respect of place – it is this last, which we call locomotion, that must be primary' (*Physics*: 260a).

Thus, for Aristotle, there are more kinds of changes than motion. The change resulting from contradiction is coming to be and passing away and is not a motion: 'Since, then, every motion is a kind of change, and there are only the three kinds of change mentioned above; and since of these three those which take the form of becoming and perishing, that is to say those which imply a relation of contradiction, are not motions' (*Physics*: 225a–b).

Change, of course, must take place in time; without the passing of time, there can be no change. Now, the emphasis on time for Aristotle is basically circular.[4] On the one hand, for Aristotle, as opposed to the Judaic–Christian tradition, the universe has always existed. It is permanent. Yet time, for Aristotle, does not really go anywhere; or rather, it tends to go in a circle. Thus, 'the same opinions appear in cycles among men not once nor twice nor occasionally, but infinitely often' (*Meteorology*: 339b). Time is forever and it is endlessly repetitive: 'The same ideas, one must believe, recur in men's minds not once or twice but again and again' (*On the Heavens*: 270b). Thus, there is no real historical development, or evolution, or progress through time as is generally understood in modern discourses.[5] Rather, things get as good as they can. They realize their potentials and actualize themselves. In that sense there is indeed a sort of development. But then things get worse, less best, less natural. There is a certain *Ecclesiastesian*-type weariness or edge to Aristotle's thought: 'In time all things come into being and pass away; for which reason some called it the wisest of all things, but the Pythagorean Paron called it the most stupid, because in it we also forget; and this was the truer view' (*Physics*: 222b). People, families and entire civilizations rise and fall; develop and degenerate.[6] So, as far as families are concerned, people who come from an old distinguished family tend unfortunately to be 'poor creatures. In the generations of men as in the fruits of the earth, there is a varying yield; now and then, where the stock is good, exceptional men are produced for a while, and then decadence sets in. A clever stock will degenerate towards

---

[4]   See, for example, Arendt (1968).

[5]   'The modern concept of process pervading history and nature alike separates the modern age from the past more profoundly than any other single idea' (Arendt, 1968: 63).

[6]   As is usually the case with Aristotle, there actually was very good empirical evidence for Aristotle's general view. Between 1150 BCE and the beginning of the 8th century there was a period of general cultural impoverishment in Greece, known as the Greek Dark Age. For example, the Linear B script of writing (and hence literacy in general) died out. So from Aristotle's perspective, history would indeed look rather cyclical; on ancient Greek history see, for example, Hammond (1986, especially Book I, Chapter 3, 'The Great Migrations'); Cartledge (1998, 'Intermezzo: Historical Outline': 54–73).

the insane type of character' (*Rhetoric*: 1390b). And so also with societal institutions, 'It is true indeed that these and many other things have been invented several times over in the course of ages, or rather times without number; for necessity may be supposed to have taught men the inventions which were absolutely required' (*Politics*: 1329b).

This emphasis on the essential circularity of time, together with Aristotle's four different types of causality, causes some real problems and difficulties in deciding what comes first in time. For example, think of a chair. The chair comes at the end of the production process in time. Yet, to make a chair, one needs to firstly think or have that as the goal at the beginning. This is similar to most all things for Aristotle, including what may be called the productions of nature.[7] Thus, 'In general, that which is becoming appears as something imperfect and proceeding to a principle; and so what is posterior in the order of becoming is prior in the order of nature' (*Physics*: 261a). Since for Aristotle the most important cause is the final cause, or the goal, in a sense this final cause is also the first cause and it comes first. Thus the final development or actuality of a thing is in a sense prior to its potential. As he explains in the *Metaphysics*

> it is also prior in substance: firstly, because the things that are posterior in becoming are prior in form and in substance, e.g. man is prior to boy and human being to seed; for the one already has its form, and the other has not. Secondly, because everything that comes to be moves towards a principle, i.e. an end. For that for the sake of which a thing is, is its principle. (1050a)[8]

Thus, in the venerable question, which comes first, the chicken or the egg, Aristotle falls down squarely on the priority of the chicken. As he explains with regards to humans, 'For the seed comes from other individuals which are prior and complete, and the first thing is not seed but the complete being, e.g. we must say that before the seed there is a man – not the man produced from the seed, but another from whom the seed comes' (*Metaphysics*: 1072b–1073a). With the development of men, 'reason and mind are the end towards which nature strives' (*Politics*: 1334b).[9]

Thus, the final cause is in a timely sense also the first cause or the principle, and hence it does come first. Aristotle actually does consider and reject what we would now consider modern secular Darwinian or evolutionary type

---

[7]   Nature is 'like an intelligent workman' (*Generation of Animals*: 731a).

[8]   Note here that Aristotle uses the term principle as the same as the goal, the end, the telos of a thing.

[9]   Note how Aristotle's analyses are always so 'normative'. I believe it is fair to say that most mainstream modern political theory, beginning with such people as Machiavelli and Hobbes, would tend to protest against this and try to write more as 'things really are' (for example, Hirschman, 1977: 12–14); most modern economic theory too.

arguments about change and natural history. 'Why', he asks, 'then should it not be the same with the parts in nature, e.g. that our teeth should come up of necessity – the front teeth sharp, fitted for tearing, the molars broad and useful for grinding down the food – since they did not arise for this end, but it was merely a coincident result; and so with all other parts in which we suppose that there is purpose?' (*Physics*: 198b). So that, 'such things survived, being organized spontaneously in a fitting way; whereas those which grew otherwise perished and continue to perish' (ibid.). Yet, Aristotle cannot go down this theoretical path: 'it is impossible that this should be the true view. For teeth and all other natural things . . . [are] not the results of chance or spontaneity' (*Physics*: 198b–199a). Most wherever he looks, Aristotle tries to use his reason to find reason, and thinks he sees reason.[10]

3.2   ON CHANGE AND THE STATE, AND OTHER PERSPECTIVES REGARDING THE STATE

There will be different types or forms of states. Each type or form of state will have its own goal or principle. Each will have a tendency to turn into its opposite, its contrary. So, for example, at one point in the *Politics* he says that there are three good or 'true' forms of governments: 'kingly rule, aristocracy, and constitutional government'. Each of these will have a tendency to turn to its opposite perverted form: kingly to tyranny; aristocracy to oligarchy; constitutional to democracy (1289a ff.). In the *Rhetoric* he succinctly summarizes the goals of some of these forms of government: 'The end of democracy is freedom; of oligarchy, wealth; of aristocracy, the maintenance of education and national institutions; of tyranny, the protection of the tyrant' (1366a). He argues that 'we should know the character of each form of government' to better persuade it. The character of a government (as with people) is learned by studying 'their acts of choice; and these are determined by the end that inspires them' (ibid.)

As touched on at various points in the previous two chapters, Aristotle is aware that households or families band together to form villages and that villages then band together to form the state (*Politics*: 1252b). Yet the emphasis in Aristotle on change and the state is not upon a historical development of the state.[11] He tends to assume that the state already exists

---

[10]   'When one man said, then, that reason was present – as in animals, so throughout nature – as the cause of the world and of all its order, he seemed like a sober man in contrast with the random talk of his predecessors' (*Metaphysics*: 984b).

[11]   I do not think Aristotle is too interested in historical time, partly because, as discussed above: (a) history is circular, endlessly repeating itself; and (b) with his four types of causes, the most important cause is the final cause, which only manifests itself at the end of the story.

in the manner that exists in Greece: the city-state. His emphasis is on how there are various forms of states with various goals and how these forms of states change into their opposites or contraries; especially how the good or best or most natural states become less good, perverted, unnatural. According to Aristotle, for example in *Politics*: 1279a:

> The conclusion is evident: that governments which have a regard to the common interest are constituted in accordance with strict principles of justice, and are therefore true forms; but, those which regard only the interest of the rulers are all defective and perverted forms, for they are despotic, whereas a state is a community of freemen.

Good, natural governments become corrupt.

Yet, let us back up now and look at other angles to the state. From another point of view, people come together to form a state partly out of friendship. Indeed justice itself derives from a form of friendship. Near the end of both the *Eudemian* and *Nicomachean Ethics* Aristotle has extensive discussions of friendship. The theme of friendship is a connecting bridge between his ethical and political theory.

Aristotle finds that there are not one but three types of friendship. The primary or true or perfect friendship is based upon excellence. 'This friendship does not exist between the bad, for the bad man feels distrust and is malignant to all, measuring others by himself. Therefore the good are more easily deceived unless experience has taught them to distrust. But the bad prefer natural goods to a friend and none of them loves a man so much as things' (*EE*: 1237b). Since bad people know they deceive, they expect others will as well; hence, they are unable to form real friendships. True friendship is the friendship of good, excellent people with each other and 'to him whom he wishes to live with merely for the sake of his company and for no other reason' (*EE*: 1240a). This sort of friendship lasts as long as the friends 'are good – and excellence is an enduring thing'; yet 'it is natural that such friendships should be infrequent; for such men are rare. Further, such friendship requires time and familiarity' (*NE*: 1156b).

Friendship can also be based upon pleasantness. This is the sort of friendship the young especially have since 'they are sensitive to pleasure; therefore also their friendship easily changes; for with a change in their characters as they grow up there is also a change in their pleasures' (*EE*:

Of course, once the modern non-circular concept of history arises, a modern Aristotelian such as Hegel will be deeply concerned with the historical process – see, for example, his *Philosophy of Right* (1952). That most Greek philosophers in general were not interested in history, see Grant (1995: 33). However, there is history in *Constitution of Athens*, which was apparently written either by Aristotle or one of his students.

1236a). This is also the sort of friendship that people tend to have who are similar to each other since 'everything too is by nature pleasant to itself' (*EE*: 1239b).

The third type of friendship for Aristotle is based upon usefulness or utility.[12] Friendship based upon utility helps to give rise to the family, the community, the state and justice. This is not the friendship of simi-larities since 'the like is useless to itself' (*EE*: 1239b). Friendships based on utility are largely economic friendships; thus, 'those who are friends for the sake of utility part when the advantage is at an end; for they were lovers not of each other but of profit' (*NE*: 1157a).[13] These largely commercial, or economic, friendships ('friendship based on utility is for the commercially minded' (*NE*: 1158a)) may frequently masquerade as superior true moral friendships; but they are not friendships of excel-lence (*EE*: 1243a). Nonetheless, this inferior form of friendship has its advantages. 'Friendship for utility's sake seems to be that which most easily exists between contraries, e.g. between poor and rich, between ignorant and learned; for what a man actually lacks he aims at, and he gives something else in return' (*NE*: 1159b). Friendship based on utility is close to or is related to commerce or exchange, the giving of something else in return. Indeed, commerce or exchange can be viewed to be a type of friendship.[14]

Marriage itself has the potential to be all three types of friendship.

> Between man and wife friendship seems to exist by nature; for man is natu-rally inclined to form couples – even more than to form cities, inasmuch as the household is earlier and more necessary than the city, and reproduction is more common to man than with the animals. With the other animals the union extends only to this point, but human beings live together not only for the sake of reproduction but also for the various purposes of life; for from the start the functions are divided, and those of man and woman are different; so they help each other by throwing their peculiar gifts into the common stock. It is for these reasons that both utility and pleasure seem to be found in this kind of friendship. But this friendship may be based also on excellence, if the parties are good; for each has its own excellence and they will delight in the fact. (*NE*: 1162a)

---

[12] Note how Aristotle makes a distinction between what is pleasant and what is useful or has utility; this distinction is conflated in modern neoclassical economic theory.

[13] Note how here utility is equated with profit.

[14] The friendly nature of commerce ('le doux commerce') was a major theme in the work of Montesquieu, and is evident in Smith. Marx enjoyed ridiculing this idea in his contempo-raries and writers in the 18th century; but it does have its source in Aristotle (see Hirschman, 1977). This idea of commerce encouraging friendship is largely lost with the neoclassical assumption of perfect competition, where the potential commercial friends become com-pletely anonymous to each other and hence totally interchangeable.

Thus, there is a sexual division of labor that Aristotle assumes which is embedded in the marriage relationship. The division of labor is also one of the main reasons people form communities. Communities are formed partly because people need each other and they form friendships based upon utilities (*NE*: 1160a).

Thus, to some extent, usefulness, and friendship based upon usefulness,[15] is the origin of the household; and of larger communities as well. Friendship based upon usefulness leads to justice. First there is private justice with friends; and then public justice. Public justice comes about when laws are written down. Private justice is basically moral; friends based upon utility ought to treat each other equitably and demand neither too much nor too little from each other. Public justice is legal:

> We speak of friendships of kinsmen, comrades, partners, the so-called 'civic friendship' . . . Civic friendship has been established mainly in accordance with utility; for men seem to have come together because each is not sufficient for himself, though they would have come together anyhow for the sake of living in company . . . The justice belonging to the friendship of those useful to one another is pre-eminently justice, for it is civic or political justice. (*EE*: 1242a)[16]

Of course, at the same time, economic considerations themselves exist for the final cause, the good life; indeed, for Aristotle this final cause is also the most important one. Thus, one should also say that there is a political basis to Aristotle's economic theory, and Aristotle's economic theory is subsumed to his political and social theory. So, people will live together for non-economic reasons since 'men even when they do not require one another's help desire to live together' (*Politics*: 1278b). People will form a state to help develop their potentialities. For Aristotle, 'The end of the state is the good life' (*Politics*: 1280b) and 'political society exists for the sake of noble actions and not of living together' (*Politics*: 1281a). Thus, for Aristotle,

> a state is not a mere society, having a common place, established for the prevention of mutual crime and for the sake of exchange. These are conditions without which a state cannot exist; but all of them together do not constitute a state,

---

[15]   Pangle: 'In friendships of utility the element of affection is much less important though it is often present. Even colleagues and business associates who would never go out of their way to see each other usually feel, if they are working well together, a mutual friendly regard that goes beyond the selfish pleasure of knowing that the other is serving one's purposes' (2003: 47).

[16]   This of course is not to say that each individual exchange leads to justice; individual exchanges can often be unjust. For a full study of Aristotle on friendship see Pangle (2003); also the perceptive review by Held (2005).

which is a community of families and aggregations of families in well-being, for the sake of a perfect and self-sufficing life. (*Politics*: 1280b)[17]

Thus, the state exists for the sake of the good life and not for mere life only, helping people to flourish, to realize or actualize their potentials, their higher souls, their excellences. 'For if what was said in the Ethics is true, that the happy life is the life according to excellence lived without impediment, and that excellence is a mean, then the life which is in a mean, and in a mean attainable by everyone, must be the best' (*Politics*: 1295a).

In trying to promote excellence, and to help people flourish, the state should promote the middle class. Indeed, the too rich, the too powerful, can be dangerous to the state and the community: 'The fact is, that the greatest crimes are caused by excess and not by necessity. Men do not become tyrants in order that they may not suffer cold' (*Politics*: 1267a); and, 'he who greatly excels in beauty, strength, birth, or wealth . . . finds it difficult to follow rational principle' (*Politics*: 1295b). There should be moderation, and a limit to the size of properties: 'Clearly, then, the legislator ought not only to aim at the equalization of properties, but at moderation in the amount' (*Politics*: 1266b). There is a need for a strong middle class: 'a city ought to be composed as far as possible, of equals and similars; and these are generally the middle classes' who 'neither plot against others, nor are themselves plotted against, they pass though life safely' (*Politics*: 1295b)

Thus, Aristotle wants a large, strong middle class, and the state should try to prevent either of the extremes (the rich and the poor) from becoming dominant. Throughout his corpus, Aristotle stresses the importance of the mean. For example, the ability for life itself to exist critically hinges upon a certain moderation, a certain meanness or average in the environment and in the living being itself. Most importantly for Aristotle, the environment and the living thing can be neither too hot nor too cold, nor too dry or too wet. Otherwise, the living thing dies. For Aristotle, at a certain fundamental level, all differences can be reduced to these two basic contraries: hot/cold, and moist/dry (*On Generation and Corruption*: 330a). The ability for a thing to live depends upon a certain mean or moderation of these two basic contraries (or four basic elements). The hot and the cold, the dry and the moist 'are properties on which even life and death are largely dependent and . . . they are moreover the causes of sleep and waking, of maturity and old age, of health and disease' (*Parts of Animals*: 648a).

---

[17] This will be contrasted with Smith's position in Part II. See Cropsey's (1957) Aristotelian criticism of Smith's work that Smith is too concerned with mere existence instead of excellence.

Similarly, Aristotle stresses the important of the mean in his ethical writings: 'moral excellence is a mean . . . it is no easy task to be good. For in everything it is no easy task to find the middle . . . that is why goodness is both rare and laudable and noble' (*NE*: 1109a). Since being good, or excellent or virtuous entails finding the mean; then being bad or having vice is not finding the mean or having an excess or a defect in relation to the mean. Hence, for example, Aristotle in the *Eudemian Ethics* has a list of 42 passions (1220b–1221a). Fourteen of these passions are good, twenty-eight are bad. For example, bravery is good; too much or excess bravery is foolhardiness and is bad; too little or deficiency is cowardice and is also bad. Liberality is good; excess is lavishness and is bad; too little or deficiency is meanness and is also bad. The just is good; excess is gain and is bad; deficiency is loss and is also bad.

In his theory of the soul and perception, Aristotle held that sense itself is a sort of mean: 'It is to this that it owes its power of discerning the objects in that field. What is in the middle is fitted to discern' (*On the Soul*: 424b).[18] Analogously, the same is true with people and social classes. Aristotle claims, 'the arbiter is always the one most trusted, and he who is in the middle is an arbiter' (*Politics*: 1297a). A government based upon a strong middle class will be able to view reality more perceptively and more accurately. Moreover, it will be a more stable one: 'Revolutions also break out when opposite parties, e.g. the rich and the people, are equally balanced, and there is little or no middle class' (*Politics*: 1304b). Just as the rich and powerful need to be limited, if possible, the poor should be brought up.

> Yet the true friend of the people should see that they are not too poor, for extreme poverty lowers the characters of the democracy . . . the proceeds of the public revenue should be accumulated and distributed among its poor, if possible, in such quantities as may enable them to purchase a little farm, or, at any rate, make the beginning in trade or farming. (*Politics*: 1320a)

So Aristotle is in favor of promoting the middle class partly by executing socioeconomic policies that to some extent take from the rich and give to the poor; taking from those with an excess and giving to those with a deficiency.

Thus, there is in Aristotle some class analysis, with emphasis on the quarrels between the rich and the poor and the importance of the middle class in mediating these quarrels. So, although for Aristotle, 'the greatest opposition is confessedly that of excellence and badness; next come that

---

[18] See Ross's commentary (1973). For a full book-length treatment on Aristotle and the sense-organs see Johansen (1998). For his interpretation of exactly how these organs should be understood as being in the mean see pp. 111 ff.

of wealth and poverty' (*Politics*: 1303b).[19] Thus, 'in the opinion of some, the regulation of property is the chief point of all, that being the question upon which all revolutions turn' (*Politics*: 1266a). For Aristotle,

> it is manifest that the best political community is formed by citizens of the middle class, and that those states are likely to be well-administered in which the middle class is large, and stronger if possible than both the other classes, or at any rate than either singly; for the addition of the middle class turns the scale, and prevents either of the extremes from being dominant. (*Politics*: 1295b)

So the purpose of the government for Aristotle is to nurture/help/ promote the character and capacities of its citizens.[20] This is what Frank (2005) calls 'a democracy of distinction',[21] and is most easily accomplished where there is a large, strong middle class. The role of the state is to help people choose wisely as they develop their characters to actualize their potentialities. As Randall points out, 'Aristotle thus stands for the omni-competence of the state. There is nothing that political government must refrain from doing, if it makes for human welfare. Aristotle thus quite literally is stating the theory of the "welfare state"' (1960: 255).[22] On the other hand, in the 20th century, Karl Popper would lament that Aristotle's theory of the role of the state could and did lead to totalitarianism via its influence on Hegel (and then to Marx).[23]

According to Aristotle, the Greek, Hellenic race was blessed by being in the middle. People in cold climates in Europe were full of spirit; they had comparative freedom but were wanting in intelligence and skill. The

---

[19] See also for example, *Politics*: 1290a: 'For a constitution is an organization of offices, which all the citizens distribute among themselves, according to the power which different classes possess (for example the rich or the poor), or according to some principle of equality which includes both.' Also *Politics*: 1291b: 'Again, because the rich are generally few in number, while the poor are many, they appear to be antagonistic, and as the one or the other prevails they form the government.'

[20] Of course, Aristotle had a theoretical defense of slavery, and he preferred that neither slaves nor women be citizens; or workers in general (see, for example, *Politics*: 1278a). The answers to questions about slavery and who should be a citizen separates Aristotle from Smith and Marx, and arguably most modern thinkers. Nonetheless, with increasing globalization, decreased communication and transportation costs, and extreme worldwide inequalities in income distribution, the question of who is allowed to become a citizen is and will doubtlessly remain a vexing controversial issue for years to come.

[21] 'If Aristotle makes no secret of his hostility to democracy, I argue that his activity oriented philosophy nonetheless harbors democratic possibilities. Indeed, it opens the way to a particularly dynamic form of democracy that can accommodate the reciprocal relation between institutions and citizens' (Frank, 2005: 8).

[22] That Aristotle's work provides a theoretical defense of the liberal welfare state, see also Nussbaum (1989, 1990).

[23] See Chapter 11, 'The Aristotelian Roots of Hegelianism' (Popper, 1945). On the dangers of what Isaiah Berlin called positive freedom or positive liberty see Berlin (1969).

Asians lived in a hotter environment. They were intelligent and inventive, but wanting in spirit; hence, they were always in a state of subjection and slavery.[24] The Hellenic race, being in the middle, were high-spirited as well as intelligent. 'Hence it continues free, and is the best-governed of any nation, and if it could be formed into one state, would be able to rule the world' (*Politics*: 1327b). Aristotle's pupil, Alexander the Great, would ruthlessly act upon this particular part of Aristotle's thought. In doing so, he would briefly become ruler of much of the then so-called known world; and he would permanently end the excellent, classical age of the Greek city-state. In a peculiar sense, Alexander the Great became an agent demonstrating Aristotle's dictum that things get as good, as excellent as they can; then they become corrupt and unnatural.

---

[24]   Here, as elsewhere, the great French Enlightenment thinker Montesquieu seems, in spite of some protestations to the contrary, to be largely following and developing Aristotle's thought. See, for example, *The Spirit of the Laws*, Part III.

PART II

Adam Smith's debate with Aristotle over
chrematistic/economic issues

4. Adam Smith on exchange value and money

4.1 SMITH ON EXCHANGE VALUE: CLARITY AMIDST THE AMBIGUITY

I think it is fair to say that Smith was quite impressed by Aristotle. Smith, who generally cannot be correctly accused of being overly generous to his predecessors,[1] writes of Aristotle: 'that great philosopher [Aristotle], who appears to have been so much superior to his master [Plato] in everything but eloquence' ('History of Ancient Logics and Metaphysics', 1980: 122fn).[2] The ethics in Smith's *Theory of Moral Sentiments* (*TMS*) seems to be heavily influenced by Aristotle's work in that field, especially in the areas of the importance of moderation and hitting upon the proper mean between contrary passions. Smith himself claims that 'It is unnecessary to observe that this [Aristotle's] account of virtue corresponds too pretty exactly with what has been said above concerning the propriety and impropriety of conduct' (*TMS*: 271).[3]

Moreover, just as Aristotle's work in *Politics* is tightly linked to his work in the *Eudemian* and *Nicomachean Ethics*, so Smith's ideas on government and jurisprudence are closely linked to Smith's ethics. At the very end of *The Theory of Moral Sentiments*, Smith promises:

> I shall in another discourse endeavour to give an account of the general principles of law and government, and of the different revolutions they have undergone in the different ages and periods of society, not only in what concerns justice, but in what concerns police, revenue, and arms, and whatever else is

---

[1] See Rashid (1998: 200–208), Chapter 9, 'The Intellectual Standards of Adam Smith's Day'. Marx, witty though nasty as usual, writes 'The Scottish proverb that if one has gained a little it is often easy to gain much, but the difficulty is to gain a little, has been applied by Adam Smith to intellectual wealth as well, and with meticulous care he accordingly keeps the sources secret to which he is indebted for the little, which he turns indeed into much' (*Critique*: 167–8).

[2] This comment comes in the middle of a long, complex, indeed bizarre footnote about, among other things, esoteric and exoteric writings; the entire footnote merits serious theoretical deconstructing.

[3] For a superb account of Smith's use of the concept propriety, which also argues that Smith is a proto-Kantian, see Montes (2004, Chapter 4, 'Adam Smith's Concept of "Propriety": Its Meaning and Philosophical Implications': 97–129).

the object of law. I shall not, therefore, at present enter into any further detail concerning the history of jurisprudence. (342)

Smith, of course, was never able to write that book. However, the end of that projected book was indeed written, and it became what we may now call his economics. It became *The Wealth of Nations*. As Smith explains in the 'Advertisement' to the 6th edition of his *Theory of Moral Sentiments*, which was published shortly before his death in 1790:

> In the last paragraph of the first Edition of the present work, I said, that I should in another discourse endeavour to give an account of the general principles of law and government, and of the different revolutions which they had undergone in the different ages and periods of society . . . In the *Enquiry concerning the Nature and Causes of the Wealth of Nations*, I have partly executed this promise; at least so far as concerns police, revenue, and arms. What remains, the theory of jurisprudence, which I have long projected, I have hitherto been hindered from executing . . . Though my very advanced age leaves me, I acknowledge, very little expectation of ever being able to execute this great work to my own satisfaction; yet, as I have not altogether abandoned the design, and as I wish still to continue under the obligation of doing what I can, I have allowed the paragraph to remain as it was published more than thirty years ago, when I entertained no doubt of being able to execute everything which it announced.

So the link for Smith, as with Aristotle, goes from his ethical to his political theory. Then for Smith (though not for Aristotle) the last part of his political work became his massive economics. Nonetheless, and perhaps somewhat surprising, in his economics, Smith appears to have more or less begun his economic story with Aristotle.[4]

By Schumpeter's reading, 'Aristotle's embryonic "pure" economics, the elements of which are to be found mainly in *Politics*, I: 8–11, and in *Ethics*, V: 5 . . . constitutes the Greek bequest, so far as economic theory is concerned. We shall follow its fortunes right to A. Smith's *Wealth of Nations*, the first five chapters of which are but developments of the same line of reasoning' (1954: 60). Actually, this slightly exaggerates the extent of Smith's indebtedness to Aristotle at the commencement of *The Wealth of Nations*. If Smith begins his *Wealth* responding to any ancient Greek, it is to Xenophon, with respect to the importance of the division of labor being constrained by the size of the market.[5]

---

[4]　On the influence of the ancient Greeks on Smith's thought in general, see Vivenza (2001). On the systematic nature of Smith's work, and attempts to tightly link up Smith's ethical and economic writings, see for example Young (1997).

[5]　See Lowry (1987) Chapter III, 'Xenophon and the Administrative Art'. That this influence may have been mediated and enriched by Medieval Persian thought, see Hosseini (1998).

In any event, Smith begins his treatise with several preliminary (though crucial) chapters on 'Of the Division of Labour', 'Of the Principle which gives Occasion to the Division of Labour' and 'That the Division of Labour is Limited by the Extent of the Market'.[6] Smith then commences his Chapter IV 'Of the Origin and Use of Money' with the following sentence: 'When the division of labour has been once thoroughly established, it is but a very small part of a man's wants which the produce of his own labour can supply' (I.iv.1). Notice here Smith alludes to both sides of what has come to be viewed as the supply and demand apparatus: we have 'wants' which can be supplied by the labor of others. Smith then proceeds to explain the development of money largely along the line delimited some two thousand years earlier by Aristotle. Money develops out of the exchange of products to overcome various technical problems with the barter of products.[7] Then, towards the end of the chapter, again following Aristotle, Smith makes a crucial distinction between use value and exchange value:

> The word VALUE, it is to be observed, has two different meanings, and sometimes expresses the utility of some particular object, and sometimes the power of purchasing other goods which the possession of that object conveys. The one may be called 'value in use'; the other, 'value in exchange'. (I.iv.13, emphasis in original)

On the last page of that chapter Smith promises that he will proceed to 'investigate the principles which regulate the exchangeable value of commodities' and show 'what is the real measure of this exchangeable value; or, wherein consists the real price of all commodities' (I.iv.14–15). The very last sentence of the chapter suggests that Smith may have felt that he did not have a full grasp of the ensuing value theory. He apologizes in advance to the reader: 'I am always willing to run some hazard of being tedious in order to be sure that I am perspicuous; and after taking the utmost pains that I can to be perspicuous, some obscurity may still appear to remain upon a subject in its own nature extremely abstracted' (I.iv.18).[8]

---

[6]   Compare this to Xenophon's, *The Education of Cyrus*, Book VIII, Chapter 2, 1–6. That Smith was a close reader of what he called 'The Expedition of Cyrus', and greatly admired Xenophon's beautiful clear, flowing writing style, see *Lectures on Rhetoric and Belles Lettres* (1983: 107–8); also, praising Xenophon's writing style, ibid.: 132–4.

[7]   See Schumpeter (1954: 62–3; and then 188).

[8]   Alternatively, one can take Smith's word for the inherent difficulty of the subject matter in Chapter V. Then Smith could be perceived as being rhetorically astute in putting off this difficult, reader unfriendly material until the fifth chapter, and beginning his story with the more easily accessible discussion of the benefits of the division of labor. In contradistinction, Marx, who notoriously began his difficult opus *Capital* immediately with value theory and

In the ensuing perplexing Chapter V, 'Of the real and nominal Price of Commodities, or of their Price in Labour, and their Price in Money',[9] as well as the rest of the work,[10] Smith presents what many readers have traditionally viewed as three rather distinct labor theories of exchange value.[11] Firstly, Smith clearly seems to have had a labor command theory of exchange value. As Smith states in the first paragraph of that chapter, 'The value of any commodity, therefore, to the person who possesses it, and who means not to use or consume it himself, but to exchange it for other commodities, is equal to the quantity of labour which it enables him to purchase or command' (I.v.1). This labor-commanded theory, how much labor your commodity can exchange for or command, will partly depend upon the price of labor, and hence upon the distribution of income. Again, Smith clearly states that 'Wealth, as Mr. Hobbes says, is power . . . The power which that possession immediately and directly conveys to him, is the power of purchasing; a certain command over all the labour, or over the produce of labour which is then in the market' (I.v.3). So here the exchange value of a commodity has to do with its power, its ability to command other labor which is in the market.

Yet, Smith has also been read to have some kind of a labor disutility theory of exchange value. For he also clearly writes, 'The real price of everything, what every thing really costs to the man who wants to acquire it, is the toil and trouble of acquiring it' (I.v.2). Thus, here the real price (and presumably value) of a good depends on disutility, psychology and largely subjective issues (toil and trouble). Or, again in the same chapter, 'Equal quantities of labour, at all times and places, may be said to be of equal value to the labourer. In his ordinary state of health, strength and spirits; in the ordinary degree of his skill and dexterity, he must always lay down the same portion of his ease, his liberty, and his happiness' (I.v.4).

Aristotle's distinction between use and exchange value, could then be viewed as rhetorically less sophisticated than Smith.

[9] 'We have been under the necessity of suspending our progress in the perusal of the *Wealth of Nations*, on account of the insurmountable difficulties, obscurity, and embarrassment in which the reasoning of the fifth chapter are involved' (Francis Horner, journal entry, 24 May 1801, *Memoirs and Correspondence of Francis Horner, M.P.*, quoted in Huekel (2000b: 317)).

[10] That Smith's work is a fascinating combination of theoretical technical difficulties glossed over by Smith, thus providing a stimulating research program for incipient economists, with quite clear and articulate public policy proposals which provide grist for the more policy-oriented or politically motivated readers, see Pack (1991) chapters 2 and 3.

[11] See for example Schumpeter (1954: 188–9 and fn. 20 on those pages). It should be noted that Schumpeter is not a very sympathetic reader of Smith. He concludes 'that, in spite of his emphasis on the labor factor, his [Smith's] theory of value is no labor theory at all' (ibid.: 189 fn. 20).

Finally, there seems to be a labor-embodied theory of exchange value in Smith.[12] As Smith clearly writes at the beginning of Chapter VI:

> In that early and rude state of society which precedes both the accumulation of stock and the appropriation of land, the proportion between the quantities of labour necessary for acquiring different objects seems to be the only circumstance which can afford any rule for exchanging them for one another. If among a nation of hunters, for example, it usually costs twice the labour to kill a beaver which it does to kill a deer, one beaver should naturally exchange for or be worth two deer. It is natural that what is usually the produce of two days or two hours labour, should be worth double of what is usually the produce of one day's or one hour's labour. (I.vi.1)

This paragraph clearly refers to some kind of pre-capitalist past or a non-capitalist society (possibly North American Native American societies?).[13] Thus, it is possible to claim that Smith did not have an embodied labor theory of value when dealing with his contemporary commercial society. Nonetheless, Smith also frequently used a labor-embodied analysis in other parts of his work. For example, he wrote, 'The proportion between the value of gold and silver and that of goods of any other kind, depends in all cases . . . upon the proportion between the quantity of labour which is necessary in order to bring a certain quantity of gold and silver to market, and that which is necessary in order to bring thither a certain quantity of any other sort of goods' (II.ii.105). Or again 'why the real price both of the coarse and of the fine manufacture, was so much higher in those antient, than it is in the present times. It cost a greater quantity of labour to bring the goods to market' (I.xi.13).[14]

Thus, Smith seems to have several conflicting labor theories of value. As Marx complained,

> Adam Smith constantly confuses the determination of the value of commodities by the labour-time contained in them with the determination of their value by the value of labour; he is often inconsistent in the details of his exposition and he mistakes the objective equalization of unequal quantities of labour forcibly brought about by the social process for the subjective equality of the labours of individuals. (*Critique*: 59)[15]

---

12 This is how David Ricardo read Smith; see Chapter I 'On Value', Section 1. Ricardo (1951) criticized Smith for confusing labor-embodied versus labor-commanded theories of value, and Ricardo went on to develop what he considered to be an embodied labor theory of value.

13 See Meek (1976).

14 See also the references in O'Donnell (1990), p. 112 and fn. 13, p. 242.

15 I think Marx's most perceptive general criticism of Smith is that 'More than once he [Smith] prefers to take the sharp edge off a problem when the use of precise definitions might have forced him to settle accounts with his predecessors' (*Critique*: 168). Marx is correct: whenever Smith really gets stuck on a technical issue, he just glosses over the problem and

There are also apparent Physiocratic residues in Smith's theory of value, where value seems to come from the earth itself. For example, at one point Smith claims that even the cattle of farmers are 'productive labourers':

> No equal capital puts into motion a greater quantity of productive labour than that of the farmer. Not only his labouring servants, but his labouring cattle, are productive labourers. In agriculture too nature labours along with man; and though her labour costs no expence, its produce has its value, as well as that of the most expensive workmen. (II.v.12)

This passage seems rather bizarre; it is difficult to reconcile it with the general tenor of Smith's work.[16] So when it comes to Smith's theory of what is value, or what produces value, we clearly have a muddle.[17]

Be that as it may, when it comes to what *measures* exchange value, Smith is crystal clear: the measure of exchange value is labor. 'Labour', writes Smith, 'therefore, is the real measure of the exchangeable value of all commodities' (I.v.1). Or, later in that same chapter Smith writes, 'But though labour be the real measure of the exchangeable value of all commodities, it is not that by which their value is commonly estimated' (I.v.4). (For Smith, commodities are in fact estimated 'by the haggling and bargaining of the market' (ibid.), and sold for money rather than their real measure labor.) Or again, 'Labour alone, therefore, never varying in its own value, is alone the ultimate and real standard by which the value of all commodities can at all times and places be estimated and compared' (I.v.7). And again, 'Labour, therefore, it appears evidently, is the only universal, as well as the only accurate measure of value, or the only standard by which we can compare the values of different commodities at all times and at all places' (I.vi.17). And finally, 'Labour measures the value not only of that part of price which resolves itself into labour, but of that which resolves itself into rent, and of that which resolves itself into profit' (I.vi.9).

So Smith may be quite ambiguous, doubtlessly confused about what is

---

moves on. In Smith's defense though, Smith was able to finish his masterpiece, *The Wealth of Nations*; that was Smith's goal (for about ten years) and he accomplished it. Marx was not able to finish *Capital* (ditto for Schumpeter's magisterial *History of Economic Analysis*).

[16]   See, for example, Hollander (1987: 156). McNally (1988, Chapter 5), largely following Marx, argues that the key analytical difficulties in Smith's work (confusion of value and wealth; the handling of fixed capital or depreciation; rent and value theory; ambiguities of productive/unproductive labor) result from a bias towards agricultural capitalist economic development.

[17]   By Marx's reading, 'Smith is very copiously infected with the conceptions of the Physiocrats, and often whole strata run though his work which belong to the Physiocrats and are in complete contradiction with the views specifically advanced by him . . . For our present purpose, we can completely disregard these passages in his writings, which are not characteristic of himself, but in which he is a mere Physiocrat' (*Theories of Surplus Value*: I, 70).

value or what creates value. Nonetheless, he is quite clear, unambiguous, indeed adamant that labor is the 'real', 'ultimate', 'universal' *measurer* of value.[18] Yet, recall the previous discussion of Aristotle on value and commensurability in Chapter 1. For Aristotle, and for a follower of Aristotle: if labor is the essential measurer of exchange value, then in some sense labor must be exchange value; and exchange value must be labor.

4.2   READING ADAM SMITH ON VALUE

Readers have often felt a certain disconnect between what seems to be Smith's theory of value, and his theory of the determination of relative prices. For example, Spiegel has written that 'Smith's labor theory of value becomes transformed into a cost-of-production theory. There is a great deal of ambivalence in all this' (1991: 250). Marx, perceptive and harsh as usual, concluded in *Theories of Surplus Value*, 'Adam's twistings and turnings, his contradictions and wanderings from the point, prove that, once he had made wages, profit and rent the constituent component parts of exchangeable value or of the total price of the product, he had got himself stuck in the mud and had to get stuck' (Part I: 103). Galbraith, though less harsh and characteristically more charitable than Marx, reaches essentially the same conclusion. By Galbraith's reading, Smith asserted 'a version of what was long to be known as the Labor Theory of Value . . . The ambiguity in which Smith finally left the question of what determines price has been endlessly debated by scholars. It is an entertainment that need not trouble us. The simple fact is that Smith himself did not decide' (1987: 66).[19]

This is not to say that Smith even consistently held to some sort of labor theory of exchange value. As noted above, his statement that the laboring cattle of a farmer should also be viewed as productive laborers is bizarre when considered in the context of the main themes of his work.[20]

---

[18] Although, even here, I must admit, Smith is not 100 percent consistent. At one point he writes that 'Woolen or linen cloth are not the regulating commodities by which the real value of all other commodities must be finally measured and determined. Corn is' (IV.v.a.23). This train of thought leads directly to Ricardo's corn theory of profit (see Sraffa's interpretation, 'Introduction', Ricardo's *Works and Correspondence*, I, xxxi–xxxii); and, as will be argued in Part III, to Marx's theory that the value of labor power is determined by what it takes to reproduce workers.

[19] For an early mathematical interpretation that Smith's theory of relative prices was theoretically indeterminate, see the late 19th century Russian mathematical economist Dmitriev (1974 [1898], Essay I).

[20] See also Alexander Gray on Smith: 'In admitting the greater productivity of agriculture, Adam Smith accepts the essence of Physiocracy. As Mr. Gonnard has well put it, Smith, in protesting against the word, accepts the idea' (1931: 136–7).

On the other hand, in recent years there has been a tendency to deny that Smith had *any* theory of value at all. The embodied labor theory of value is relegated to the irrelevant pre-capitalist era,[21] the labor disutility theory is ignored[22] and the labor-commanded theory of value is viewed as merely a means to measure value. So, for example, O'Donnell, arguing from a Sraffian perspective, claims that Smith did not confuse a labor-commanded versus a labor-embodied measure of value. However, 'In explaining changes in value brought about by changes in methods of production Smith frequently related the change in value to the change in the quantity of *labour* used in production' (1990: 112, emphasis in original). Thus, in O'Donnell's reading, Smith *seems* to have a labor-embodied theory even though he does not. Hueckel (2000a) harshly criticizes O'Donnell for supposedly promoting yet another Sraffian-inspired rationally reconstructed 'legend'. Nonetheless, Hueckel basically agrees with O'Donnell that Smith's 'labour-commanded expression' is a 'unit of measure and no more – as the markings on a thermometer expressing the "heat" of exchange value' (2000a: 483).[23] Hueckel also claims that 'it is now widely agreed' that Smith understood the difference between a measure and a regulator of value (2000b: 318), and Smith basically uses labor command as a price index. Hueckel finds that

> there is indeed in Smith's measure a 'beauty of . . . systematical arrangement' that is breathtaking in its compass, if we can but grasp the 'connecting chain' that gives it form. If the synthesis proposed here can withstand scrutiny, perhaps future students will not feel impelled to . . . flee the beauty of Smith's thought 'to something more agreeable because more easy'. (2000b: 343)[24]

I do not want to here get into a discussion of what Smith did or did not 'understand'.[25] I will simply make two points. First, from the strong rhetoric Smith uses, that only labor is the 'real', 'ultimate', 'universal', 'accurate' measure of exchange value, it does not appear as if Smith is merely using labor as 'a choice to employ the wage as deflator, expressing

---

[21]   However, for a recent careful study contesting this trend in Smithology, and arguing that Smith did indeed have a 'rudimentary' labor theory of value applicable even in a commercial society, particularly useful to measure changes in exchangeable values, see Peach (2009b).

[22]   Smith himself tended to do this in most of his text.

[23]   On the ambiguities as to the uses of Smith's 'real measure of exchange value' see Peach (2009a).

[24]   Here is just another case of a contemporary economist who is overly sympathetic to the magnificence of Smith's work; and overindulging in the inconsistencies in Smith's thought. On this large problem see Rashid (1998).

[25]   On the difficulty of knowing an author's intention in general, and Smith's in particular, see Brown (1994).

value magnitudes in labor units' (ibid.: 319).[26] Second, and more important, from an Aristotelian perspective, if Smith is so adamant that only
labor is the real measure of exchange value, then that must mean that
for Smith, in some sense, labor must be exchange value. It would seem
that Smith must have had or been groping towards some kind of labor
theory of exchange value. Labor is what makes all goods commensurable
in terms of value. Certainly a reader such as Marx, who intimately knew
his Aristotle, would be inclined to read Smith that way (as will be shown
below in Part III). Yet it would not only be someone such as Marx who
would be tempted towards this sort of reading. For, as Theodor Gomperz
has written:

> Even those who have no acquaintance with the doctrines and writings of the
> great masters of antiquity, and who have not even heard the names of Plato
> and Aristotle are, nevertheless, under the spell of their authority. It is not only
> that their influence is often transmitted to us by their followers, ancient and
> modern: our whole mode of thinking, the categories in which our ideas move,
> the forms of language in which we express them, and which therefore govern
> our ideas, – all these are to no small extent the products of art, in large measure
> the art of the great thinkers of antiquity. A thorough comprehension of these
> origins is indispensable if we are to escape from the overpowering despotism of
> their influence. (1896: pp. 528–9; quoted in Lowry, 1987: 5)

Also, as Lowry has pointed out, 'Most of the formally educated
nineteenth-century economists made explicit their interest in and recognition of the perspectives inherited from the Greeks' (1987: xiv). So, at either
the conscious or unconscious level, most of Smith's nineteenth century
readers would have been tempted to give an Aristotelian reading to Smith's
work. Any reader who somewhere in the crevasses of his or her brain knew
or felt their Aristotle, upon reading in Smith so clearly that labor is the
absolutely correct measure of value, would no doubt be tempted to think
that Smith had some sort of labor theory of exchange value.[27]

Hence, the recent commentator who is most discerning concerning
Smith's value theory is perhaps Murray Rothbard. Viewing Smith from
a self-consciously Austrian perspective, Rothbard argues that 'Adam
Smith's doctrine on value was an unmitigated disaster' (1995: 448).
Rothbard claims that 'It was, indeed, Adam Smith who was almost
solely responsible for the injection into economics of the labour theory of
value' (453). 'Adam Smith, in addition, muddied the waters still further
by putting forward, side by side with the labour-cost theory of value, the

---

[26] Indeed, how can we 'choose' what is real, ultimate, accurate and universal?
[27] On the influence of Greek thought in Victorian Britain see Turner (1981).

very different "labour-command" theory' (454). 'Modern writers have tried to salvage the unsalvageable labour theory of value of Adam Smith by asserting that, in a sense he did not really mean what he was saying but was instead seeking to find an invariable standard with which he could measure value and wealth over time' (456). Smith turned to 'the erroneous and pernicious labour theory of value' (457).[28]

I think in many ways Rothbard is absolutely correct.[29] Certainly any reader who knew their Aristotle on value and commensurability, at a conscious or unconscious level, would be sorely tempted to conclude that Smith indeed had, or was muddling towards, some kind of a labor theory of exchange value. From an Aristotelian perspective, if labor is the true measure of exchange value, then in some sense labor is exchange value; and exchange value is labor. Thus, if one wants to be able to measure, count, or tally value, then it would seem from an Aristotelian reading of Smith that one would need some kind of a labor theory of exchange value.

---

[28] Rothbard felt that the labor theory of value was pernicious since 'Smith's labour theory of value did inspire a number of English socialists before Marx, generally named "Ricardian" but actually "Smithian" socialists, who decided that if labour produced the whole product, and rent and profit are deductions from labour's produce, then the entire value of the product should rightfully go to its creators, the labourers' (p. 456). That Marx read Smith as saying that workers are the source of surplus value and property income see Engels (1967: 8–10).

[29] For my full views on Rothbard's interpretation of Smith, see Pack (1998).

5. Adam Smith on money and capital

5.1 THE USE OF MONEY (OR VALUE) TO PRODUCE (OR ACQUIRE) MORE MONEY (OR REVENUE)

It was pointed out in the last chapter that for Smith, following Aristotle, money developed out of the exchange of products. The precious metals gold and silver over time became money. People appreciated these metals for their utility, beauty and scarcity.[1] Moreover, they were durable, and could be divided and re-united easily. The metals were originally used in rude bars without stamp or coinage. At this time, they had to be weighed and assayed as to their quality. Over time, the metals were stamped, attesting to their goodness or fitness. This was done by governments. Finally, coinage arose, where the government attested to both the fineness and the weight of the metal (I.iv.3–9).

Thus, Smith generally assumes that money is a produced commodity. Therefore the value of money (or the general price level) will be determined in some sense by what it costs to produce the money commodity. Sometimes, as discussed earlier, Smith reduces this to labor: 'Labour, it must be remembered, is the ultimate price which is paid for everything' (I.xi.e.34). In any event, the value of money itself should really be measured by labor: 'Labour, it must always be remembered, and not any particular commodity or set of commodities, is the real measure of the value both of *silver* and of all other commodities' (I.xi.e.26, emphasis added). The value of money, gold and silver, is high, and gold and silver tend to be scarce. But they are scarce because they are in some sense difficult or hard or expensive to produce. The line of causation for Smith is not, as with neoclassical economic theory, from scarcity to high value. Rather, it is from difficult to produce to high value to scarcity:

> They [gold projectors] did not consider that the value of those metals has, in all ages and nations, arisen chiefly from their scarcity, and that their scarcity

---

[1] 'These qualities of utility, beauty and scarcity, are the original foundation of the high price of those metals . . . This value was antecedent to and independent of their being employed as coin, and was the quality which fitted them for that employment' (I.xi.c.31).

has arisen from the very small quantities of them which nature has any where deposited in one place, from the hard and intractable substances with which she has almost every where surrounded those small quantities, and consequently from the *labour and expense* which are every where necessary in order to penetrate to and get at them. (IV.vii.a.19, emphasis added)

In practice, money itself becomes both a means of exchange and a measure of value. That is, although Smith asserts that labor is or ought to be the real measure of value, in practice we do measure the value of a product by its price in money: how much it sells for.[2] This leads to confusions. People are led to believe that the wealth of a country consists in money, in gold and silver, rather than in what is actually produced in the country – either by labor, or by labor and the land.[3]

That wealth consists in money, or in gold and silver, is a popular notion which naturally arises from the double function of money, as the instrument of commerce, and as the measure of value. In consequence of its being the instrument of commerce, when we have money we can more readily obtain whatever else we have occasion for, than by means of any other commodity. The great affair, we always find, is to get money. When that is obtained, there is no difficulty in making any subsequent purchase. In consequence of its being the measure of value, we estimate that of all other commodities by the quantity of money which they will exchange for. (IV.i.1)

So there is an asymmetry between money and all other products. It is easier to buy a product with money than it is to 'purchase' money with another product.[4] Thus, as a means of instrument, or universal equivalent, 'money is the known and established instrument of commerce, for which everything is readily given in exchange but is not always with equal readiness to be got in exchange for every thing' (IV.i.18).

Hence, as with Aristotle, money can be used to circulate goods, and 'the great wheel of circulation [i.e. money] is altogether different from the goods which are circulated by means of it' (II.ii.14). On the one hand, Smith can boldly assert that 'the sole use of money is to circulate

---

[2] Recall above in Chapter 1, that Aristotle also considered the idea that money itself makes goods commensurable since all goods are indeed sold for money; Smith insists that beneath this appearance the real measure of value is labor.

[3] As usual, Smith is not clear on this issue. Compare the first sentence of the treatise 'The annual labour of every nation is the fund which originally supplies it with all the necessaries and conveniences of life which it annually consumes' (I.1, in 'Introduction and Plan of the Work') to for example, 'The real wealth of the country, the annual produce of *its land* and labour' (I.xi.n.9, emphasis added). Smith's writing style is such that each particular *sentence* is clear; the entire analysis is frequently anything but clear.

[4] Keynes would later emphasize this aspect of money, calling the demand for money a preference for liquidity.

consumable goods' (II.iii.23). On the other hand, still following Aristotle, for Smith, money can also be used with the goal of acquiring more money.[5] Unlike Aristotle, Smith calls products used to acquire more money, not chrematistics, but capital. Money may be used as capital: 'Money, no doubt, makes always a part of the national capital' (IV.i.17); and 'Money, therefore, the great wheel of circulation, the great instrument of commerce, like all other instruments of trade, though it makes a part and a very valuable part of the capital' (II.ii.23).

Now we should back up a bit and take a closer look at what Smith calls capital. For Smith, capital is a subset of a person's 'stock'. Part of a person's stock is set aside to be consumed. But another part of it will be used to generate 'revenue' or income. Smith: 'His whole stock, therefore, is distinguished in two parts. That part which he expects, is to afford him this revenue, is called his *capital*. The other is that which supplies his immediate consumption' (II.i.2, emphasis added). And, 'whatever part of his stock a man employs as a capital, he always expects it to be replaced with a profit' (II.iii.6). So, as with Aristotle, a part of a person's property can be used to generate an income.[6] This capital, for Smith, is used, basically by definition, to support and employ 'productive labour'. That is, capital 'must have been employed, as all capitals are, in maintaining productive labour' (V.iii.47).[7]

It seems that there is always a certain amount of controversy in economic theory as to whether capital is merely physical goods (a stock of capital), or also money. For Smith, capital can be money. Indeed, capital, in the form of money wages, is spent to hire productive workers: 'almost the whole capital of every country is annually distributed among the inferior ranks of people, as the wages of productive labour' (V.ii.k.43). Workers need a certain stock of goods which can support them while they make and sell products. This stock of goods can be supplied by themselves or by another.[8] When it is supplied by another, it becomes capital:

---

[5]   Again, Smith was either unaware of, or he purposely glossed over, this differentiation in the uses of money.

[6]   'In all countries where there is tolerable security, every man of common understanding will endeavour to employ whatever stock he can command in procuring either present enjoyment or future profit' (II.i.30).

[7]   On confusions in Smith concerning productive versus unproductive labor, see, for example, Dobb (1973: 59–61) or Schumpeter (1954: 192n; 628–31).

[8]   See Dobb: 'What Smith may well have derived from his French visit . . . is the notion of capital as involving an "advance" in time – in advance, that is, of production or at least of its completion: a notion which implicitly contained all the essentials of capital theory as subsequently developed, so far as this has treated the crux of the problem of capital and its investment as revolving on time. At any rate, the notion of capital as consisting essentially of wage-advances to labourers ran through classical Political Economy in England' (1973: 42).

> In all arts and manufactures the greater part of the workmen stand in need of a
> master to advance them the materials of their work, and their wages and main-
> tenance till it be completed. He *shares in the produce of their labour, or in the
> value which it adds to the materials upon which it is bestowed*; and in this share
> consists his profit. (I.viii.8, emphasis added)

Notice that in this formulation, the workers themselves (and not machinery or other physical equipment) are generating or producing the profits,
the produce, or the value of their produce which are then 'shared' with
their 'master'. In a sense then, the workers are creating value and surplus
value which is then appropriated by their master. As Smith says at another
point, 'The value which the workmen add to the materials, therefore,
resolves itself in this case into two parts, of which the one pays their wages,
the other the profits of their employer upon the whole stock of materials
and wages which he advanced' (I.vi.5). So in a controversial sense capital
generates the capitalist, who then lives off profits or surplus value created
by the workers. As will be seen in Part III, Marx will develop this potentially radical strain of thought which can be found in Smith's writings.[9]

If the workers are creating the stock, the capital, that capital itself is
nonetheless hiring or 'demanding' workers. For Smith, basically, it is
capital that employs the worker, not the other way around: 'Stock cul-
tivates land; stock employs labour' (V.ii.f.6). As the amount of capital
in society goes up, the demand for productive workers goes up, and the
wealth of nations increases. That is, for Smith, 'the number of its productive labourers, it is evident, can never be much increased, but in consequence of an increase of capital, or of the funds destined for maintaining
them' (II.iii.32). So here the increase in capital is the funds destined for
maintaining productive workers. And 'the increase in the quantity of
useful labour actually employed within any society, must depend altogether upon the increase of the capital which employs it' (IV.ix.36).

As will be seen below, Marx will fundamentally object to all of this.
Since for Marx the capital is created by the workers, it is as if dead labor
hires or consumes the living labor. The dead labor then sucks surplus
value created by the live labor, vampire-like. The capital hires the workers,
and the more capital there is in society, the more workers will be hired by

---

[9]   Schumpeter noted this connection. Marx's 'preconceptions about the nature of the
relations between capital and labor, in particular, he simply took from an ideology that was
already dominant in the radical literature of his time. If, however, we wish to trace them
further back, we can do so without difficulty. A very likely source is the *Wealth of Nations*.
A. Smith's ideas on the relative position of capital and labor were bound to appeal to him,
especially as they linked up with a definition of rent and profits – as "deductions from the
produce of labour" (Book I, ch. 8, "Of the Wages of Labour") – that is strongly suggestive of
an exploitation theory' (1954: 389).

capital. So it is as if the workers are ruled by their products; as indeed they largely are.

Yet, we are getting ahead of ourselves a bit, and anticipating how Marx will read and develop Smith's magnum opus. Now, I would like to turn back, to how Smith seems to be responding to Aristotle's strictures on the unnaturalness of using money to acquire more money.

5.2 SMITH'S INSISTENCE ON THE NATURALNESS OF USING MONEY TO ACQUIRE MORE MONEY

Actually, when people use their capital to hire workers to acquire a profit, Smith does not call these employers capitalists. Moreover, he does not call a society which is largely based upon using capital to produce profits a capitalist society; these are Marx's terms. Rather, Smith's choice of terminology centers upon trade. He tends to emphasize that people in his society are merchants, and that his society is a commercial or trading society:

> When the division of labour has been once thoroughly established, it is but a very small part of a man's wants which the produce of his own labour can supply. He supplies the far greater part of them by exchanging that surplus part of the produce of his own labour, which is over and above his own consumption, for such parts of the produce of other men's labour as he has occasion for. Every man thus lives by exchanging, or becomes in some measure a *merchant*, and the society itself grows to be what is properly a *commercial society*. (I.iv.1, emphasis added)

Of course, retail trade, trading with the goal of acquiring a profit,[10] using money in general with the goal of acquiring more money, and by implication an entire society based largely upon these activities and goals: these are exactly the activities and goals which Aristotle condemned! They corrupted people; Aristotle called them unnatural. Viewed in this light, Smith's answer to Aristotle is largely one of repetition, repetition, repetition: Smith insists that these activities, and this type of society, are quite natural.

Thus, we may read Smith as initially following and then responding to Aristotle.[11] Yet note: unlike Aristotle, Smith finds absolutely nothing

---

[10] Here, following Smith, I am eliding the distinction between trading because one has a surplus of one good and a deficit of another (which Aristotle approved of and considered natural) with trade with the goal of making a profit.

[11] That Smith of course knew of Aristotle's distinctive use of the concept of nature and the natural, see 'History of the Ancient Logics and Metaphysics' (1980: 126–7); also 'History of the Ancient Physics' (1980: 115).

wrong or improper about using a thing to acquire more of itself. In fact, here and elsewhere, or perhaps more accurately, here and everywhere, Smith persistently presents exchange value and developments arising from the exchange of objects as perfectly natural. Thus, as seen above, 'If among a nation of hunters, for example, it usually costs twice the labour to kill a beaver which it does to kill a deer, one beaver should *naturally* exchange for or be worth two deer' (I.vi.1, emphasis added).[12] At this point in his story Smith is assuming no accumulation of stock or capital and no rent. Here a simple labor theory of value apparently holds so that 'It is *natural* that which is usually the produce of two days or two hours labour, should be worth double of what is usually the produce of one day's or one hour's labour' (ibid., emphasis added). And 'If the one species of labour should be more severe than the other, some allowance will *naturally* be made for this superior hardship' (I.vi.2, emphasis added). And, in a key move, 'As soon as stock has accumulated in the hands of particular persons, some of them will *naturally* employ it setting to work industrious people, whom they will supply with materials and subsistence, in order to make a profit by the sale of their work' (I.vi.5, emphasis added). So, as opposed to Aristotle, for Smith wage labor, that is, working for someone else, is natural.

For Smith, 'There is in every society or neighbourhood an ordinary or average rate both of wages and profit in every different employment of labour and stock. This rate is *naturally* regulated' (I.vii.1, emphasis added). And in a one sentence paragraph, 'These ordinary or average rates may be called the *natural* rates of wages, profit, and rent, at the time and place in which they commonly prevail' (I.vii.3, emphasis added). And in the next one sentence paragraph,

> When the price of any commodity is neither more nor less than what is sufficient to pay the rent of the land, the wages of the labour, and the profits of the stock employed in raising, preparing, and bringing it to market, according to their *natural* rates, the commodity is then sold for what may be called its *natural* price. (I.vii.4, emphasis added)

In a sense we have here a dogmatic refutation of Aristotle by affirmation (or perhaps by definition) and repetition. It is as if Smith is in a debate with Aristotle, and his strategy is to win the debate by making the same point over and over and over again.

---

[12]   Actually, in a sense this passage is quite perplexing, since we now know from Smith's *Lectures on Jurisprudence* that Smith was well aware that normally people do not exchange their products in a hunting and gathering society. However, I think this well-known passage is quite rhetorically effective in promoting the idea that exchange is natural as opposed to unnatural – which was no doubt one of Smith's goals.

Thus, we read that market price 'may either be above, or below, or exactly the same with its *natural* price' (I.vii.7, emphasis added), and we find that 'the quantity of every commodity brought to market *naturally* suits itself to the effectual demand' (I.vii.12, emphasis added); thus, 'the *natural* price therefore, is, as it were, the central price, to which the prices of all commodities are continually gravitating' (I.vii.15, emphasis added).

Indeed, claims Smith, the whole commercial system of exchange is natural: 'The whole quantity of industry annually employed in order to bring any commodity to market *naturally* suits itself in this manner to the effectual demand. It *naturally* aims to bringing always that precise quantity thither which may be sufficient to supply and no more than supply, that demand' (I.vii.16., emphasis added). If we read Smith as responding to Aristotle, it is a monotonous, hypnotizing, yet soothing argument by repetition: 'The *natural* price itself varies with the *natural* rate of each of its component parts, of wages, profit, and rent' (I.vii.33, emphasis added). Smith endeavours to explain 'what are the circumstances which *naturally* determine the rate of profit' (I.vii.35, emphasis added).

The rate of profit itself is naturally determined: 'The increase of stock, which raises wages, tends to lower profit. When the stocks of many rich merchants are turned into the same trade, their mutual competition *naturally* tends to lower its profit' (I.ix.2, emphasis added).[13] As opposed to Aristotle, it is also perfectly natural to lend money for interest: 'The increase of those particular capitals from which the owners wish to derive a revenue, without being at the trouble of employing them themselves, *naturally* accompanies the general increase of capitals; or, in other words, as stock increases, the quantity of stock to be lent at interest grows gradually greater and greater' (II.iv.7, emphasis added). Or again, as opposed to Aristotle, when people lend out money, 'Part of that profit *naturally* belongs to the borrower, who runs the risk and takes the trouble of employing it; and part to the lender, who affords him the opportunity of making this profit' (I.vi.18, emphasis added).

Actually, the word natural is even in the title of the first book of *The Wealth of Nations*: 'Of the Causes of Improvement in the productive Powers of Labour, and of the Order according to which its Produce is *naturally* distributed among the different Ranks of the People' (emphasis added)). Indeed, the word nature is also in the title of the second book: 'On the *Nature*, Accumulation, and Employment of Stock' (emphasis added). In fact, if we go back and take a look at the full title of Smith's economic

---

[13]   I interpret this passage to mean the rate of profit; arguably, it is ambiguous whether Smith is referring to the rate or the mass of profit.

treatise, we see that the word nature is in that very title: *An Inquiry into the* Nature *and Causes of the Wealth of Nations* (emphasis added).

Truly, one could pick out quotes from Smith with the word nature or natural in it ad nauseam. Yet, that would be tedious, and I think the point has been adequately made. One can read Smith as responding to Aristotle's assertion that the use of money to acquire more money, and by implication a form of society based upon the use of money to make more money (what Smith termed a commercial society, what Aristotle called chrematistics) is unnatural. Smith's response is based largely on a numbing, repetitive denial of Aristotle's view that there is anything unnatural about the commercial system.

Of course, what Smith is doing is using the word 'natural' in a different way than Aristotle.[14] Smith usually uses the word natural to be normal or ordinary or necessary, or some variant thereof. So, for example, Smith writes that 'this equality in the whole of the advantages and disadvantages of the different employments of labour and stock, can take place only in the *ordinary* or what may be called the *natural* state of those employments' (I.x.b.44, emphasis added). Puro (1992), in his careful study of 'Uses of the Term "Natural" in Adam Smith's *Wealth of Nations*', found eight distinct uses of the term 'natural'; not one of those uses was the Aristotelian use to mean the best or excellent, or the goal or end of a thing.[15]

There are several other implications from Smith's repetitive, hypnotic, insistent, and for many soothing, calming, yes, convincing claim that the use of money to acquire more money, and the resulting commercial society based upon that use, is quite natural. Consider that the opposite to the natural is not merely the unnatural; it may also be the supernatural. Smith's insistence in *The Wealth of Nations* (as well as in *Theory of Moral*

---

[14] Temple-Smith emphasizes this discrepancy between Smith and Aristotle's use of the word nature to conclude that 'Smith's claim of correspondence between his and Aristotle's doctrine of moral virtue cannot be sustained' (2007: 43); this reading is, I believe, hyperbolic. It is true that Humean as Smith is, he emphasizes the importance of the passions and sentiments compared to Aristotle's emphasis on human reason. Yet, I think Smith in *The Theory of Moral Sentiments* is largely trying to systematize, organize, and unify Aristotle's work on ethics through the concepts of sympathy (or what we would now call empathy) and the impartial spectator. Recall that for Smith, 'Philosophy is the science of the connecting principles of nature . . . Philosophy, by representing the invisible chains which bind together all these disjointed objects, endeavours to introduce order into this chaos of jarring and discordant appearances, to allay this tumult of the imagination, and to restore it, when it surveys the great revolutions of the universe, to that tone of tranquility and composure, which is most suitable to its nature' ('History of Astronomy' 1980: 45). Smith's main criticism of Aristotle is that Aristotle was too disconnected, disjointed in the presentation of his works; hence, insufficiently 'philosophical'. See *Lectures on Rhetoric and Belles Lettres* (1983: 144–6).

[15] For a demonstration that Smith did not necessarily approve of what he called 'natural' or 'nature' see Pack (1995a). Also, that according to Smith the natural desire to better one's condition does not always better one's condition (or that of society), see Paganelli (2008).

Sentiments) that he was dealing with natural phenomena, would suggest to some readers that he was not dealing with supernatural phenomena. This would open up space for Smith to conduct an analysis relatively free from religious powers who would tend to be more concerned with supernatural (or 'revealed') issues. At a time when Smith's great friend David Hume could not obtain a university teaching position because he had offended the religious powers that be,[16] this may have been no small consideration.

Also note that the opposite to the natural may be the social. Smith's insistence that money being used to acquire more money, and the resulting commercial or capitalist society is natural, would suggest to many readers that commercial or capitalist society is not social. This implication particularly irked Karl Marx, who, for example, argued that:

> One thing, however, is clear: nature does not produce on the one hand owners of money or commodities, and on the other hand men possessing nothing but their own labour-power. This relation has no basis in natural history, nor does it have a social basis common to all periods of human history. It is clearly the result of a past historical development, the product of many economic revolutions, of the extinction of a whole series of older formations of social production. (*Capital*: 273)

As will be seen below, from a Marxist perspective, the language of the naturalness of commercial or capitalist society would tend to legitimize or normalize the status quo. It would inhibit efforts to transcend this level of socioeconomic development.

Finally, Smith's abandonment of Aristotle's use of the natural to mean the final or the best or the most perfect opens himself up to the Straussian (and ultimately Aristotelian) charge that Smith privileges mere existence over excellence. As Cropsey perceptively lamented, 'Is it at last true that *nature* prescribes no norm of existence except existence itself; or is there such a thing as excellence, standing as a norm by which existence itself may be judged and qualified?' (1957: 99, emphasis in original). Smith's emphasis that the natural is the normal would suggest to some readers that he was insufficiently concerned with the promotion of the excellent, the best.

---

[16] Hume's argument (1955 [1748]) that people could believe in miracles, but it was a bit of a miracle that they do, did not win him many friends in orthodox religious circles. Also, the first year Smith attended Glasgow College as a student, Smith's great teacher, 'the never-to-be-forgotten Hutcheson', was prosecuted by 'the local Presbytery' for his theological teachings (Rae, 1965 [1895]: 11–13).

6.   Adam Smith on character

6.1   FOLLOWING ARISTOTLE ON CHARACTER

Smith largely follows Aristotle on the importance and the development of character.[1] For example, with regards to virtue, Smith agrees with Aristotle that virtue is excellence (*Theory of Moral Sentiments* (*TMS*): 25). Also, for Smith as for Aristotle, it is important to hit the mean to be virtuous (for example, *TMS*: 27); for both, virtuous actions are a sort of mean between two opposite vices, one of excess, one of defect (for example, *TMS*: 270–72). In his lecture course on *Rhetoric and Belles Lettres*, Smith, sounding much like Aristotle, counsels that 'it is chiefly the character and disposition of a man that gives rise to his particular conduct and behaviour' (p. 78). For Smith, as for Aristotle, character is largely a function of upbringing. Thus, for example, Smith claims that people who:

> have had the misfortune to be brought up amidst violence, licentiousness, falsehood, and injustice; lose, though not all sense of the impropriety of such conduct, yet all sense of its dreadful enormity . . . They have been familiarized with it from their infancy, custom has rendered it habitual to them, and they are very apt to regard it as, what is called, the way of the world, something which either may, or must be practiced, to hinder us from being the dupes of our own integrity. (*TMS*: 200–201)

As with Aristotle, habits and experience will have a large effect upon the development of a person's character. Thus, 'the objects with which men in the different professions and states of life are conversant, being very different, and habituating them to very different passions, naturally form in them very different characters and manners. We expect in each rank and profession, a degree of those manners, which, experience has taught us, belong to it' (*TMS*: 201). Character, as with Aristotle, while formed by habit, over time becomes a sort of second nature. Thus:

> a man born to a great fortune . . . The situation of such a person naturally disposes him to attend rather to ornament which pleases his fancy, than to profit for which he has so little occasion. The elegance of his dress, of his equipage,

---

[1]   See, for example, Calkins and Werhane (1998); also Hanley (2006).

of his house, and household furniture, are objects which from his infancy he has been accustomed to have some anxiety about. The turn of mind which this habit naturally forms . . . (III.ii.7)

Thus, a person born rich will, in a sense, naturally have a certain type of character. This character may be called natural, but, of course, it is also social, or is largely socially determined. The division of labor itself will also lead to different characters, due to differing habits, experiences and educations. Thus, 'the difference of natural talents in different men is, in reality, much less than we are aware of; and the very different genius which appears to distinguish men of different professions, when grown up to maturity, is not upon many occasions so much the cause, as the effect of the division of labour' (I.ii.4).

Also, as with Aristotle, people of use or utility to each other will tend to form a kind of friendship. Therefore,

Colleagues in office, partners in trade, call one another brothers; and frequently feel towards one another as if they were really so. Their good agreement is an advantage to all; and, if they are tolerably reasonable people, they are naturally disposed to agree. We expect that they should do so; and their disagreement is a sort of small scandal. (*TMS*: 224)

So, in all these positions, Smith seems to be largely following, or simply be largely in agreement, with Aristotle.[2] However, where Smith parts in striking fashion from Aristotle is in his view of the type of characters formed by commercial or chrematistic society. In sharp contradistinction to Aristotle, Smith generally admired them!

6.2 SMITH'S FAVORABLE ATTITUDES TOWARDS CHARACTERS FORMED IN COMMERCIAL SOCIETY

By Schumpeter's reading of Smith's character, Smith was quite at home and in synchronization with the spirit of his times:

And it was Adam Smith's good fortune that he was thoroughly in sympathy with the humors of his time. He advocated the things that were in the offing,

---

[2] Some key differences between Smith and Aristotle on character development would include differing relative weights to the role of emulation (more for Smith), reason (probably less for Smith, although this is a complicated issue), imagination (more for Smith) and empathy (or what Smith calls sympathy and is one of the key unifying concepts of his theoretical system of morals).

and he made his analysis serve them. Needless to insist on what this meant both for the performance and success: where would the *Wealth of Nations* be without free trade and laissez-faire? Also, the 'unfeeling' or 'slothful' landlords who reap where they have not sown, the employers whose every meeting issues in conspiracy, the merchants who enjoy themselves and let their clerks and accountants do the work, and the poor laborers who support the rest of society in luxury – these are all important parts of the show. It has been held that A. Smith, far ahead of his time, braved unpopularity by giving expression to his social sympathies. This is not so. (1954: 185–6)

I think Schumpeter is quite right on this score. Indeed, the impression given by the various biographers of Smith,[3] and in his *Correspondence*, is that Smith was someone who was relatively quite at ease in his commercial society; indeed, he generally appreciated it. This, of course, showed up in his writings. On the good side of commercial, manufacturing countries, Smith held that:

> Third, and lastly, commerce and manufactures gradually introduced order and good government, and with them, the liberty and security of individuals, among the inhabitants of the country, who had before lived almost in a continual state of war with their neighbours, and of servile dependence upon their superiors. This although it has been the least observed, is by far the most important of all their effects. Mr. Hume is the only writer who, so far as I know, has hitherto taken notice of it. (III.iv.12)

Commerce and manufactures, the capitalist/wage laborer relation, is what Smith approves of and thinks is beneficial for society. It generally encourages both the employer and the employee to work hard. In a commercial society, the way to obtain wealth is not by seizing the wealth of neighbors, but by working, or creating, or producing wealth. To paraphrase a popular saying from another era, Smith felt that people should make money, not war.[4] This also points to another major difference between Smith and Aristotle. For Aristotle, there are various ways to *acquire* things: hunting, farming, commerce, and so on. For Smith, things (or wealth) are *created* or *produced* by laborers, particularly when they are in the capitalist/wage laborer relation. To take another example:

> The proportion between those different funds [i.e. for servants/unproductive workers or productive workers] determines in every country the general

---

[3]   Probably most important Rae (1965 [1895]); but see also Stewart ('Account of Adam Smith' in Smith 1980: 269–351), Scott (1965), and most recently, the thorough Ross (1995).

[4]   I mean money, of course, in the sense of representing value or wealth (the two being generally conflated in Smith); not in the literal sense of printing or minting money.

character of the inhabitants as to industry or idleness. We are much more industrious than our forefathers; because in the present times the funds destined for the maintenance of industry, are much greater in proportion to those which are likely to be employed in the maintenance of idleness, than they were two or three centuries ago. Our ancestors were idled for want of a sufficient encouragement to industry. (II.iii.12)

So, according to Smith, merchant and manufacturing towns will tend to be industrious, sober and thriving. In court towns, the inferior ranks of people will generally be idle, dissolute and poor. 'The proportion between capital and revenue, therefore, seems every where to regulate the proportion between industry and idleness. Wherever capital predominates industry prevails; wherever revenue, idleness' (II.iii.13). So, the goal of using property to create or accumulate more property makes people industrious, hard-working, and productive of wealth. This is generally true of the employer as well as the laborer. Workers will particularly work hard in an advancing commercial society where high pay 'increases the industry of the common people. The wages of labour are the encouragement of industry, which, like every other human quality, improves in proportion to the encouragement it receives' (I.viii.44).

In general then, for Smith a commercial society is good. With properly structured social institutions and policies, it will produce industrious, hard-working people.[5] So, how did the policy of Europe contribute,

> to the present grandeur of the colonies of America? In one way, and in one way only . . . It bred and formed the men who were capable of achieving such great actions, and of laying the foundation of so great an empire; and there is no other quarter of the world of which the policy is capable of forming, or has ever actually and in fact formed such men. The colonies owe to the policy of Europe the education and great views of their active and enterprising founders; and some of the greatest and most important of them, so far as concerns their internal government, owe to it scarce anything else. (IV.vii.b.64)

So a commercial society can form great, enterprising men.[6] Moreover, as Eric Schliesser has convincingly argued, Smith felt that philosophers themselves could thrive in a commercial society. Professional thinkers (or

---

[5] See Mark Blaug: 'So frequently accused of *Harmonielehre*, the vulgar doctrines of the spontaneous harmony of interests, Smith instead seems to be forever emphasizing that the powerful motive of self-interest is only enlisted in the cause of the general welfare under definite institutional arrangements' (1978: 63, emphasis in original). This includes the protection of property rights, and the prohibition of such things as slavery and polygamous marriages.

[6] Note the casual sexism here; no mention of great women! On Smith's problematic relationship to 18th century feminist concerns, see for example Kay (1986) and Kuiper (2006); to women in general, see Justman (1993).

'men of letters') such as David Hume (and by implication himself) could 'enjoy the rewards of friendship in this life and immortality after their death if they were benefactors to humanity' (Schliesser, 2003: 328).[7]

In particular, according to Smith, small property owners would develop the characters and abilities to help develop a prosperous, growing society. For example, in discussing small landowners, Smith writes, 'A small proprietor, however, who knows every part of his little territory, who views it with all the affection which property, especially small property, naturally inspires, and who upon that account takes pleasure not only in cultivating but in adorning it, is generally of all improvers the most industrious, the most intelligent and the most successful' (III.iv.19). So, in general Smith can be viewed to be pro small businessmen: these people will tend to be alert, attentive and hard-working as they studiously watch over their relatively small properties.

Moreover, as was noted in the previous section, the division of labor itself makes for different characters and that in itself is good. People need each other's expertise. As Smith remarks about our canine friends, 'Nobody ever saw a dog make a fair and deliberate exchange of one bone for another with another dog. Nobody ever saw one animal by its gestures and natural cries signify to another, this is mine, that yours; I am willing to give this for that' (I.ii.2). Yet, the division of labor in humans creates different characters: 'without the disposition to truck, barter, and exchange, every man must have procured to himself every necessary and conveniency of life which he wanted. All must have had the same duties to perform, and the same work to do, and there could have been no such difference of employment as could alone give occasion to any great difference of talents' (I.ii.4). So the division of labor not only increases productivity and eventually gives us a variety of products; it also gives us a variety of characters. By Smith's modest reckoning, 'The difference between the most dissimilar characters, between a philosopher and a common street porter, for example, seems to arise not so much from nature, as from habit, custom and education' (ibid.).[8]

Note two things about this famous quote: one is the radical

---

[7]   This article contains a close reading of Smith's 'Letter from Adam Smith, LL.D. to William Strahan, Esq' which was carefully crafted to be published with Hume's autobiography 'My Own Life'. The letters exchanged between Hume, Smith, Alexander Wedderburn, William Strahan and others over what to do concerning Hume's posthumous public reputation gives fascinating evidence of what may be conceived to be Smith's prudence; or his slipperiness. That philosophers can thrive in commercial societies, see also Schliesser (2006b).

[8]   Given Smith's relatively modest background, the fact that his father died before he was born, and that he was a single child raised by a single mother, I suspect that Smith may have indeed been thinking about himself.

egalitarianism of Smith.[9] As far as nature goes, people are pretty much alike: no doubt much more so than in Aristotle's view.[10] On the other hand, for Smith, the things which ultimately form and determine the contrasting characters of philosophers and street porters are actually the same things stressed by Aristotle: habit, custom and education.

6.3   NONETHELESS: PROBLEMS WITH THE CAPITALISTS/MERCHANTS/MASTERS AND THEIR MANAGERS

Yet, while Smith often painted a positive side to the characters formed in commercial society, there was also a deep pessimism or unease in Smith about the major character-types found therein.[11] For Smith, there will arise three separate 'orders' or classes of people: landlords, workers and capitalists.[12]

> The whole annual produce of the land and labour of every country, or what comes to the same thing, the whole price of that annual produce, naturally divides itself, it has already been observed, into three parts; the rent of land, the wages of labour, and the profits of stock; and constitutes a revenue to three different orders of people; to those who live by rent, to those who live by wages, and to those who live by profit. These are the great, original and constituent orders of every civilized society, from whose revenue that of every other order is ultimately derived. (I.xi.p.7)

There will be issues or problems with each of these broad character-types; let us first turn to the capitalists/merchants/masters.

---

[9]   Schumpeter, astutely, picks up on this side of Smith: 'A judiciously diluted Rousseauism is also evident in the equalitarian tendency of his economic sociology' (1954: 186). On the relationship between Rousseau and Smith see Pack (2000); Dawson (1991–92); Schliesser (2006b); also Force (2003). For the first book-length analysis of the relations between Rousseau and Smith, heavily weighted to Smith's answers to Rousseau's critique of commercial society, see Rasmussen (2008).

[10]   Aristotle, of course, developed a theoretical argument in defense of slavery: some people were so naturally inferior to others that they deserved and needed to be the slaves to other superior humans. At the same time, Aristotle was no doubt well aware that most slaves were not 'natural' slaves; they were merely the unfortunate survivors of the losing side of a war. That there are, of course, alternative interpretations of Aristotle on human nature and choice stressing different aspects of Aristotle's work, see Duhs (2008).

[11]   I go into more detail on this issue in my book on Smith (Pack, 1991, Chapter 8: 138–65), which I call the downside of Smith's system of capitalism.

[12]   In today's 21st century corporate managerial system, would it make more sense to separate the orders or classes into rentiers, managers and workers (see, for example, Galbraith's last book *The Economics of Innocent Fraud*, Chapter 2, 'The Renaming of the System', 2004: 3–9)? More on this below in Part IV.

6.3.1   General Problems

The main problem with this rank or class is that in pursuit of their economic self-interest they lie, dissimulate and mislead the public:

> Merchants and master manufacturers are . . . the two classes of people who commonly employ the largest capitals, and who by their wealth draw to themselves the greatest share of the public consideration. As during their whole lives they are engaged in plans and projects, they have frequently more acuteness of understanding than the greater part of country gentlemen. As their thoughts, however, are commonly exercised rather about the interest of their own particular branch of business, than about that of the society, *their judgment, even when given with the greatest candour (which it has not been upon every occasion)* is much more to be depended upon with regard to the former of these two objects, than with regard to the latter. Their superiority over the country gentleman is, not so much in their knowledge of the public interest, as in their having a better knowledge of their own interest than he has of his. It is by this superior knowledge of their own interest that they have frequently imposed upon his generosity, and persuaded him to give up both his own interest and that of the public, from a very simple but honest conviction, that their interest, and not his, was the interest of the public. (I.xi.p.10, emphasis added)

So, these clever, astute, hard-working big businessmen have an unfortunate tendency to dupe the other sectors of society. In our current age where, for example, the fossil fuel industry appears to support bogus scientists and set up bogus research institutes to convince us that human 'consumption' of their products is not causing global climate change; or when firms hire the most brilliant psychologists to convince us to purchase their products which may be detrimental to our health – this would seem to be a remarkably prescient, pertinent and relevant point made by Smith.[13]

It is often forgotten, I think, that the system Smith railed against, mercantilism, was designed by and for the merchants. Moreover, it was a system Smith named himself, against his theoretical opponents, the spokespeople for this merchant class.[14] According to Smith,

> of the greater part of the regulations concerning the colony trade, the merchants who carry it on, it must be observed, have been the principal advisers. We must not wonder, therefore, if, in the greater part of them, their interest

---

[13]   More on this below in Part IV.

[14]   Now here is an interesting rhetorical strategy employed by Smith. He holds that we are all now traders, and to some extent merchants, and we live in a commercial society which is basically good as well as natural. Yet, the theoretical system thought up by the merchants is not called, for example, commercialism. Rather, it is called mercantilism, and is bad. So, commercial society is good; yet mercantilism is bad. I wonder if Smith's reputation and success would have been different if he labeled his opponents commercialists.

has been more considered than either that of the colonies or that of the mother country. (IV.vii.b.49)

The strategy employed by the merchants was largely one of promoting monopolistic practices, so they could reduce output and increase their prices and profits: 'That it was the spirit of monopoly which originally both invented and propagated this doctrine, cannot be doubted, and they who first taught it were by no means such fools as they who believed it' (IV.iii.c.10).[15] For Smith, 'the traders of both countries [France and Great Britain] have announced, with all the passionate confidence of interested falsehood, the certain ruin of each, in consequence of that unfavourable balance of trade, which, they pretend, would be the infallible effect of an unrestrained commerce with the other' (IV.iii.c.13).

So merchants and manufacturers[16] pretend, they exude passionate confidence in their self-serving falsehoods. They are also big complainers about anything which may affect their profits, but become quite quiet concerning their own gains:

> Our merchants and master-manufacturers complain much of the bad effects of high wages in raising the price, and thereby lessening the sale of their goods both at home and abroad. They say nothing concerning the bad effects of high profits. They are silent with regard to the pernicious effects of their own gain. They complain only of those of other people. (I.ix.24)

And again, hundreds of pages later, Smith makes basically the same point:

> Our merchants frequently complain of the high wages of British labour as the cause of their manufactures being undersold in foreign markets; but they are silent about the high profits of stock. They complain of the extravagant gain of other people; but they say nothing of their own. (IV.vii.c.29)

This leads to another problem for Smith concerning the character of this class: it is important that profit rates not be too high. High profit rates wreck their character; and through their poor example, that of the whole country:

> The high rate of profit seems every where to destroy that parsimony which in other circumstances is natural to the character of the merchant. When profits are high, that sober virtue seems to be superfluous, and expensive luxury to suit

---

[15] Later, in that same paragraph, Smith argues that 'the interested sophistry of merchants and manufacturers' had 'confounded the common sense of mankind'.

[16] In the quote above, 'traders' is used by Smith to refer to both merchants and manufacturers.

better the affluence of his situation. But the owners of the great mercantile capitals are necessarily the leaders and conductors of the whole industry of every nation, and their example has a much greater influence upon the manners of the whole industrious part of it than that of any other order of men. If his employer is attentive and parsimonious, the workman is very likely to be so too; but if the master is dissolute and disorderly, the servant who shapes his work according to the pattern which his master prescribes to him, will shape his life too according to the example which he sets him. (IV.vii.c.61)

High profit rates lead to copious, profligate expenditures by the employing class; to their detriment, the employee class emulates this behavior.[17]

Smith has a huge problem with his merchants and manufacturers, and his dream, vision, or ideal of the potentialities of commerce and commercial society.[18] He wants to believe that 'Commerce, which ought naturally to be, among nations, as among individuals, a bond of union and friendship'. Here let us interrupt Smith to make two points. One, is this necessarily true; is commerce necessarily a bond of union and friendship? Or does it depend more on the nature of the commercial transactions? Does there not need to be more specificity, and perhaps cataloguing of the various types of commercial transactions? For example, I shudder when I recall the experiences I have personally had in the landlord/renter relationship: they were rarely ones of friendship (and I have experienced this relationship as both a tenant and a landlord). Or, to take another example, is the current world oil trade generating bonds of union and friendship? If so, these are indeed peculiar friendships.

Secondly, note that on this point Smith is to an extent indeed following Aristotle. Aristotle says that people who are of use to each other indeed do form a type of friendship. Moreover, trade amongst people is not something that Aristotle is against per se. Aristotle is against trade amongst people for profit: the professional merchant whose goal, whose aim, is to acquire more money. This is what is for Aristotle unnatural, and corrupting. Let us now give Smith his full position:

> Commerce, which ought naturally[19] to be, among nations, as among individuals, a bond of union and friendship has become the most fertile source of discord and animosity. The capricious ambition of kings and ministers has not, during the present and the preceding century, been more fatal to the repose of Europe, than the impertinent jealousy of merchants and manufacturers. The violence and injustice of the rulers of mankind is an ancient evil, for which, I

---

[17] For evidence that this seems to be happening in contemporary society see Bowles and Park (2005); Park (forthcoming).

[18] Dare we call this a contradiction? Or, would that confuse the issue?

[19] There is that ubiquitous word (or variant) again: naturally!

am afraid, the nature of human affairs can scarce admit of a remedy. But the mean rapacity, the monopolizing spirit of merchants and manufacturers, who neither are, nor ought to be the rulers of mankind, though it cannot perhaps be corrected, may very easily be prevented from disturbing the tranquility of any body but themselves. (IV.iii.c.9)

So, Smith feels that theoretically, commerce between nations should lead to international friendliness. Yet, in actuality, in practice, in the last century or two, international commerce had led to discord and animosity.[20] Moreover, Smith blames this on the impertinent jealousy, mean rapacity and monopolizing spirit of the merchants and manufacturers, who were acting in their narrow economic self-interest. Yet, is not this just the sort of scenario that Aristotle might predict from people whose goal is to make a profit, to use money to acquire more money? Corrupted by their goal, would not these people behave despicably? Moreover, note that Smith feels merchants and manufacturers are not and should not be the political rulers. Yet, in the 21st century, are not many commercial or capitalist or mercantile countries now being ruled by their businessmen; or their hired disreputable representatives? To the extent they are, then by Smith's own reckoning these countries are being ruled in the interest of the business class, most likely to the detriment of the general public interest.

6.3.2 Problems with the Pursuit of Money

As seen above in section 6.2, in general Smith, as opposed to Aristotle, does not *appear* to be too concerned that using money or capital to acquire more money makes people too greedy, or is in anyway in itself bad, corrupting, or unnatural. Indeed, in contradistinction to Aristotle, he repeatedly insists that it is quite natural. Nonetheless, as seen above in subsection 6.3.1, the master manufacturers and merchants do have a nasty tendency to lie and mislead the public in pursuit of their narrow own self-interest. Perhaps the problem for Smith is not so much the use of money or capital to acquire more value and wealth. Perhaps it is the pursuit of money itself that is the problem. After all, Smith's whole diatribe against the mercantilist system[21] can largely be reduced to the fact that the mercantilists tend to think that the wealth of nations consists in the physical money in a country, rather

---

[20] Also, due to disparities in power between the European and some non-European nations, international commerce had led to the outright plundering and domination of many non-European nations; not friendly.

[21] Smith officially spends hundreds of pages describing (or more accurately, to some extent creating) and critiquing the mercantilist system in Book IV, chapters one through eight. However, he is also critiquing it in various places all through *The Wealth of Nations*.

than what that country can produce. That is their theoretical mistake. Their economic policies that follow from that erroneous theory are to create a batch of rules and regulations designed to bring more money into the country and let less leave. So the money commodity itself does trick people. The desire for physical money, for gold and silver, can lead people to do crazy, extravagant things. So, for example, consider Columbus:

> In consequence of the representations of Columbus, the council of Castile determined to take possession of countries of which the inhabitants were plainly incapable of defending themselves. The pious purpose of converting them to Christianity sanctified the injustice of the project. But the hope of finding treasure of gold there, was the sole motive which prompted to undertake it; and to give this motive the greater weight it was proposed by Columbus that the half of all the gold and silver that should be found there belong to the crown. (IV.vii.a.15)

So the pursuit of the money commodities themselves, gold and silver, led to the occupation of these lands by a European power. Notice, according to Smith, this occupation was covered up by lies; in this case religious lies. Pretending to bring Christianity to the Native Americans, they merely plundered them. Focusing on the fiscal side of the issue, Smith writes, 'As long as the whole or the far greater part of the gold, which the first adventurers imported into Europe, was got by so very easy a method as the plundering of the defenceless natives, it was not perhaps difficult to pay even this heavy tax' (IV.vii.a.16).

So the adventurous search for gold and silver led to the plundering of the natives of Hispaniola. This, combined with the uneven distribution of power between Europe and these natives of the Western Hemisphere, led to their destruction. Smith continues, 'All the other enterprises of the Spaniards in the new world, subsequent to those of Columbus, seem to have been prompted by the same motive. It was the *sacred* thirst of gold' (IV.vii.a.17, emphasis added). Note how Smith imports religious terminology into his discourse, as if the search for gold had, or could have, religious connotations.[22] Smith concludes that:

> A project of commerce to the East Indies, therefore, gave occasion to the first discovery of the West. A project of conquest gave occasion to all the establishments of the Spaniards in those newly discovered countries. The motive which

---

[22] On the other hand, the worship of gold, of money, can be viewed as just another form of idolatry – arguably the most prevalent form of idolatry in contemporary society. If, as Marx would argue, the value of gold is merely embodied abstract human labor, then the worship of the value of gold is really the worship of abstract human labor: of what humans can make (and buy).

excited them to the conquest was a project of gold and silver mines. (IV.vii.b.21, emphasis added)

So the lure of gold and silver mines 'excites' people to do extravagant things; in this case it led to conquest. Other Europeans followed suit, with the same motives: 'The first adventurers of all the other nations of Europe, who attempted to make settlements in America, were animated by the same chimerical views; but they were not equally successful' (IV.vii.b.22).

So it was the lure of the money commodities, gold and silver, which prompted the Europeans to invade and occupy the Western Hemisphere. Let us briefly return to the fiscal side of this issue once again. By Smith's account, 'The crown of Spain, by its share of the gold and silver, derived some revenue from its colonies, from the moment of their first establishment. It was a revenue too, of a nature to excite in human avidity the most extravagant expectations of still greater riches' (IV.vii.b.7).

Thus, the form of revenue, that it came to Spain in the form of the money commodities themselves, gold and silver, created a craving, desire, greed for more gold and silver. This suggests, then, that for Smith the problem of greed, and the desire for more money, may not so much arise from the use of money or capital to acquire more wealth; rather it may arise from the mere existence of money itself.

Yet, there is another major problem with a basic character-type in a commercial society. This is the cheating managers hired by large commercial or capitalist enterprises.

6.3.3 Problems with the Managers

The basic problem with managers in a commercial or capitalist society is that they have an unfortunate tendency to become abusive, wasteful, fraudulent and to rob their owners. One of the few people to pick up on this side of Smith's work was John Kenneth Galbraith:

Considerably less influential has been Smith's warning as to the institution that, along with the state itself, might destroy competition. This was the state-chartered company – in modern terms, the corporation. Where it has monopoly privileges, as in the colonial era, he was especially critical. But he also thought little of its efficiency. Returning today, he would be appalled at a world where, as in the United States, a thousand corporations dominate the industrial, commercial and financial landscape and are controlled by their hired management, something Smith thought especially to be deplored. (1987: 71)[23]

---

[23] See also his *The Culture of Contentment* where he argues that 'Modern advocates of free enterprise would find Smith's attack on corporations deeply disconcerting' (1992: 99–100).

According to Smith, the English East India Company was run by managers and this would necessarily be wasteful: 'all the extraordinary waste which the fraud and abuse, inseparable from the management of the affairs of so great a company, must necessarily have occasioned' (IV. vii.c.91). Among other things, managers will have the tendency to wrack up exorbitant expenses:

> The directors of such companies, however, being the managers rather of other people's money than of their own, it cannot be be expected, that they should watch over it with the same anxious vigilance with which the partners in a private copartnery frequently watch over their own. Like the stewards of a rich man, they are apt to consider attention to small matters as not for their master's honour, and very easily give themselves a dispensation from having it. Negligence and profusion, therefore, must always prevail, more or less, in the management of the affairs of such a company. (V.i.e.18)

Or again, in discussing the South Sea Company, Smith wrote that 'they had an immense capital divided among an immense number of proprietors. It was naturally to be expected, therefore, that folly, negligence, and profusion should prevail in the whole management of their affairs' (V.i.e.22). And later he comments on the same company, 'the loss occasioned by the negligence, profusion, and malversation of the servants of the company' (V.i.e.25).[24] Later, returning to the English East India Company,[25] he comments that 'The great increase of their fortune had, it seems only served to furnish their servants with a pretext for greater profusion and a cover for greater malversation' (V.i.e.26).

Sometimes the managers will be supported in their crookedness and plundering of the corporation by the owners themselves:

> It might be more agreeable to the company that their servants and dependants should have either the pleasure of wasting, or the profit of embezzling whatever surplus might remain, after paying the proposed dividend of eight per cent. . . The interest of those servants and dependants might so far predominate in the court of proprietors, as sometimes to dispose it to support the authors of depredations which had been committed, in direct violation of its own authority. With the majority of proprietors, the support even of the authority of their own court might sometimes be a matter of less consequence, than the support of those who had set that authority at defiance. (V.i.e.27)

---

[24]   Smith uses basically the same terms in V.i.e.30: 'It is merely to enable the company to support the negligence, profusion, and malversation of their own servants'.

[25]   Or to be more precise, 'in 1708, they were, by act of Parliament perfectly consolidated into one company by their present name of The United Company of Merchants trading to the East Indies' (V.i.e.26).

This may be a major problem now with our 21st century system of corporate or managerial capitalism. As long as managers provide a minimum return,[26] they get to cream off much of the rest.[27]

6.4   CHARACTER OF LANDLORDS

There are also some major character flaws with the order or class of landlords, those who live by rent. We saw above (section 6.1) that according to Smith rich landlords are not accustomed to worrying their brains about how to successfully run a commercial or manufacturing enterprise (III. ii.7). These people are generally not good at investing for profit, which requires skills and habits which they tend not to develop.[28] They tend to be more concerned with how they and their property look than with their personal or proprietary productivity. Due to too easy living, these landlords often do not even know what public policies promote their own economic interests since:

> They are the only one of the three orders whose revenue costs them neither labour nor care, but comes to them, as it were, of its own accord, and independent of any plan or project of their own. That indolence, which is the natural effect of the ease and security of their situation, renders them too often, not only ignorant, but incapable of that application of mind which is necessary in order to forsee and understand the consequences of any publick regulation. (I.xi.p.8)

Thus, because of their indolence and intellectual slothfulness, they are easily tricked and misled by the more clever, cunning, merchants and manufacturers. This would seem to be another rather major problem with the types of character 'naturally' developed in commercial societies.

---

[26]   Or sometimes even a non-negative return; or at other times, as long as the company is not completely bankrupt; or even, apparently, not so very occasionally, when the corporation is technically bankrupt. In such circumstances, of course, the managers are generally helping themselves not just to the revenues of the firm but to its assets, or to money owed to its creditors.

[27]   I will go into this in more detail below in Part IV.

[28]   According to Smith, they generally cannot even successfully invest in their own land: 'To improve land with profit, like all other commercial projects, requires an exact attention to small savings and small gains, of which a man born to a great fortune, even though naturally frugal, is very seldom capable' (III.ii.7).

6.5   CHARACTER OF WORKERS

As is relatively well-known, for Smith there will also most likely be major character flaws with the workers.[29] These problems arise from the division of labor itself. What is most curious[30] is that Smith begins his book accentuating the positive side of increases in the division of labor in society: that it is the key to increasing worker productivity and hence increasing the wealth of nations. While Smith scatters references to the problems an extensive division of labor causes to the character of the workers throughout his work, the bulk of his discussion is buried deep in the text, where the casual (or perhaps weary) reader could overlook it.[31]

As with the landlords, the workers tend not to be able to know what is in their own economic interests. Here though, the problem is not because they lead too privileged and soft a life. Just the opposite: it is because they tend to work too long and hard. Thus, 'the labourer . . . is incapable either of comprehending that interest, or of understanding its connection with his own. His condition leaves him no time to receive the necessary information, and his education and habits are commonly such as to render him unfit to judge even though he was fully informed' (I.xi.p.9). Notice, once again, as with Aristotle, the importance of education and habits. Thus, according to Smith, when it comes to government policy, 'In the publick deliberations, therefore, his voice is little heard and less regarded, except upon some particular occasions, when his clamour is animated, set on, and supported by his employers, not for his, but their own particular purposes' (ibid.).

Note several points about this. One, clearly, Smith does not think too much of the character developed by the workers. Yet, also, as with the landlord class, the workers tend to be deceived and misled by the capitalists. The workers, when they get aroused, end up supporting the economic interests of their employers more than their own interests.

In any event, it is clear that Smith should not be considered a full-fledged democrat. For example, in commenting on the corn laws, and arguing that there should be free trade in foodstuffs, Smith makes an interesting comparison between food and religion:

---

[29]   I go into this in more detail in my book on Smith (Pack, 1991, Chapter 8). See also Heilbroner (1975) and Rosenberg (1990).

[30]   Or perhaps devious.

[31]   In Book V, 'Of the Revenue of the Sovereign or Commonwealth'; Chapter I, 'Of the Expenses of the Sovereign or Commonwealth'; Part III, 'Of the Expence of publick Works and publick Institutions'; Article Two, 'Of the Expence of the Institutions for the Education of Youth'. In the Glasgow edition, this section is pp. 758–88; in this edition the main text runs to 947 pages.

The laws concerning corn may every where be compared to the laws concerning religion. The people feel themselves so much interested in what relates either to their subsistence in this life, or to their happiness in a life to come, that government must yield to their prejudices, and, in order to preserve the publick tranquility, establish that system which they approve of. It is upon this account, perhaps, that we so seldom find a reasonable system established with regard to either of those two capital objects. (IV.v.b.40)[32]

With regards to religion, it would be agreeable to see 'that pure and rational religion, free from every mixture of absurdity, imposture, or fanaticism, such as wise men have in all ages wished to see established'. Unfortunately, this is not likely to occur due to the interests and concerns of the common people: 'such a positive law has perhaps never yet established, and probably never will establish in any country: because, with regard to religion, positive law always has been, and probably always will be, more or less influenced by popular superstition and enthusiasm' (V.i.g.8).[33]

The habits of a worker will help to determine the worker's character. So, for example, a country workman who is a jack of all trades will develop slothfulness:

The habit of sauntering and of indolent careless application, which is naturally, or rather necessarily acquired by every country workman who is obliged to change his work and his tools every half hour, and to apply his hand in twenty different ways almost every day of his life; renders him almost always slothful and lazy, and incapable of any vigorous application even on the most pressing occasions. (I.i.7)

Nonetheless, country workers in general, especially farm workers, will tend to have a greater understanding of the world in general than, say, that highly productive worker in that pin plant extolled by Smith in the beginning of his work (I.i.3). Indeed, even a common ploughman's 'understanding, however, being accustomed to consider a greater variety of objects, is generally much superior to that of the other, whose whole attention from morning till night is commonly occupied in performing one or two very simple operations' (I.x.c.24).

The problem is the division of labor itself. In a remarkable paragraph Smith writes:

---

[32] Also on the workers' intellectual dimness: 'The common people of England, however, so jealous of their liberty, but like the common people of most other countries never rightly understanding wherein it consists' (I.x.c.59).

[33] For more on this, see the next section, 6.6. Note that the word enthusiasm was a rather common derogatory term in the 18th century for the excessive religious zeal (or fanaticism) of the early Methodists, etc. It denoted ill-regulated or misdirected religious emotion by what we would not call puritanical or fundamentalist religious movements.

> In the progress of the division of labour, the employment of the far greater part of those who live by labour, that is, of the great body of the people, comes to be confined to a few very simple operations; frequently one or two. But the understandings of the greater part of men are necessarily formed by their ordinary employments. The man whose whole life is spent in performing a few simple operations, of which the effects too are, perhaps, always the same, or very nearly the same, has no occasion to exert his understanding, or to exercise his invention in finding out expedients for removing difficulties which never occur. He naturally loses, therefore, the habit of such exertion, and generally becomes as stupid and ignorant as it is possible for a human creature to become. (V.i.f.50)

In the same paragraph Smith claims the worker's mind becomes torpid; he cannot take part in or enjoy rational conversation; he becomes incapable of just judgments concerning either his private life or the interests of the country; the uniformity of his stationary life makes him a coward and corrupts his body too. He concludes the paragraph by saying, that the worker's

> dexterity at his own particular trade seems, in this manner, to be acquired at the expence of his intellectual, social, and martial virtues. But in every improved and civilized society this is the state into which the labouring poor, that is, the great body of the people, must necessarily fall, unless government takes some pains to prevent it. (ibid.)

It does seem quite odd that Smith waits until Book V, the last book of *The Wealth of Nations*, to elaborate upon this downside to the division of labor which he so fulsomely praises at the beginning of the work.[34]

In the next paragraph Smith writes that 'all the nobler parts of the human character may be, in a great measure, obliterated and extinguished in the great body of the people' (V.i.f.51). The problem is that there is generally too much work and it is too tedious: 'That trade too is generally so simple and uniform as to give little exercise to the understanding; while, at the same time, their labour is both so constant and so severe, that it leaves them little leisure and less inclination to apply to, or even to think of anything else' (V.i.f.53). In the final paragraph to that section, Smith writes of the 'gross ignorance and stupidity which, in a civilized society, seem to frequently benumb the understandings of all the inferior ranks of people' (V.i.f.61).

Hence, the government needs to take some pains and expense to educate the youth of the country, among other reasons so the workers do not fall too much under the influence of severe religious enthusiasts and superstitions (ibid.).

---

[34] Marx calls this praise an 'apotheosis' (*Capital*: 220, fn. 29).

6.6   RELIGION AND CHARACTER

There is a remarkable discussion of religion and character in Smith which has absolutely no counterpart in the work of Aristotle. According to Smith, there will tend to be two types of religion or morality: one strict or austere, the other loose or liberal. The common people will tend to adopt the former; the relatively wealthy or 'people of fashion' the latter. The major difference between the two will be the degree to which people will disapprove of what Smith calls vices of levity. These are vices which arise from economic prosperity, and from too much gaiety and good humor. The loose system will tolerate much mirth, the pursuit of pleasure to some degree of intemperance, and 'the breach of chastity, at least in one of the two sexes, and etc. provided they are not accompanied with gross injustice' (Vi.g.10). The austere system will look upon these vices with abhorrence and detestation. As is often the case for Smith, there is a brilliant economic explanation for these differences: 'The vices of levity are always ruinous to the common people, and a single week's thoughtlessness and dissipation is often sufficient to undo a poor workman for ever, and to drive him through despair upon committing the most enormous crimes' (ibid.). Hence, according to Smith, the wiser of the common people will abhor such excess which 'their experience tells them are so immediately fatal to people of their condition' (ibid.)

However, these sorts of excesses tend not to be such a big deal for the wealthier 'people of fashion'. They can indulge in these excesses for several years and not be economically ruined. Hence, it is acceptable to indulge in some degree of excess 'as one of the privileges which belong to their situation' (ibid.). These sorts of vices are either not censored or only slightly.[35]

Hence, austere, severe religious sects will almost always originate with the common people. For Smith, these sects can go too far in their austerity, and pose a danger to society. 'Many of them, perhaps the greater part of them, have even endeavoured to gain credit by refining upon this austere system, and by carrying it to some degree of folly and extravagance; and this excessive rigour has frequently recommended them more than anything else to the respect and veneration of the common people' (V.i.g.11).

These austere, or excessively austere, sects will appeal to poor people, especially those in large cities. There the poor will likely be anonymous. In the country, people will know the poor person, and he will need to be careful how he acts. Not so in the city: 'as soon as he comes into a great

---

[35]   So, for example, in 21st century US, the punishment/reward to a young rich person who drunkenly wrecks a new car . . . is frequently another new car. Not so for a poor youth.

city, he is sunk in obscurity and darkness. His conduct is observed and attended to by nobody, and he is therefore very likely to neglect it himself, and to abandon himself to every sort of low profligacy and vice' (V.i.g.12). To counteract this anomie, the poor person may become a member of a religious sect. Then he is observed by the other members of the sect who are interested in his behavior, and will expel him if his behaviour is deemed inadequate. Thus, 'In little religious sects, accordingly, the morals of the common people have been almost always remarkably regular and orderly; generally much more so than in the established church. The morals of those little sects, indeed, have frequently been rather disagreeably rigorous and unsocial' (ibid.).

According to Smith, there is a role for the government to correct these possibly unsocial, disagreeably rigorous morals. The government should encourage the study of science and philosophy. In a sense, there is competition between science/philosophy and austere religious sects, since 'Science is the great antidote to the poison of enthusiasm and superstition' (V.i.g.15). Notice that here Smith is explicitly equating the austere religious sects to enthusiasm; and enthusiasm to poison. Smith also writes of the 'melancholy and gloomy humour which is almost always the nurse of popular superstition and enthusiasm' (V.i.g.15). Again, in both these passages, Smith is linking enthusiasm with austere religious sects and then to superstition.

In general, it is important to keep the religious authorities in check.[36] For Smith, it is the religion of the poor, the austere sects, which tend to be most dangerous, and one needs to beware of 'popular and bold, though perhaps stupid and ignorant enthusiasts' (V.i.g.1). As Smith points out in his *Theory of Moral Sentiments*, humans will generally do really awful, morally misguided deeds only under the influence of false notions of religious duty:

> False notions of religion are almost the only causes which can occasion any very gross perversion of our natural sentiments in this way; and that principle which gives the greatest authority to the rules of duty, is alone capable of distorting our ideas of them in any considerable degree. In all other cases, common sense is sufficient to direct us, if not to the most exquisite propriety of conduct, yet to something which is not very far from it. (176)

---

[36] This is stressed in V.i.g. 16–19. Yet, really it is one of the major themes of the entire Article III, 'Of the Expense of the Institutions for the Instruction of People of all Ages', V.i.g. 1–42; pp. 788–814 in the Glasgow edition. As with the previous article 'Of the Expence of the Institutions for the Education of Youth', I think its placement buried deep within the text may have reduced the attention which it merits. When one writes a book of this length, placement certainly matters.

So, by and large, it is only religion that can get us to do really awful things, if we are at all trying to be morally responsible.[37] In the 18th century, Smith called the followers of possibly overly austere religions enthusiasts. In the 21st century, I think we might reasonably call them fundamentalists: as in Fundamentalist Moslems; and Fundamentalist Christians. From Smith's point of view, these sorts of people can cause a lot of trouble.[38] From this point of view, Fundamentalist Moslems and putatively Fundamentalist Christians such as George W. Bush are in a sense not really opponents; rather, they are on the same side!

6.7 CONCLUSION

Smith's relation to Aristotle on the issue of character is indeed complex. On one hand, Smith is largely following Aristotle in such things as (among others) the importance of character in making choices; the importance of upbringing, experience, habits and education in forming characters; and the importance of moderation, that virtues are a sort of mean, and vices are extreme excesses or deficiencies.

On a second hand, Smith clearly departs from Aristotle on the issue of the use of money, stock or capital to acquire more money and property. Aristotle calls this chrematistics and thinks it is corrupting and unnatural. It wrecks character by making people too greedy. Smith disagrees almost (but not quite) completely. Smith insists the use of money, stock or capital to acquire more property is perfectly natural, and is a foundation of civilized, commercial society. The goal for Smith in *The Wealth of Nations* is 'What encourages the progress of population and improvement, encourages that of real wealth and greatness' (IV.vii.b3). To the extent that the business class saves and invests their profits, they will promote wealth and greatness; and 'the populousness of every country must be in proportion to the degree of improvement and cultivation' (IV.vii.b7). So, an increase in stock, an increase in capital, will increase output, population and the wealth of the nation.

Also, the workers, as both wage laborers and relatively intelligent consumers in a modern commercial society, are independent, as opposed to earlier class societies. So, for example, compared to a shepherding society such as the Tartars:

---

[37] Following the above quote, Smith gives a very favourable description of Voltaire's play *Mahomet* (*TMS*: 177).
[38] This will be discussed in further detail below, in Part IV.

In an opulent and civilized society, a man may possess a much greater fortune, and yet not be able to command a dozen people. Though the produce of his estate may be sufficient to maintain, and may perhaps actually maintain, more than a thousand people, yet as those people pay for everything which they get from him, as he gives scarce any thing to any body but in exchange for an equivalent, there is scarce any body who considers himself as entirely dependent upon him, and his authority extends only over a few menial servants. (V.i.b.7)

So exchange is good. Once the exchange is completed, you do not owe anybody anything.[39]

On a third hand,[40] a close reading of Smith shows that he had severe reservations concerning the character types of all three major classes in commercial society. Perhaps particularly problematic is the character type of the capitalists. The master manufacturers and merchants, that is capitalists, out of greed will lie and try to mislead the public. This seems to be precisely the sort of corruption of a person's character that someone such as Aristotle would expect. So, in this sense, Smith, apparently without realizing it, is again actually following down Aristotle's path. Smith says we live in a commercial society, and we are to some extent all merchants. Yet, the actual policy put forth by the merchants, which Smith names mercantilism, rather than, say, commercialism, is one based upon greed. Moreover, their overly zealous pursuit of their narrow economic self-interest is at the expense of the public. How Aristotelian.

Yet, I do not want to end this chapter on Smith and character on such a sour note. In defense of Smith, he may be viewed to be deeply pragmatic. His basic understanding of human nature is that people will not work very hard, either as employers or employees, or entirely outside of the wage labor/capitalist relationship, unless they are forced to. Moreover, the best way to force people to work hard, to be diligent, is through competition. That is, people will not naturally act 'professional'. So, for example, Smith wrote a letter to a colleague arguing against a proposal to regulate and restrict the supply of medical degrees. As far as the schools are concerned,

The monopoly of medical education which this regulation would establish in favour of Universities would, I apprehend, be hurtful to the lasting prosperity of such bodies-corporate. Monopolists very seldom make good work, and a lecture which a certain number of students must attend, whether they profit by it or no, is certainly not likely to be a good one. (*Correspondence*: 174)

---

[39]   On Smith and dependent social relations see Perelman (1989).
[40]   Ian Steedman once called me the first three handed economist he ever met. So be it.

As for the medical doctors themselves, 'That in every profession the fortune of every individual should depend as much as possible upon his merit, and as little as possible upon his privilege, is certainly for the interest of the public' (ibid.: 178).

Finally, implicit in Smith's analysis of human characters in a developed commercial society is a deeply humane view of the world. We should enjoy each other's characters. We cannot do all, everything in life. At this stage of society, the division of labor will necessarily give rise to a wonderful, interesting diversity of characters. For example, as philosophers and social theorists, as economists, even as historians of economic thought, we cannot know or do or be everything in even our own limited fields of endeavor. Hence, we should enjoy and appreciate the insights, diversity and differences of people. This is something that people, even economists, do not always seem to understand. Do not be like the imagined artisan in Smith's 'History of Astronomy' essay, who laughs at others not of his trade, others who have difficulty following and understanding what he does (1980: 44). Rather, appreciate, empathize with the other, and imagine what it would be like to be in that person's shoes. As with material production, the diversity and differences of characters produced in a commercial society can be treasured; and even shared.

7. Adam Smith on government and change

Smith departs from Aristotle on the issues of the role of the government, and social change. Unlike Aristotle, Smith is not a wholehearted proponent of what we would now call the social welfare state. Also, he did not view change in general, or historical change in particular, as essentially circular. Rather, there is evolutionary change and development. These are big differences.

7.1 SMITH ON THE ROLE OF THE GOVERNMENT

7.1.1 On Mercantilist Policies

Smith's position on the proper role of the government is complex.[1] In the first place, Smith was clearly against many (or most) of the governmental rules and regulations in his time. He claimed these rules constituted a system, which he named the mercantilist system. Obviously, Smith opposed this system. As Warren Samuels and Steven Medema succinctly argued in a recent article,

> If government and law seem anathema in the *Wealth of Nations*, it is because of Smith's opposition to the direction of certain *activities* of government at the time. The point of the *Wealth of Nations* is not that government is bad, but that government was doing bad things in promulgating mercantilist policy. This does not negate the centrality of government and law. (2005: 225, emphasis in original)

---

[1] Perhaps somewhat paradoxically, I think the complexity of his argument, both here and elsewhere, is obscured by the clarity of his writing style and the smoothness of his exposition. Schumpeter, for one, was taken in by this, actually arguing that 'He [Smith] never moved above the heads of even the dullest readers. He led them on gently, encouraging them by trivialities and homely observations, making them feel comfortable all along' (1954: 185). Partly for this reason, I think professional philosophers during most of the 20th century generally had a difficult time taking Smith seriously. In more recent years, this has changed, and much of the most interesting work on Smith is currently being done by the professional philosophers. See for example Griswold (1999), Fleischacker (1999, 2004), Darwall (1998, 1999), the young philosophers in Schliesser and Montes (2006), Schliesser (forthcoming).

As discussed in the previous chapter, this particular system of government policies was basically constructed by and for the interests of the capitalist class. As Smith concluded, 'It cannot be very difficult to determine who have been the contrivers of this whole mercantile system; not the consumers, we may believe, whose interest has been entirely neglected; but the producers whose interest has been so carefully attended to; and among this latter class our merchants and manufacturers have been by far the principal architects' (IV.viii.54). They developed these policies to promote their own narrow economic interests; a system run by and for the rich and powerful. Not surprisingly, 'It is the industry which is carried on for the benefit of the rich and powerful, that is principally encouraged by our mercantile system. That which is carried on for the benefit of the poor and the indigent, is too often, either neglected, or oppressed' (IV.viii.4).

The laws they helped to get enacted could be crueler than any tax laws. Indeed, in Smith's view,

> the cruellest of our revenue laws, I will venture to affirm, are mild and gentle, in comparison of some of those which the clamour of our merchants and manufacturers has extorted from the legislature, for the support of their own absurd and oppressive monopolies. Like the laws of Draco, these laws may be said to be all written in blood. (IV.viii.17)

As discussed in the previous chapter, a fundamental problem with these capitalists is they lie, dissimulate and deceive:

> The proposal of any new law or regulation of commerce which comes from this order, ought always to be listened to with great precaution, and ought never to be adopted till after having been long and carefully examined, not only with the most scrupulous, but with the most suspicious attention. It comes from an order of men, whose interest is never exactly the same with that of the publick, who have generally an interest to deceive and even to oppress the publick, and who accordingly have, upon many occasions, both deceived and oppressed it. (I.xi.p.10)[2]

So the capitalists have the potential to be liars and oppressors. As will be seen below in Part III, this side of Smith is actually not too different from Marx. In discussing the British Empire, Smith acerbically writes:

> To found a great empire for the sole purpose of raising up a people of customers, may at first sight appear a project fit only for a nation of shopkeepers. It is, however, a project altogether unfit for a nation of shopkeepers; but extremely fit for a nation whose government is influenced by shopkeepers. Such

---

[2] These are the concluding two sentences of Book I of *The Wealth of Nations*.

statesmen, and such statesmen only, are capable of fancying that they will find some advantage in employing the blood and treasure of their fellow citizens, to found and to maintain such an empire. (IV.vii.c.63)

Thus, as Samuels and Medema pointed out, 'Smith clearly opposed mercantilism'. The question then becomes 'whether or not this opposition to mercantilism is extended to oppose other forms of government "activism"'; and, of course, 'The answer is, quite clearly, "no"' (2005: 221).

7.1.2   A Positive Role for Government

For Smith, the role of the government appears to be largely (although not entirely) to make a commercial society function smoothly and more or less efficiently in the production of material goods, or national wealth. As Smith explains, 'In almost all countries the revenue of the sovereign is drawn from that of the people. The greater the revenue of the people, therefore, the greater the annual produce of their land and labour, the more they can afford to the sovereign. It is his interest, therefore, to increase as much as possible that annual produce' (IV.vii.c.102).[3]

Yet, recall above that Smith had also intended to write a book on the 'general principles of law and government, and of the different revolutions they have undergone in the different ages and periods of society . . . in what concerns justice' (*TMS*: 342). That book was never written. If it was, it would have been the discourse which explicitly linked up his *Theory of Moral Sentiments* with *The Wealth of Nations* which did discuss in detail 'police, revenue, and arms' (ibid.).[4] Thus, there is no book by Smith on the role of government in the promotion of justice, and we do not really know what his system of justice would be.[5] Samuel Fleischacker, the philosopher who has probably written the most extensively on this subject, correctly concludes, I think, that Smith has *no* developed theory of justice.[6] Fleischacker essentially follows my position

---

[3]   'Smith discusses the economic role of government here only insofar as he deems necessary for his particular purpose: the elaboration of a program to promote the increase of national wealth against the backdrop of the extant mercantilist system' (Samuels and Medema, 2005: 221–222).

[4]   Note that by police Smith means economic policy.

[5]   This is not to say that we know nothing about his views on justice; see for example Witztum (1997), Pack and Schliesser (2006), Schliesser (2006a).

[6]   2004, Part IV, 'Justice': 145–226. He also argues persuasively that attempts to ream Smith into some kind of natural jurisprudence tradition (for example Haakonssen 1981; 1996, Chapter 4) are quite mistaken. In my view, attempts to pigeonhole Smith into any one tradition (unless it is arguably the entire Western intellectual tradition) are indeed misguided and unduly simplify Smith's work. Smith is much too encyclopaedic, systematic and original a thinker to be manhandled in this way.

when I earlier argued that 'In many (although not quite all) ways, Smith's position on the role of the state in a capitalist society was close to that of a modern twentieth century US liberal democrat' (Pack, 1991: 1). In Fleishacker's restatement, Smith's 'general approach to the functions of the state may well be closer, in fact, to welfare state liberalism than to libertarianism' (2004: 145). Fleischacker is quite correct, I think, as long as it is emphasized that Smith was *neither* a full-fledged theorist of the welfare state nor a libertarian.

As for Smith not being a libertarian, that is easy enough to dispel. For Smith, taxation is necessary. Indeed, it is a sign of freedom: 'Every tax, however, is to the person who pays it a badge, not of slavery, but of liberty. It denotes that he is subject to government, indeed, but that, as he has some property, he cannot himself be the property of a master' (V.ii.g.11). Also, recall that Smith was the son of a tax collector, and that Smith himself became a tax collector after he wrote *The Wealth of Nations*.[7]

That Smith was not a strict, dogmatic advocate of laissez-faire policies is also quite clear. As I and others have stressed,[8] there are many things the government can and ought to do. Among other things, the government should take steps to ensure the integrity of the money-commodity through coinage; just as it has taken steps to ensure the quality of other key commodities such as woolen and linen cloth. Special regulations on the banking industry concerning bank reserves and the proper issuance of bank notes are needed. Just as the government enforces the building of fire walls to prevent the spread of physical fires, so here special regulations are needed to help prevent the spread of financial fires and panics.[9] Usury laws in Smith's time at about 4 or 5 percent to discourage money from being lent to prodigals and projectors were quite appropriate. Hence, the government should have and enforce usury laws.[10] The government should encourage schooling through the administration of various tests people must pass before they may enter a trade or liberal profession, or be any kind of political candidate; subsidize the production of teachers to encourage their high supply, and hence their low wages and thus the

---

[7]   Specifically, he was one of the 'Commissioners of His Majesty's Customs in Scotland' (Stewart, 1793: 325). For an unfortunate attempt to paint Smith as a libertarian by someone who clearly knew better, see George Stigler's (1988) Adam Smith lecture to the National Association of Business Economists; a truly sleazy performance.

[8]   See for example Viner (1928); Rosenberg (1979); Muller (1995).

[9]   Writing in the summer of 2008, it does seem most unfortunate that Alan Greenspan and other US financial (mis)regulators did not pay more attention to Smith on this issue.

[10]   Given the current debacle in the US (or with securitization, really global) subprime mortgage markets, and various problems in the personal credit card markets, it may very well be time for the US to heed Smith's advice and reintroduce federal usury laws; actually, past time!

relative cheapness of a literary education; encourage the production of other commodities and goods and services which have positive externalities; own land for parks and gardens; use the tax system to discourage various activities such as rents in kind, or to encourage such things as technological change; and use high tariffs to protect important industries such as shipping and defense.[11]

Smith is in many ways in favor of laws, rules and regulations which aid the poor and the working class. He is for a higher standard of living for the working class.[12] Hence, for example, he can be in favor of higher taxes upon the rich, for example:

> A tax upon house-rent, therefore, would in general fall heaviest upon the rich; and in this sort of inequality there would not, perhaps, be any thing very unreasonable. It is not very unreasonable that the rich should contribute to the publick expense, not only in proportion to their revenue, but something more than in that proportion. (V.ii.e.6)[13]

Most of the rules and regulations in his time were in favor of the wealthy and powerful, not the poor or the workers. So, for example, 'We have no acts of parliament against combining to lower the price of work; but many against combining to raise it' (I.viii.12). And 'Whenever the law has attempted to regulate the wages of workmen, it has always been rather to *lower* them than to *raise* them' (I.x.c.34, emphasis added). Nonetheless, in Smith's estimation, whenever laws were passed in favor of the workers, these laws did tend to be just and equitable. Thus,

> Whenever the legislature attempts to regulate the differences between masters and their workmen, its counselors are always the masters. When the regulation, therefore, is in favour of the workmen, it is always just and equitable; but it is sometimes otherwise when in favour of the masters. Thus the law which obliges the masters in several different trades to pay their workmen in money and not in goods, is quite just and equitable. It imposes no real hardship upon the masters. It only obliges them to pay that value in money, which they pretended to pay, but did not always really pay, in goods. (I.x.c.61)

---

[11] Pack (1991, Chapter 4, 'Obvious *Wealth of Nations* Lessons: The Questions of Laissez-Faire and Regressive Taxation': 51–72) goes into all of these examples in much more detail.

[12] 'Smith was not biased in favour of the rich and powerful. If his biases were toward anyone, they tended to be pro-worker' (Pack, 1991: 4). Rothschild (2001) and Fleischacker (2004) reach basically the same conclusion.

[13] See also V.i.d.5, although elsewhere Smith argued for proportional, not progressive taxation. For a fuller discussion, see Pack (1991: 64–9). That Smith argued that 'improvement in the circumstances of the lower ranks of the people' was an advantage to society, see I.viii.36.

Indeed, Betsy Jane Clary (2009) has recently forcefully argued that were Adam Smith alive today, he very likely would support the living wage movement, as well as other public policies which might better ensure the achievement of a living wage for workers. Used with discretion, for Smith, the government can actually make all kinds of rules and regulations to promote the wellbeing of society. For example, in talking about the cowardice which the modern division of labor typically induces in workers in commercial societies, he writes:

> Even though the martial spirit of the people were of no use towards the defence of the society, yet to prevent that sort of mental mutilation, deformity and wretchedness, which cowardice necessarily involves in it, from spreading themselves through the great body of the people, would still deserve the most serious attention of government; in the same manner as it would deserve its most serious attention to prevent a leprosy or any other loathsome and offensive disease, though neither mortal nor dangerous, from spreading itself among them; though, perhaps, no other publick good might result from such attention besides the prevention of so great a publick evil. (V.i.f.60)

This sort of pronouncement by Smith opens the door to all sorts of government policies to promote the public welfare and which would violate strict, dogmatic notions of laissez-faire. The key is discretion, judgment[14] and fairness on the part of the public authorities. Smith is actually most clear (yet vague) on this topic in his *Theory of Moral Sentiments*, where he argues that the government should even legislate that people be beneficent to each other:

> A superior may, indeed, sometimes, with universal approbation, oblige those under his jurisdiction to behave, in this respect, with a certain degree of propriety to one another. The laws of all civilized nations oblige parents to maintain their children, and children to maintain their parents, and impose upon men many other duties of beneficence. The civil magistrate is entrusted with the power not only of preserving the public peace by restraining injustice, but of promoting the prosperity of the commonwealth, by establishing good discipline, and by discouraging every sort of vice and impropriety; he may prescribe rules, therefore, which not only prohibit mutual injuries among fellow-citizens, but command mutual good offices to a certain degree . . . Of all the duties of a law-giver, however, this, perhaps, is that which it requires the greatest delicacy and reserve to execute with propriety and judgment. To neglect it altogether exposes the commonwealth to many gross disorders and shocking enormities,

---

[14] Fleischacker (1999) is good on this point. He correctly points out that Smith and Kant should be seen as the two greatest followers and developers of David Hume's thought. Montes' work (2004) also draws links between Smith and Kant (and draws attention to Aristotelian roots in Smith's work).

and to push it too far is destructive of all liberty, security, and justice. (*TMS*: 81)

A theoretical system that says the government can, or actually must, to some extent, force people[15] to be kind, charitable or beneficial would seem to be a far cry from what most people would consider to be a laissez-faire type government. So, why do so many people misread Smith on this issue?

7.1.3   The Misreading of Smith as Pro Laissez-Faire

People misread Adam Smith as being pro laissez-faire for several reasons. One is that, as noted above, in *The Wealth of Nations* Smith only wrote about the economic policies the government should undertake to promote the more or less smooth running of the economy. He never wrote about what the government should do to promote justice in general. Yet, more than this, Smith does oversimplify his own position when writing about the necessary duties and hence expenses of the sovereign or commonwealth. He does this at the very end of Book IV of *The Wealth of Nations* when introducing or transitioning to the last Book V which is titled 'Of the Revenue of the Sovereign or Commonwealth'. According to what he calls his own

> *system of natural liberty*, the sovereign has only three duties to attend to; three duties of great importance, indeed, but plain and intelligible to common understandings: first, the duty of protecting the society from the violence and invasion of other independent societies; secondly, the duty of protecting, as far as possible, every member of the society from the injustice or oppression of every other member of it, or the duty of establishing an exact administration of justice; and thirdly, the duty of erecting and maintaining certain publick works and certain publick institutions, which it can never be for the interest of any individual, or small number of individuals, to erect and maintain; because the profit could never repay the expence to any individual or small number of individuals, though it may frequently do much more than repay it to a great society. (IV.ix.51, emphasis added)

So there it is; in his own prelude to the necessary responsibilities of the government, no talk of usury laws, other regulations on the financial services industry, special laws to help the working poor, and so on. Smith is to some extent his own vulgarizer.

---

[15] And presumably corporations too, although in general, as discussed above, Smith would most likely be against nearly all corporations. As Samuels puts it, 'coercion for Alpha is correlative to freedom for Beta, and vice versa, and . . . government produces both – directly and indirectly' (1995: 441).

Moreover, Smith also stresses the utter, crucial importance of the protection of private property for economic growth. This, in addition to an extensive market (as well as peace), really is the key for increasing the wealth of nations. Thus, for example, in remarking on England's relative prosperity, Smith credits, 'above all, that equal and impartial administration of justice which renders the rights of the meanest British subject respectable to the greatest, and which, by securing to every man the fruits of his own industry, gives the greatest and most effectual encouragement to every sort of industry' (IV.vii.c.54). This may be contrasted to the relative poverty of Spain and Portugal, which has several reasons but 'above all, that irregular and partial administration of justice . . . which makes the industrious part of the nation afraid to prepare goods for the consumption of those haughty and great men, to whom they dare not refuse to sell upon credit, and from whom they are altogether uncertain of repayment' (IV.vii.c.53). So for Smith, an extensive market, peace and protection of private property will in themselves go a very long way to promoting economic growth.

In addition, Smith's methodological position and rhetorical style contribute to thinking he is laissez faire. Smith is one smooth person,[16] thinker and writer. He tries to write a smooth, engaging, comforting story to win over readers to his position. He holds that in general successful scientific theories make sense of the world to ease our surprise and wonder, to soothe our imagination and calm ourselves.[17] Particularly in the first two books of *The Wealth of Nations*, Smith shows how a commercial system can theoretically work as a self-regulating system. For most readers, Smith successfully removes the surprise and wonder that the seeming chaotic tumult of commercial society can potentially be a largely self-regulating system; and this calls forth our admiration for that very system. This is similar to the success of Newton's theory of nature, which causes us to admire nature, and also calms the tumult of our imagination. According to Smith, Newton's theoretical system replaces surprise and wonder at nature with admiration, which is what Smith tried and largely succeeded in doing *vis-à-vis* commercial society.[18]

---

[16] I think this is quite evident in his *Correspondence*. He particularly writes great letters of recommendation; as well as condolence.

[17] See Pack (1996a).

[18] For more detail on my position, see Pack (1991, Chapter 6, 'Rhetoric, Science and Smith's *Wealth of Nations*': 104–18). On Smith's methodology and philosophy of science, see, for example, Schliesser (2005a, 2005b); Montes (2004, especially Chapter 5, 'Smith and Newton: Some Methodological Issues Concerning General Economic Equilibrium Theory: 130–64); but also Cremaschi (1981, 1989). On Smith's rhetoric, see for example Bazerman (1993); Griswold (1991, 1999 especially Chapter 1). The main debate among interpreters of

96 *Aristotle, Adam Smith and Karl Marx*

Finally, there is indeed, I think, a streak of suspicion of government in general which does manifest itself in Smith, even as he makes various suggestions throughout his work on positive things which the government may (and often ought) to do. So, for example, in commenting upon the propensity to save, Smith writes that 'Great nations are never impoverished by private, though they sometimes are by publick prodigality and misconduct' (II.iii.30). Compared to private individuals, governments frequently foul things up: 'The uniform, constant, and uninterrupted effort of every man to better his condition . . . is frequently powerful enough to maintain the natural progress of things toward improvement, in spite both of the extravagance of government, and of the greatest errors of administration' (II.iii.31). Indeed, along the same vein, 'It is the highest impertinence and presumption, therefore, in kings and ministers, to pretend to watch over the economy of private people, and to restrain their expence either by sumptuary laws, or by prohibiting the importation of foreign luxuries' (II.iii.36).

Smith has a view of natural liberty that he nowhere fully explicates, or details,[19] but is hesitant to violate. Thus, for example, in speaking against restraints on the free trade of food, he writes 'both laws were evident violations of natural liberty and therefore unjust' (IV.v.b.16). Furthermore, due to limitations of knowledge, there should be a limited role for government: 'the law ought always to trust people with the care of their own interest, as in their local situations they must generally be able to judge better of it than the legislator can do' (ibid.).

So: due to limits of knowledge on the part of government; the fact that the government is so often ruled by the rich and powerful; that the merchants and manufacturers are so clever and devious that most rules in a commercial society are no good and dysfunctional to the economic system and economic growth; then laissez-faire may be indeed be pictured as a viable second best solution.

> That security which the laws in Great Britain give to every man that he shall enjoy the fruits of his own labour, is alone sufficient to make any country flourish, notwithstanding these and twenty other absurd regulations of commerce; and this security was perfected by the revolution . . . The natural effort of every individual to better his own condition, when suffered to exert itself with freedom and security, is so powerful a principle, that it is alone, and without any assistance, not only capable of carrying on the society to wealth and prosperity, but of surmounting a hundred impertinent obstructions with which the

Smith's 'science' is probably on the degree to which Smith should be seen as a skeptic (as well as exactly what it means to be a skeptic).

[19] Although, as seen above, he does ingeniously (or cleverly) label his own theoretical system, *the* system of natural liberty. Similar to a putative 'Patriot Act', it may be difficult for many people to oppose a system of natural liberty.

folly of human laws too often encumbers its operations . . . In Great Britain industry is perfectly secure; and though it is far from being perfectly free, it is as free or freer than in any other part of Europe. (IV.v.b.43)

The above pretty much sums up Smith's views on his government. Although there are lots of rules and regulations which the government could and ought to provide, in practice many of the government's rules and regulations are impertinent obstructions. Why this streak of antipathy towards government in general? I think because, in some key ways, Adam Smith has what may be termed a Marxist theory of the State.

7.1.4   Smith's 'Marxist' Theory of the State

The careful reader, plodding along Smith's masterpiece,[20] may be surprised upon coming to Book V, the last book of *The Wealth of Nations*. In explicitly discussing the necessary expenses of the state, Smith suddenly introduces a four stage theory of socioeconomic development. In explaining the expenses of defense and justice[21] it turns out that, according to Smith, government arises at a definite stage in history, with the development of private property. Indeed, the origin of government is to protect private property, particularly that of the rich. Thus,

> Among nations of hunters, as there is scarce any property, or at least none that exceeds the value of two or three days labour; so there is seldom any established magistrate or any regular administration of justice. Men who have no property can injure one another only in their persons or reputations. But when one man kills, wounds, beats, or defames another, though he to whom the injury is done suffers, he who does it receives no benefit. (V.i.b.2)

Note here that Smith seems to have a peculiar definition of benefit, where he restricts benefits in general to material benefits. One would think, depending upon the situation, that a killer, wounder, beater or defamer may very well receive psychic benefits from these energizing activities. Anyway, for Smith,

> It is otherwise with the injuries to property. The benefit of the person who does the injury is often equal to the loss of him who suffers it. . . . avarice and ambition in the rich, in the poor the hatred of labour and the love of present ease

---

[20]   See Morrow's (1928) charming description of that mythical reader who actually read the *Wealth of Nations* from cover to cover.

[21]   In Book V, 'Of the Revenue of the Sovereign or Commonwealth'; Chapter I, 'Of the Expences of the Sovereign or Commonwealth'; Part First, 'Of the Expence of Defense' and Part II, 'Of the Expence of Justice'; pp. 689–723 of the Glasgow Edition.

and enjoyment, are the passions which prompt to invade property, passions much more steady in their operation, and much more universal in their influence. Wherever there is great property, there is great inequality. For one very rich man, there must be at least five hundred poor, and the affluence of the few supposes the indigence of the many. The affluence of the rich excites the indignation of the poor, who are often driven by want, and promoted by envy to possessions. It is only under the shelter of the civil magistrate that the owner of that valuable property, which is acquired by the labour of many years, or perhaps of many successive generations, can sleep a single night in security. He is at all times surrounded by unknown enemies, whom though he never provoked, he can never appease, and from whose injustice he can be protected only by the powerful arm of the civil magistrate continually held up to chastise it. The acquisition of valuable and extensive property, therefore, necessarily requires the establishment of civil government. Where there is no property, or at least none that exceeds the value of two or three days labour, civil government is not so necessary. (ibid.)

Thus, this is pretty much what we would now[22] call the Marxist theory of the state. The state arises at a definite stage (or level) of socioeconomic development. Its function is basically to protect private property, to protect the rich from the poor.[23] According to Smith, 'Civil government, so far as it is instituted for the security of property, is in reality instituted for the defence of the rich against the poor, or of those who have some property against those who have none at all' (V.i.b.11). Yet, unlike Marx, Smith thinks this is good. The rise of private property and the state which protects this property is basically desirable; it is at least as good or desirable as is possible for such a frail creature as humans. It would be worse to not have a state.

Thus, Smith in these sections employs a four stage theory of socioeconomic development: the hunting, shepherding, agriculture and commercial stages of society. The state will have different functions depending upon the stage of socioeconomic development. While the state, for Smith, is necessary in post-hunting societies, there is still in him, I think, a deep distrust of government in general, government throughout its entire history; the state had always protected the property classes.[24] We saw, in an earlier embedded quote, that Smith wrote 'The violence and injustice of

---

[22] Or at least in the 20th century. With the break up of the Soviet Union, I suppose there is a chance that people in the 21st century will soon even forget what the Marxist theory of the state was. But for reasons explained below in Part IV, I doubt that will happen.

[23] The clearest introduction to the Marxist theory of the state may be Engels' *The Origin of the Family, Private Property, and the State* (1972 [1884]).

[24] Once again, we see the deep influence of Rousseau on Smith's thought. See Pack (2000); also Smith's 'A Letter to the Authors of the *Edinburgh Review*' with the 'Appendix: Passages quoted from Rousseau' (1980: 242–56); and 'Considerations Concerning the First Formation of Languages' (1983: 201–26).

the rulers of mankind is an ancient evil, for which, I am afraid, the nature of human affairs can scarce admit of a remedy' (IV.iii.c.9).[25] In writing of the feudal landlords, Smith held that 'All for ourselves, and nothing for other people, seems, in every age of the world, to have been the vile maxim of the masters of mankind' (III.iv.10).[26]

This deep distrust of government in general prevents Smith from being, as with Aristotle, a fully committed theorist of the welfare state.[27] Also, Smith parts company with Aristotle on the emphasis of the forms of government. Recall that Aristotle was keenly concerned with the various forms of government, and how good natural forms of government changed into corrupt, unnatural forms of government. Indeed, even Montesquieu, writing earlier in the 18th century in *The Spirit of the Laws* (1989 [1748]), emphasized the different forms of government. For Montesquieu, no doubt influenced by Aristotle, different forms of government, republic (including democracy and aristocracy), monarchy and despotism, will each have its own principle which determines the type of law needed for that society. Not so for Smith. In contradistinction, Smith historicizes the different types of society based upon what Aristotle called the mode of acquisition: hunting, shepherding, agriculture and commercial. For Smith, economics, the mode of acquisition, becomes crucial: that is what largely determines the type of government the society will have and need. Hence, history itself for Smith also becomes crucial, because the stages of socioeconomic development will tend to succeed each other, and to take place in historical time. Recall that in the discourse which he did not write, Smith was to, among other things, 'give an account of the general principles of law and government, and of the different revolutions they have undergone in the *different ages and periods of society*' (*TMS*: 342, emphasis added). Thus, in the unwritten book on the general principles of law and government, unlike in Aristotle (but as in Marx), history, largely non-reversible historical change, would have been key.

---

[25] This was part of a longer quote concerning capitalists' character; see above Chapter 6, subsection 6.3.1.

[26] Feudal landlords, of course, had governmental authority; see, for example, III.iv.9.

[27] So, for example, in dealing with agricultural issues, 'The principal attention of the sovereign ought to be to encourage, by every means in his power, the attention both of the landlord and of the farmer; by *allowing both to pursue their own interest in their own way*, and according to *their own judgment*; by giving to both the most perfect security that they shall enjoy the full recompence of their own industry; and by procuring to both the most extensive market for every part of their produce, in consequence of establishing the easiest and safest communications, both by land and by water, through every part of his own dominions, as well as the most unbounded freedom of exportation to the dominions of all other princes' (V.ii.c.18, emphasis added).

7.2   SMITH ON CHANGE

7.2.1   Historical Change Largely Caused by the Unintended Consequences of Human Action

In *The Wealth of Nations*, with his emphasis on the natural, and his early memorable story of beaver-killers in a hunting society exchanging their kill in a 'natural' exact proportion with that of their associated deer-killers (I.vi.1), one would naturally think Smith was always conceptualizing about a commercial society, and that he imagined a commercial, capitalist-like society to have always existed. One would think that Smith had a sort of one dimensional approach to history, or a radical flattening of historical change and the different epochs of human society. Yet, this interpretation would ultimately be wrong. Rather abruptly, in explicitly discussing the role of government and the need to provide for defense, Smith introduces a four stage theory of socio-economic development. In dealing with the issue of government and defense Smith finally specifies that he is indeed writing about a specifically commercial society. This type of society has a lot more need for defense and to train people in the military than hunting societies, whose peoples Smith calls 'savages'; shepherding societies, whose peoples Smith labels 'barbarians'; and agricultural societies. In these previous types of societies, the bulk of the people were already more or less accustomed to working outdoors, to fighting, and could fairly readily participate in the defense of the nation. This is not the case for the typical worker in a commercial society (V.i.a).

There is, I am afraid, a certain amount of trickery going on here with Smith's presentation, or a game of bait and switch.[28] Commercial society, which Smith insists is so natural, actually did not always exist in the past. Rather, Smith has a four stage theory of socioeconomic development which he apparently derived from Aristotle. The key difference is that for Aristotle these different types of society co-exist in time. For Aristotle, some nations live by hunting, some are shepherds, most are farmers, some traders (*Politics*: 1256a–b). Smith takes Aristotle's categories and historicizes them. Smith has an evolutionary or developmental conception of history where, basically, a shepherding society may develop out

---

[28]   That Smith was not above a certain amount of caginess is evident, I think, in his handling of his eminent predecessor in political economy, James Stewart. See, for example, Smith's letter to William Pulteney, where he writes, 'I have the same opinion of Sir James Stewart's Book that you have. Without once mentioning it, I flatter myself, that every false principle in it, will meet with a clear and distinct confutation in mine' (*Correspondence*: 164). Sweet.

of a hunting society, a farming society may develop from a shepherding society, and finally a commercial society may arise.[29]

Note that Smith discusses hunting and shepherding societies as savage and barbarian societies respectively, as if he is using these terms in a scientifically objective way. For Smith, savages are simply people living at the stage of hunting, and barbarians are at the stage of shepherding. Given the pejorative nature of these terms,[30] Smith's choice of nomenclature is, to say the least, quite unfortunate. It will make some contemporary readers think that Smith is disgustedly Eurocentric.

Anyway, unlike Aristotle, for the most part Smith believes in historical evolution or development,[31] although there are occasional hints of circularity or at least stagnation in Smith's discourse. For example, he writes that 'It is now more than two hundred years since the beginning of the reign of Elizabeth, a period as long as the course of human prosperity usually endures' (III.iv.20). Or again, 'The course of human prosperity, indeed, seems scarce ever to have been of so long continuance as to enable any great country to acquire capital for all those three purposes; unless, perhaps, we give credit to the wonderful accounts of the wealth and cultivation of China, of those of antient Egypt, and of the ancient state of Indostan' (II.v.22).[32]

Moreover, until the invention of firearms, there was always the very real danger of shepherding societies overrunning farming and commercial societies. Smith calls the invention of gunpowder 'a mere accident' (V.i.a.43) and writes that:

> In modern war the great expence of fire-arms gives an evident advantage to the nation which can best afford that expence; and consequently, to an opulent and civilized, over a poor and barbarous nation. In antient times the opulent and civilized found it difficult to defend themselves against the poor and barbarous nations. In modern times the poor and barbarous find it difficult to defend themselves against the opulent and civilized. The invention of fire-arms, an

---

[29] This emphasis on historical development is particularly evident in the student lecture notes of his course on jurisprudence 'Report of 1762–3', *Lectures on Jurisprudence*: 5–394. These remarkable lecture notes were first published in 1978. On these lectures see, for example, Meek (1976, 1977); Nyland (1993).

[30] Both then and now; see the examples of usage in the *Oxford English Dictionary* under savage and barbarian.

[31] This evolution or development even extends to human speech. See, for example, his article 'Considerations Concerning the First Formation of Languages' first published in *The Philological Miscellany* (1761) and Lecture 3, *Lectures on Rhetoric and Belles Lettres*: 9–13, where he considers a time before humans even had a shared language. See also Berry's excellent early article on this topic (1974).

[32] The three purposes for the use of capital that Smith is referring to are investments in agriculture, manufacturing and foreign trade.

invention which at first sight appears to be so pernicious, is certainly favourable both to the permanency and to the extension of civilization. (V.i.a.44)

So before the invention of gunpowder and firearms, there was indeed some historical circularity as shepherding nations could and did overrun and destroy richer civilizations.[33] Nonetheless, the emphasis in Smith is on historical evolution and historical change; change which goes somewhere and not merely in circles.

Hence, compared to Aristotle, there is relatively little in the way of goals or telos in Smith's work. It is rather more like a Darwinian story of evolution and survival. Indeed, for Smith, 'Every species of animals naturally multiplies in proportion to the means of their subsistence, and no species can ever multiply beyond it' (I.viii.39); and the demand for people regulates their production (ibid.).[34] In *The Theory of Moral Sentiments*, in explaining how the murder of new-born infants in ancient Greece was influenced by custom, although the general tenor of morals and behavior could never be so horrid, Smith explicitly gives an argument based upon mere physical survival:

> There is an obvious reason why custom should never pervert our sentiments with regard to the general style and character of conduct and behaviour, in the same degree as with regard to the propriety or unlawfulness of particular usages. There never can be any such custom. No society could subsist a moment, in which the usual strain of men's conduct and behaviour was of a piece with the horrible practice I have just now mentioned (*TMS*: 211)

So like Darwin's later theory of biological evolution, Smith's theory of historical evolution is not guided by planning.[35] Smith replaces Aristotle's emphasis on goals, planning and human reason with his own theory of unintended consequences of human action.[36] In contradistinction to Aristotle, it is the unintended consequences of human action which largely drives human history, and creates real unidirectional historical change.[37]

---

[33] As apparently happened in ancient Greece, leading to a pre-Aristotelian Greek 'dark age'.
[34] Actually, Smith writes that 'the demand for men, *like that for any other commodity*, necessarily regulates the production of men' (I. viii. 40, emphasis added). It seems odd (or a theoretical slip) that Smith would write that people are commodities, as if they were produced with the goal of being exchanged in the market and that they are slaves.
[35] On Darwin's later dependence on Smith, see Schweber (1977, 1994).
[36] As Hayek (1967) points out, Smith is following up on the insights of the second volume of Mandeville's *Fable of the Bees* (1924 [1729]).
[37] Hegel would later take Smith's theory of unintended consequences, give human history a goal, and denote it the cunning of reason. On the relationship between Smith and Hegel, see, for example, Henderson and Davis (1991).

So, for example, near the very beginning of *The Wealth of Nations*, in writing about the division of labor, which gives rise to greater output, increased productivity of labor, increases in the wealth of nations, and so on, Smith explicitly stresses that it is not the result of human wisdom, planning, or rationality. It is rather the unintended result of 'the propensity to truck, barter, and exchange one thing for another' (I.ii.1). This urge to trade is probably a consequence of 'reason and speech' (I.ii.2). So, human reason and speech probably gave rise to the urge to trade, which in turn gave rise to the division of labor and increased productivity. Yet, it was not human reason itself which figured all this out.[38] People never said, let us trade so we may increase the division of labor and hence our productivity and wealth. People did reason that we should trade so that each may acquire what we need; unintended consequences followed.

A delightful example of the unintended consequence of human action as a prime motor in directing historical change is Smith's story of the introduction of commerce and cheap commodities to the countryside of feudal Europe. The undoing of the feudal landlords was 'gradually brought about' by 'the silent and insensible operation of foreign commerce and manufactures. These gradually furnished the great proprietors with something for which they could exchange the whole surplus produce of their lands, and which they could consume themselves without sharing it either with tenants or retainers' (III.iv.10). The lords spent their money on frivolities. 'For a pair of diamond buckles perhaps, or for something as frivolous and useless, they exchanged the maintenance, or what is the same thing, the price of the maintenance of a thousand men for a year, and with it the whole weight and authority which it could give them' (ibid.). Thus, getting rid of the dependents, 'for the gratification of the most childish, the meanest and the most sordid of all vanities, they gradually bartered their whole power and authority' (ibid.). So,

> having sold their birth-right, not like Esau for a mess of pottage in time of hunger and necessity, but in the wantonness of plenty, for trinkets and baubles, fitter to be the play-things of children than the serious pursuits of men, they became as insignificant as any substantial burgher or tradesman in a city. A regular government was established in the country as well as in the city'. (III. iv. 15)

Thus, the lords spent their money on trinkets. They got rid of their dependents, and the lords became insignificant. Thus was the unintended

---

[38] As pointed out in the preceding footnote, Hegel would call this the cunning of reason; Smith did not.

consequence of cheap commodities in the countryside: the disintegration of traditional feudal relationships.[39]

7.2.2   Aristotelian Residues and the Temporality of Species

Human history then for Smith[40] becomes one of real change, development and evolution, largely arising from the unplanned results of human actions. This is in contradistinction to Aristotle's emphasis on the ultimate circularity to history, and the importance of goals, ends, the final cause. Nonetheless, there is a distinctly Aristotelian concept which is then smuggled into Smith's concept of human history. Aristotle says that if we know a dog, then we know a puppy, given the right conditions, will naturally grow and develop into a dog. Similarly, if we know a tree, then we know, given the right conditions, an acorn will naturally grow and develop into a tree. This idea of a natural development is to some extent taken by Smith and applied to the idea of human history; an application that Aristotle himself did not do.[41] This is particularly evident in Book III of *The Wealth of Nations*.

In that book Smith argues, among other things, that the countryside should develop before the cities since, 'As subsistence is, in the nature of things, prior to conveniency and luxury, so the industry which procures the former, must necessarily be prior to that which ministers to the latter' (III.i.2).[42] Smith here is like Aristotle in that there is a natural growth or change to things, though here applied to human history, which would occur in the absence of violent change: 'Had human institutions, therefore, never disturbed the natural course of things, the progressive wealth and increase of the towns would, in every political society be consequential, and in proportion to the improvement and cultivation of the territory or country' (III.i.4). Thus, for Smith, there appears to be a natural order,

---

[39] Smith makes basically the same point in Book V near the end of *The Wealth of Nations*: 'For the sake of an inferior pageantry of the same kind, his nobles dismiss their retainers, make their tenants independent, and become gradually themselves as insignificant as the greater part of the wealthy burghers in his dominions' (V.iii.3).

[40] And eventually, I think, for most secular people in the modern era.

[41] As will be seen below, this idea will be extensively developed by Marx. Hegel took the idea of history as development, gave it a goal, the unfolding of reason on earth, the efficient cause being called the cunning of reason. For what is an essentially Hegelian reading of Smith, that is that interprets Smith as a sort of proto-Hegel, see Evensky's careful, yet overly sympathetic (to Smith) work (2005). Hegel's teleological view of history develops and follows Kant's speculations on universal history. See the surprisingly clear and polemical essays collected in his *Perpetual Peace and Other Essays* (1983 [1784–95]).

[42] The first chapter of this third book is significantly titled 'Of the natural Progress of Opulence'.

growth, change and evolution in human history.[43] Hence, 'according to the natural course of things, therefore, the greater part of the capital of every growing society is, first directed to agriculture, afterwards to manufactures, and last of all to foreign commerce. This order of things is so very natural' (III.i.8). Unfortunately, due partly to poor government policies 'though this natural order of things must have taken place in some degree in every such society, it has, in all the modern states of Europe been, in many respects, entirely inverted' (III.i.9). The result is 'an unnatural and retrograde order' (ibid.). Not good!

Nonetheless, one of the main reasons Smith wrote *The Wealth of Nations* was to change the policy of the government. Smith in a letter characterized his book as containing 'a very violent attack I had made upon the whole commercial system of Great Britain' (*Correspondence*: 251). In Smith's view, the laws, customs, interests and prejudices which favored the position of the towns over the country in Europe were contrary to the order of nature and, eventually, of reason. Hence they should be changed: 'Laws frequently continue in force after the circumstance, which first gave occasion to them, and which could alone render them reasonable, are no more' (III.ii.4). Smith felt that if these laws were changed, the wealth of the European nations could grow faster and history would evolve, or revert towards a more 'natural' direction.

So Smith's story, as with most of the moderns, is history as one of development and evolution; not circularity as with Aristotle and the ancients.[44] The reasons for this shift in perspective are complex and deep-rooted. Yet one that I think has been relatively underappreciated was the role of species extinction. For Plato, the forms were eternal. Similarly, for Aristotle, animal species, animal forms, were also eternal. Yet, I suspect that Smith most likely knew they were not. Smith wrote in *The Wealth of Nations* that:

> The Cori, something between a rat and a rabbit, and supposed by Mr. Buffon to be the same with the Aperea of Brazil, was the largest viviparous quadruped in St. Domingo. This species seems never to have been very numerous, and the dogs and cats of the Spaniards were said to have long ago almost entirely extirpated it, as well as some other tribes of a still smaller size. (IV.vii.a.11)

Note, Smith wrote that the Cori was almost entirely extirpated, not completely wiped out. Also, writes Smith, it was almost completely exterminated only in St. Domingo. Yet, I think the handwriting was on the

---

[43] This teleological aspect of Smith's thought actually rests uneasily with the dominant explanation he usually gives, stressing the unintended results of human actions.

[44] See Hannah Arendt (1968).

wall. Recall also that the last record of a living dodo bird was in 1662 or 1681 (Fuller, 2002: 25). So by the time Smith wrote *The Wealth of Nations* the dodo bird had been extinct for a hundred years or so. Smith himself took a keen interest in travel works, as well as biology.[45] So my guess is that Smith probably knew (or strongly suspected) that the dodo bird was extinct. Moreover, the last (or possibly one of the last) surviving stuffed dodos was in the collection of the Ashmolean Museum in Oxford when Smith was attending Oxford.[46] In 1755 it was destroyed except for the head and right foot (Strickland and Melville, 1848: 32; Fuller, 2002: 28).[47]

So, if Smith knew that the dodo bird or other species were extinct, then he knew Aristotle was wrong. Species are not eternal. If a species could be completely wiped out, then history could not be circular. The dodo bird was not coming back. It was gone; forever. No more humans will ever again supper upon fresh succulent dodo meat. The idea of human history as circular had to be replaced with history as really changing, evolving, developing, going somewhere. Eventually the idea of social evolution, as used by people such as Smith, would lead to the idea of biological evolution as well. If old species could be wiped out, then new ones could also be formed, or developed, or evolved. Eventually, Darwin in a sense would replace Aristotle's hierarchical ordering of plants to animals to humans with a historical, evolutionary ordering based upon development in time. Animals will develop after plants; the human animal will eventually develop from previous advanced animal species. The hierarchical ordering envisioned by Aristotle will largely manifest itself in historical time.

---

[45]   See, for example, 'Letter to Edinburgh Review' (1980: 248–9). For evidence that Smith studied botany while he was working on *The Wealth of Nations*, see *Correspondence* (1977, Letter 208: 252).

[46]   Smith studied at Oxford for six years, from 1740 to 1746.

[47]   All current stuffed dodos in museums are fake.

PART III

Karl Marx's modern return to Aristotle

8. Karl Marx on exchange value and money

8.1 INTRODUCTORY COMMENTS

We saw above in Part II that for Smith, largely following Aristotle, the exchange of products will necessarily generate money. Again, following Aristotle, money may be used to acquire more money. Smith considered this to be perfectly natural and basically good; it largely formed the basis of what he termed commercial society, which was the society Smith lived in. Here Smith parted company from Aristotle. Aristotle felt the use of money to acquire more money, which he termed chrematistics, was unnatural. It was a corrupt use of money and would tend to wreck the character of people who used money in this way.[1]

Marx admired Smith greatly, knew Smith's work extremely well,[2] and no doubt considered Smith to be a worthy adversary. The subtitle to Marx's *Capital* was *A Critique of Political Economy*. *Capital* was a massive development of his earlier 1859 *Contribution to the Critique of Political Economy*. Marx considered Smith to be perhaps political economy's chief, most able spokesperson.[3] Thus:

> Political economy had achieved a certain comprehensiveness with Adam Smith; to a certain extent he had covered the whole of its territory . . . Smith himself moves with great naivete in a perpetual contradiction. On the one hand he traces the intrinsic connection existing between economic categories or the obscure structure of the bourgeois economic system. On the other, he simultaneously sets forth the connection as it appears in the phenomena of competition and thus as it presents itself to the unscientific observer, just as to him who is actually involved and interested in the process of bourgeois production. One of

---

[1] For some, Aristotle can be seen as providing the basis for a successful critique of capitalist society and of mainstream modern economic theory; see, for example, Murray (1997: 69–71; also 'General Introduction': 1–7).

[2] This is perhaps most apparent in *Theories of Surplus Value*, Parts I and II (1963, 1968). Yet, Marx referred extensively to Smith throughout all his mature economic work. See, for example, the careful and extensive discussion of Smith's views on fixed and circulating capital, and reproduction in *Capital*, Vol. II, Chapters X and XIX (1967a: 189–214; 360–89).

[3] Though analytically, of course, inferior to Ricardo.

these conceptions fathoms the inner connection, the physiology, so to speak, of the bourgeois system, whereas the other takes the external phenomena of life as they seem and appear and merely describes, catalogues, recounts and arranges them under formal definitions . . . his task was indeed a twofold one. On the one hand he attempted to penetrate the inner physiology of bourgeois society but on the other, he partly tried to describe its externally apparent form of life for the first time. . . The one task interested him as much as the other, and since both proceeded independently of one another, this results in completely contradictory ways of presentation: the one expresses the intrinsic connections more or less correctly, the other . . . expresses the *apparent* connections without any internal relation. (*Theories of Surplus Value* (*TSV*), Part II: 165, emphasis in original)

Marx recognizes Smith as the great systematizer of political economy. Thus, 'Adam Smith's contradictions are of significance because they contain problems which it is true he does not solve, but which he reveals by contradicting himself. His correct instinct in this connection is best shown by the fact that his successors take opposing stands based on one aspect of his teaching or the other' (*TSV* Part I: 151). Marx, I think, also had a good sense of Smith's temperament, at one point accusing him of being immoderately moderate: 'When moreover Adam Smith says of the Physiocrats: "Their works have certainly been of some service to their country", this is an immoderately moderate statement' (*TSV* Part I: 344).[4] Touché.

In critiquing political economy, Marx may be viewed as returning to and developing Aristotle's critique of chrematistics.[5] Also, in methodology, he is rather Aristotelian. As with Aristotle, Marx begins with the surface appearance of things.[6] So, for example, in the first sentence of *Capital* he writes that 'The wealth of societies in which the capitalist mode of production prevails *appears* as an "immense collection of commodities"' (1976: 125, emphasis added).[7] Yet, Marx feels that he is able to get beneath the surface appearance or presentation of things to grasp their essential attributes. Thus, according to Marx, 'The forms of appearance are reproduced directly and spontaneously, as current and usual modes of

---

[4]   No one, I think, would ever make that accusation of Marx himself.

[5]   See McCarthy (1990, especially chapter 2: 57–119 and chapter 6: 247–96; 1992 ed., especially the articles by DeGolyer (1992) and Miller (1992); 2003, chapter 1: 15–63). Urquhart (2008) calls Marx a 'Left-Aristotelian'. On the dialectical relationship between Aristotle, Smith and Marx (and Polanyi) see Kozel, chapters 2, 3 and 4 (2006: 17–80). Here and elsewhere in this work, I generally use dialectical in the sense meaning dialogical; a dialog.

[6]   Laurence Berns notes 'one of the cardinal excellences of Aristotle's way of inquiry: the way he describes things as they naturally present themselves, while he makes his way towards uncovering their own inner articulation' (1994: 74, fn.5).

[7]   Marx is quoting himself from the first sentence of the *Critique* (1970: 27). In that work, he writes that 'The wealth of bourgeois society, *at first sight, presents itself*' (emphasis added).

thought; the essential relation must first be discovered by science' (*Capital*: 682).[8] So, in a sense Marx is an Aristotelian essentialist, in that he believes he can get to the essence, or bottom, or true objective reality of things. So for example,

> the way in which the *immanent* laws of capitalist production manifest themselves in the external movement of the individual capitals, assert themselves as the coercive laws of competition, and therefore enter into the consciousness of the individual capitalist as the motives which drive him forward . . . a scientific analysis of competition is possible only if we can grasp the inner nature of capital, just as the apparent motion of the heavenly bodies are intelligible only to someone who is acquainted with their real motions, which are not perceptible to the senses. (*Capital*: 433, emphasis added)

As the great theologian Karl Barth wrote about Hegel's philosophy, Karl Marx's critique is the critique of self-confidence.[9] In *Capital*[10] Marx writes as if there is indeed an essence to the capitalist mode of production; and that he has firmly, nay, brilliantly, grasped it.[11]

8.2 MARX ON VALUE AND EXCHANGE VALUE

Marx consciously begins his mature economic analysis with Aristotle.[12] The first paragraph of his 1859 *Critique* ends with a reference and a

---

[8] See also, for example, *Capital* (1976: 710): 'In our presentation of accumulation, then, we assume no more than is assumed by the actual process of accumulation itself. . . . An exact analysis of the process, therefore, demands that we should, for a time, disregard all phenomena that conceal the workings of its inner mechanism'. Unless I explicitly note otherwise, this and all other references to *Capital* will be to Volume I, sub-subtitled, *The Process of Production of Capital*.

[9] 1973: Chapter 10, 'Hegel': 384–421. The sentence, 'Hegel's philosophy is the philosophy of *self-confidence*' is on p. 391 (emphasis in original).

[10] And in his earlier *Critique*. For interpretations that Marx was not an Aristotelian essentialist, and worked out of a very complex overdetermined methodology, see, for example, the work of Althusser (1969); Althusser and Balibar (1979); and Resnick and Wolff (1987). In my reading, in Marx's mature, 'economistic' works, he definitely writes as if he has access to, and has indeed grasped the essence of the capitalist mode of production. For an advanced introduction to Marx and historical changes in interpreting his work see Reuten (2003).

[11] For a criticism of essentialism in economics because it leads to an anti-empirical tendency, seeking to solve problems by the use of definitions instead of looking at empirical data, and hence produces theories which are extremely difficult to falsify, see Blaug (1980: 34–5), also Popper's work criticizing essentialism (see 1957: 26–34; 1962: 31–4; 1976: 17–21).

[12] See Pack (1985b), Appendix D, 'Aristotle and Marx on the Origins of Capital': 126–31. As we saw above, Smith basically did too in *The Wealth of Nations*. According to Theocarakis, Marx 'is, however, the most Aristotelian of all economists. He argues as if Aristotle had lived in a capitalist society' (2006: 44).

quote from Aristotle's *Politics*: 1257a. As noted above, the middle of the first sentence of Volume I of *Capital* then footnotes this first page of his *Critique*.[13] Marx's emphasis, here and elsewhere in his work, is on contradictions, not contraries.[14] Marx claims in the *Critique*, 'Every commodity, however, has a twofold aspect – *use-value and exchange-value*' (27, emphasis in original). Marx will work out what he perceives to be the contradictions between use and exchange value, since there is an 'opposition between use-value and value' (*Capital*: 199).[15] Thus, a commodity is a unity of use-value and value, and 'there is an antithesis, *immanent* in the commodity, between use-value and value, between private labour which must simultaneously manifest itself as directly social labour' (*Capital*: 209, emphasis added).

For Marx, 'a use-value has value only in use, and is realized only in the process of consumption' (*Critique*: 27). Immediately, there is a concern with measurement and the proper measuring rod: 'Different use-values have different measures appropriate to their physical characteristics; for example, a bushel of wheat, a quire of paper, a yard of linen' (ibid.). But then he writes 'To be a use-value is evidently a necessary prerequisite of the commodity, but it is immaterial to the use-value whether it is a commodity. Use-value as such, since it is independent of the determinate economic form, lies outside the sphere of investigation of political economy' (*Critique*: 28).[16]

Not so for exchange-value. At the surface level of appearances, 'Exchange-value seems at first to be a *quantitative relation*, the proportion in which use-values are exchanged for one another' (ibid., emphasis in original). Again there is a concern with measurement, and a common denominator so that commodities may be compared, 'take one another's place in the exchange process, are regarded as equivalents, and despite

---

[13] Part One of *Capital*, 'Commodities and Money', pp. 125–244, is largely a reworking of his earlier *Critique*. In some places, Marx condenses the discussion of the previous work. This, I think, is one of the main reasons the beginning of *Capital* is so difficult to follow; it is too condensed. In other places, Marx elaborates and develops the *Critique's* discussion. I do not think there are any significant differences in the two works in content and will use them interchangeably when dealing with Marx's analysis of commodities and money. In form, *Capital* dispensed with the three separate sections dealing with extended discussions of Marx's predecessors. Marx himself in the 'Preface to the 1st Edition' of *Capital* wrote that *Capital* was a continuation of the *Critique* (1976: 89).

[14] Recall that for Aristotle (and no doubt for Marx too), a contradiction has no intermediate; a contrary does.

[15] As will be seen below, for Marx the value of a commodity can only manifest or show itself as exchange-value, the exchange of one commodity for another in definite quantities.

[16] That is, use values are omnipresent. They do not distinguish one form of economic organization from another. Marx, of course, basically wants to restrict the subject matter of political economy to the capitalist mode of production.

their motley appearance have a common denominator' (ibid.). Marx then makes a significant leap. He claims that 'as objectification of social labour, all commodities are crystallizations of the same substance. The specific character of this substance, i.e. of labour which is embodied in exchange-value' (*Critique*: 29). So labor is the substance of value. Therefore, 'as exchange-value they represent the same homogeneous labour, i.e. labour in which the individual characteristics of the workers are obliterated. Labour which creates exchange-value is thus *abstract general* labour' (ibid., emphasis in original).

Thus, 'regarded as exchange-values all commodities are merely definite quantities of *congealed labour-time*' (*Critique*: 30, emphasis in original). This is Marx's answer to what is value, and why commodities can be exchanged in certain proportions. Hence, 'Labour is reduced to simple labour, labour so to speak, without any qualitative attributes' (*Critique*: 30). Following Aristotle, Marx wants to know what it is that is being measured, claiming, 'the common factor in the exchange relation, or in the exchange-value of the commodity, is therefore its value' (*Capital*: 128). And it is 'labour that forms the substance of value' (*Capital*: 129). Therefore, as with Aristotle being concerned with what makes goods commensurate, Marx believes he has finally (over two thousand years later) discovered the answer: 'we reduce them to the characteristic they have in common, that of being the expenditure of human labour-power, of human labour in the abstract' (*Capital*: 166). Thus, 'as exchange-values of different magnitudes they represent larger or smaller portions, larger or smaller amounts of simple, homogeneous, abstract general labour, which is the substance of exchange-value' (*Critique*: 29).[17]

Once again, there lurks the issue of how to measure this exchange value: 'The question now arises, how can these amounts be measured? . . . Just as motion is measured by time, so is labour by *labour-time*' (*Critique*: 29–30, emphasis in original). So, in both following and answering Smith from an Aristotelian perspective,[18] Marx holds that 'Labour-time . . . is the quantitative aspect of labour as well as its inherent measure. The labour-time materialized in the use-values of commodities is both the substance that turns them into exchange-value and therefore into commodities and the standard by which the precise magnitude of their value is measured' (*Critique*: 30). That is, according to Marx, labor is both the substance

---

[17] See also *Capital*: 293: 'We know that the value of each commodity is determined by the quantity of labour materialized in its use-value'. It is, of course, abstract, socially necessary labor.

[18] Marx follows Smith because he agrees that labor time is the measure of value. He answers Smith from an Aristotelian perspective because if labor time is the measure of value, then labor itself in its congealed form must also be value.

(or material) and the measure of value; labor causes commodities to have value, and its time measures the value of the commodity.[19]

According to Marx, 'during the labour process, the worker's labour constantly undergoes a transformation, from the form of unrest into that of being, from the form of motion into that of objectivity' (*Capital*: 296). That is to say, it goes from labor power or labor potential, to actual labor which gets crystallized (or actualized) in the resulting product. The result is that 'definite quantities of product . . . now represent nothing but definite quantities of labour, definite masses of crystallized labour-time' (*Capital*: 297). So, the expenditure of human labor-power, or humans who have the capacity or potential to labor, may be viewed as the actualization of human labor-power; and the actualization of this human labor-power crystallizes or becomes embodied in commodities. Note how Aristotelian is this notion of going from the potential of a thing to its actualization.

Marx relentlessly works out what he sees as the contradiction between use value and exchange value. So, for example, 'Whereas labour positing exchange-value is *abstract universal* and *uniform* labour, labour positing use-values is concrete and distinctive labour, comprising infinitely varying kinds of labour as regards its form and the material to which it is applied' (*Critique*: 36, emphasis in original). And, 'Since it is not a use-value to its owner, it must be a use-value to owners of other commodities' (*Critique*: 42). Thus, commodities must be traded, since 'A commodity can only therefore become a use-value if it is realized as an exchange-value' (*Critique*: 43). Furthermore, 'Definite historical conditions are involved in the existence of the product as a commodity. In order to become a commodity, the product must cease to be produced as the immediate means of subsistence of the producer himself' (*Capital*: 273). So commodities arise only at specific times in history.

As opposed to neoclassical theory, for Marx the value of a good is not at all due to its productivity (of either utility or other goods). Therefore,

'What matters is not the service it renders, but the service rendered to it in the course of its production. Thus, the exchange-value of a machine, for instance, is determined not by the amount of labour-time which it can replace, but by the amount of labour-time expended in its production and therefore required for the production of a new machine of the same type. (*Critique*: 37)

---

[19] 'Since labour time is the substance and the inherent measure of value' (*Critique*: 82). See also *Capital*: 675: 'But what is the value of a commodity? The objective form of the social labour expended in its production. And how do we measure the quantity of the value? By the quantity of the labour contained in it.'

In Marx's theoretical system, it turns out that 'things which in and for themselves are not commodities, things such as conscience, honor, etc., can be offered for sale by their holders . . . hence a thing can, formally speaking have a price without having a value. The expression of price is in this case imaginary, like certain quantities in mathematics' (*Capital*: 197). In similar fashion is 'the price of uncultivated land, which is without value because no human labour is objectified in it' (ibid.).[20]

In comparing the values of two commodities, say, a coat and linen, Marx holds that 'As values the coat and the linen have the same substance, they are the objective expressions of homogeneous labour' (*Capital*: 134). Note that Marx here uses the word objective, and he may be said to have an objective theory of value. Marx holds that 'the values coat and linen, however, are merely congealed quantities of homogeneous labour' (*Capital*: 135–6). Because they are made of the same substance, they may be compared quantitatively. Generalizing, 'since the magnitude of the value of a commodity represents nothing but the quantity of labour embodied in it, it follows that all commodities, when taken in certain proportions, must be equal in value' (*Capital*: 136).[21]

Marx claims that 'things only become comparable in quantitative terms when they have been reduced to the same unit. Only as expressions of the same unit do they have a common denominator, and are therefore commensurable magnitudes' (*Capital*: 141). So as with Aristotle, Marx is searching for some common unit, common to all commodities. He claims he has found it in that all commodities are created by labor-power, or labor potential, or labor capacity.[22]

According to Marx, 'the same labour, therefore, performed for the same length of time, always yields the same amount of value, independently of any variations in productivity' (*Capital*: 137). So here, as opposed to Smith, there is a clear distinction between value and wealth. To clarify this distinction, let us briefly consider a one output world, say a Ricardian corn model.[23] Say, for example, in one year 100 workers can produce 100 units of corn. Suppose the next year there is an increase of 10 percent of workers, each working the same number of hours, with the same intensity, and so

---

[20]   In contemporary accounting terms, 'good will' is also an example of something having a price but no value.

[21]   Marx writes labor, but he means abstract, homogenized labor.

[22]   Although, as noted above, in Marx's system some things such as honor, conscience and uncultivated land may assume the form of a commodity, be for sale and have a price, without having value; a complication.

[23]   I realize that some purists may object that in a one output world there can be no exchange of commodities with each other, hence, no exchange values, and so on. However, the example easily demonstrates that for Marx, as opposed to Smith's various endeavors, the close link between values and wealth is clearly severed.

on. Yet, suppose due to bad weather, climate change, whatever, in spite of the increase of 10 percent in the number of labor hours, the actual output of the society declined by 10 percent. In this case, by Marx's system, the value of the output would have increased by 10 percent; yet, the mass of output, or the 'wealth of the nation' had decreased by 10 percent. Hence, for Marx, the monotonic connection between changes in the quantity of value produced and the quantity of wealth produced is severed; total value may go up even as total wealth produced goes down – and vice versa.

According to Marx, 'human labour-power in its fluid state, or human labour, creates value, but is not itself value. It becomes value in its coagulated state, in objective form' (*Capital*: 142).[24] So, human labor power is humans, in their capacity or potentiality to labor – a very Aristotelian conception with its emphasis on the distinction between the potential and the actualization of a thing.[25] When people labor they are creating value, and the value becomes embodied in the commodity. Thus, every commodity produced by human labor can be exchanged for every other commodity in determinate quantities. For Marx then, any apparent 'superficial' market prices determined by short run supply and demand considerations are merely variations around true, objective, underlying values.[26] Hence, the value of, say, linen is in a way in the linen, and in a way not, since it can show itself only as exchange value, only when the linen is exchanged for another commodity. That is, 'the value of the linen as a congealed mass of human labour can be expressed only as an objectivity, a thing which is materially different from the linen itself and yet common to the linen and all other commodities' (ibid.).

So, for Marx, 'the equation 20 yards of linen = 1 coat, or 20 yards of linen are worth 1 coat, presupposes the presence in 1 coat of exactly as much of the substance of value as there is in 20 yards of linen' (*Capital*: 144–5). Marx is considering (as we saw above with Aristotle) what makes things equivalent when we measure, and exactly what is it that we are measuring. So, for example, in weighing a sugar-loaf on a scale against units of iron, 'Just as the body of the iron, as a measure of weight, represents weight alone, in relation to the sugar-loaf, so in our expression of

---

[24]   Marx repeats himself at *Capital*: 677: 'Labour is the substance, and the immanent measure of value, but it has not value itself'.

[25]   'Man himself, viewed merely as the physical existence of labour-power, is a natural object, a thing, although a living, conscious thing, and labour is the physical manifestation of that power' (*Capital*: 310).

[26]   I am ignoring here, as Marx does, issues which result from the transformation of values into Marxian prices of production. Those issues are dealt with in the posthumously published third volume of *Capital* which was edited by Engels from Marx's notes. I will address some of them below in Part IV.

value, the body of the coat represents value alone' (*Capital*: 149). That is, the weight of iron measures the weight of a sugar-loaf. Nonetheless, it appears as if it is the iron itself measuring the weight of the sugar-loaf. Yet, really it is the weight of the iron measuring the weight of the sugar-loaf. Similarly, when comparing values, the body of the equivalent seems to be or apparently 'figures as the embodiment of abstract human labour' (*Capital*: 150). The physical body of the commodity in the equivalent form of value (which in Marx's further discussion will become the money form) appears to represent pure value.

Marx explicitly turns to Aristotle for clarification on these measurement and commensurability issues. He writes that we should 'go back to the great investigator who was the first to analyse the value-form, like so many other forms of thought, society and nature. I mean Aristotle' (*Capital*: 151).[27] Marx then quotes from Book V, Chapter V of the *Nicomachean Ethics*, dealing with the exchange of beds for a house and the issue of their commensurability.[28] Marx interprets Aristotle as not being able to complete his analysis of what makes commodities commensurate because of 'the lack of a concept of value' (ibid.). Marx claims that Aristotle was unable to realize that human labor is 'the homogeneous element, i.e. the common substance, which the house represents from the point of view of the bed' (ibid.) because Aristotle lived in a slave society. According to Marx:

> Greek society was founded on the labour of slaves, hence had as its natural basis the inequality of men and of their labour-powers. The secret of the expression of value, namely the equality and equivalence of all kinds of labour because and in so far as they are human labour in general, could not be deciphered until the concept of human equality had already acquired the permanence of a fixed popular opinion. This however becomes possible only in a society where the commodity-form is the universal form of the product of labour . . . Aristotle's genius is displayed precisely by his discovery of a relation of equality in the value-expression of commodities. Only the historical limitation inherent in the society in which he lived prevented him from finding out what 'in reality' this relation of equality consisted of. (*Capital*: 152)[29]

So, for Marx, in capitalism the 'dominant social relation is the relation between men as possessors of commodities' (ibid.).[30] Since that was not the case in Aristotle's society, Aristotle could not discover that what really

---

[27] Elsewhere, Marx calls Aristotle 'the greatest thinker in antiquity' (*Capital*: 532).
[28] Discussed above in Chapter 1, Section 1.2.
[29] It is not clear to me why Marx puts 'in reality' in quotes.
[30] As with Smith, notice the casual sexism; as well as the privileging of a male point of view.

enabled commodities to be exchanged in definite proportions was that they were produced by human labor.[31]

Hence, for Marx, commodities have a use value or are an object of utility, and a value. Yet, value only manifests, shows, or expresses itself as exchange value – that is, in the commodity's ability to exchange in definite quantities with other commodities. The value itself is socially necessary abstract homogeneous labor. Therefore,

> When at the beginning of this chapter, we said in the customary manner that a commodity is both a use-value and an exchange-value, this was, strictly speaking, wrong. A commodity is a use-value or object of utility, and a 'value'. It appears as the twofold thing it really is as soon as its value possesses its own particular form of manifestation which is distinct from its natural form. This form of manifestation is exchange-value. (Ibid.)

For Marx, a commodity indeed has an objective value which manifests itself as exchange value.[32] From an explicitly Aristotelian perspective,[33] we can say that labor power actually working is the efficient cause of value. The embodied crystallized labor, the socially necessary abstract homogenized labor in the commodity, is the material cause. The value itself will acquire various forms, such as the commodity form, or the form of money.[34] The goal, in a capitalist society, to produce surplus value, is the final cause. This final cause, however, will not explicity be developed by Marx until later in his work when he gets to capital itself. Now, we are still at the stage where the exchange of commodities generates money.

8.3 MARX ON THE DEVELOPMENT OF THE MONEY FORM

For Marx, as with Aristotle and Smith, the generalized exchange of commodities will eventually necessarily generate money, or what Marx considers to be the money form of value, value being embodied or crystallized

---

[31] See also the *Grundrisse* where it is held that labor time 'regulates exchange values and indeed is not only the inherent measure of exchange values but their substance as well (for, as exchange value, commodities have no other substance, no natural attributes)' (1973: 169).

[32] See also *Theories of Surplus Value*, Part III (1971b: 141–4) where Marx criticizes the relativistic theory of value in Samuel Bailey's *Critical Dissertation on the Nature, Measures and Causes of Value*.

[33] As opposed to the largely implicit Aristotelian perspective which is in Marx's text. I suspect that for rhetorical reasons, Marx would not have wanted to overly stress the Aristotelian nature of his analysis.

[34] See especially, *Capital*, Chapter I, section 3, 'The Value-Form or Exchange-Value': 138–63; this will be discussed in the next section.

labor. On the final page of the *Critique*, at the end of a long section criticizing the work of all his predecessors, Marx concludes that their difficulties arise because 'Generally speaking these writers do not first of all examine money in its abstract form in which it develops within the framework of simple commodity *circulation*' (187, emphasis added). This, of course, is what Marx himself tries to do.[35]

According to Marx's distinctly original analysis, money develops originally from the simple, isolated, or accidental form of value where one commodity equals or is worth another commodity; to the total or expanded form of value where one particular commodity equals or is worth a series of other commodities; to the general form of value where the equation is turned around and this series of other commodities now equals or is worth one equivalent commodity.[36] For Marx, this is when 'a particular kind of commodity acquires the form of universal equivalent' (*Capital*: 160). The money form of value is where all particular commodities express their value in the specific commodity gold, so the money form is not really different from the general form of value.[37]

Thus, 'universal labour-time finds its expression in a universal product, a *universal equivalent*' (*Critique*: 32). Therefore 'the commodity which has been set apart as universal equivalent acquires a dual use-value. In addition to its particular use-value as an individual commodity it acquires a universal use-value' (*Critique*: 47). This universal use-value is to express or reveal or manifest the immanent values of all the other commodities. It 'arises from the specific role which this commodity plays as a result of the universal action exerted on it by the other commodities in the exchange process' (ibid.). This commodity becomes a universal medium of exchange, thereby becoming 'the embodiment of universal labour-time' (*Critique*:

---

[35] And several times too. See, for example, his 'Postface to the 2nd edition of *Capital*' (1976: 94). Note also, that at this stage in his analysis, Marx is working at the level of circulation, not the production of commodities. See, for example, Pack (1985b: 126–7).

[36] See *Capital*: 138–62. I think on this issue Marx is correct in the high estimation of his own work. As far as I know, no one before Marx attempted to work out the generation of money in such detail, particularly with an Aristotelian emphasis that money arises out of the change of *forms* of value. As Albritton correctly writes, 'It is Marx's theory of the commodity form that most fundamentally places his theoretical achievement far above those of all other economic theorists' (2007: 21). Of course, this is because Aristotle's formal cause is never even considered by most mainstream economists.

[37] Since 'throughout this work I assume that gold is the money commodity, for the sake of simplicity' (*Capital*: 188). For a contrary interpretation stressing that value for Marx has no existence without money see Reuten (2005). Reuten's reading minimizes the importance of Marx's discussion in *Capital* I, Chapter One, Section Three, 'The Value-Form, or Exchange-Value', as well as the crucial importance of Aristotle to this part of Marx's work. Marx here is clearly responding to issues which Marx interprets as being raised, but not solved, by Aristotle. See also Moseley (2005: 15–16).

48). Marx concludes, 'The particular commodity which thus represents the exchange-value of all commodities, that is to say, the exchange-value of commodities regarded as a particular, exclusive commodity, constitutes *money*' (ibid., emphasis in original).

So there is the exchange of commodities through the medium of money, where one commodity is sold for money which then buys another commodity, or C–M–C in Marx's notation.[38] This exchange, for Marx, is really a change in the form of value, from private labour to social labor; particular concrete labor, to abstract universal labor, back to concrete labor. Thus, following Aristotle and Smith, but developing their analyses in much more detail,[39] Marx concludes that 'Money necessarily crystallizes out of the process of exchange . . . The historical broadening and deepening of the phenomenon of *exchange* develops the opposition between use-value and value which is latent in the nature of the commodity' (*Capital*: 181, emphasis added).[40] That is, the commodity has both a use value and a value, which value reveals itself as exchange value when it is exchanged.

Money becomes a universal measure of value 'because all commodities, as values, are objectified human labour, and therefore in themselves commensurable, their values can be communally measured in one and the same specific commodity' . . . (*Capital*: 188). Thus, 'money as a measure of value is the necessary form of appearance of the measure of value which is immanent in commodities, namely labour-time' (ibid.). So, in agreement with Smith, Marx claims that 'the real measure of commodity and gold is labour itself' (*Critique*: 66).

Following Aristotle, Marx argues that money comes about with exchange between communities. 'In fact, the exchange of commodities evolves originally not within primitive communities, but on their margins, on their borders' (*Critique*: 50). Indeed, Marx here footnotes Aristotle, noting that 'Aristotle makes a similar observation with regard to the individual family considered as the primitive community. But the primitive form of the family is the tribal family, from the historical dissolution of which the individual family develops' (ibid.).

---

[38]   Or commodity–money–commodity. This comes, of course, from Aristotle's orginal analysis in *Politics*.

[39]   And with an emphasis on a complex dialectical analysis stressing contradictions (not contraries). For more on the importance of contradictions and change for Marx, see below, Chapter 10.

[40]   Again, note that throughout this stage in Marx's analysis, he is stressing the exchange of commodities. Marx is not here really dealing with production at all. Production only arises later in his analysis. The Japanese and Canadian Unoite Marxists are excellent at stressing the importance of this aspect of Marx's work. See Uno (1980), Sekine (1984, 1986) and Albritton (1986, 2007).

Furthermore, Marx follows Aristotle's analysis[41] in arguing that it is an illusion 'to suppose that money makes commodities commensurable. On the contrary, it is only the commensurabiliy of commodities as material-ized labour-time which converts gold into money' (*Critique*: 68). Marx once more footnotes Aristotle and claims 'Aristotle does indeed realize that the exchange-value of commodities is antecedent to the prices of com-modities' (ibid.). Again, for Marx, Aristotle cannot get to a labor theory of value, and hence to what makes commodities commensurable, because he lived in a slave society: 'Aristotle is aware of the fact that the different things measured by money are entirely incommensurable magnitudes. What he seeks is the oneness of commodities as exchange values, and since he lived in ancient Greece it was impossible for him to find it' (ibid.).

So money acts as a medium of exchange between commodities (or perhaps more accurately, from Marx's viewpoint, as a medium of the circulation of commodities) and a measurer of value. As gold, money has value. Gold bullion can be coined by the state and at first, 'the only difference between coin and bullion lies in their physical configuration, and gold can at any time pass from one form to the other' (*Capital*: 222). However, over time, the coins will become worn down and contain less gold than they stand for. The metallic money can be replaced with tokens, which become mere symbols of value. Eventually, even these tokens may be replaced with paper money. For Marx, 'Paper money is a symbol of gold, a symbol of money' (*Capital*: 225). With paper money, this 'symbol of money must have its own objective social validity. The paper acquires this by its forced currency. The state's compulsion can only be of any effect within that internal sphere of circulation which is circumscribed by the boundaries of a given community' (*Capital*: 226). Thus, 'gold circu-lates because it has value, whereas paper has value because it circulates' (*Critique*: 121).[42]

Marx claims that Aristotle 'understood that gold coin is a symbol or token of value' (*Critique*: 117).[43] In a long footnote, he first quotes *Nicomachean Ethics*: 1133a on this issue. Marx then quotes from *Politics*: 1257a and 1257b to argue that Aristotle showed that as a result of barter between different communities one commodity which has value is turned into money; but then the money may be coined and eventually become a mere symbol or token of value (ibid.).

---

[41]   Or it may be more accurate to say this is Marx's interpretation of Aristotle.

[42]   With paper money, the quantity theory of exchange/inflation becomes relevant. If only gold is money (or presumably were one on a strict gold standard) then the general price level is determined by the value of the gold/money commodity. See, for example, *Capital*: 224–5; *Critique*: 118–22.

[43]   Plato, too.

The money commodity, gold, becomes 'universal wealth in an individual form' (*Critique*: 125). In time, 'Since money does not reveal what has been tranformed into it, everything, commodity or not, is convertible into money. Everything becomes saleable and purchaseable . . . Just as in money every qualitative difference between commodities is extinguished, so too for its part, as a radical leveller, it extinguishes all distinctions' (*Capital*: 229).

The money itself may be hoarded. This is accomplished by selling without buying. With the hoarding of money, there is a change in the end, the goal. As with Aristotle, money gets desired for itself, to be accumulated. Since, 'the quantitative delimitation of exchange-value conflicts with its qualitative universality, and the hoarder regards the limitations as a restriction, which in fact becomes also a qualitative restriction, i.e. the hoard is turned into a merely limited representation of material wealth' (*Critique*: 131–2). As with Aristotle, because the money commodity gold can buy most anything, it has no limits, and the formation of hoards becomes an unending process.

> The hoarding drive is boundless in its nature. Qualitatively or formally considered, money is independent of all limits, that is it is the universal representative of material wealth because it is directly convertible into any other commodity. But at the same time every actual sum of money is limited in amount . . . This contradiction between the quantitative limitation and the qualitative lack of limitation of money keeps driving the hoarder back to his Sisyphean task: accumulation. He is in the same situation as a world conqueror, who discovers a new country with each country he annexes. (*Capital*: 230–31)

So we are once again back to Aristotle. Yet there does seem to be a slight difference. For Marx, it is money itself, because it is the universal equivalent, because it can purchase anything for sale, which generates the greed. Whereas Aristotle says that there is a proper way to use money, to facilitate the handy transfer of things from those with an excess to those with a deficit, Marx emphasizes that it is the existence of money itself which will generate the goal, the desire, to accumulate it.[44]

There arises now an issue where Marx does indeed go beyond Aristotle.[45] Previously, we have always been assuming spot purchases, where a

---

[44] 'The passion of enrichment by contrast with the urge to acquire particular material wealth, i.e. use values, such as clothes, jewelry, herds of cattle, etc., becomes possible only when general wealth as such is represented by a specific thing and can thus be retained . . . Money therefore appears both as the object and the source of the desire for riches' (*Critique*: 132).

[45] And I believe Smith too. Although see his discussion of the Scottish banking system and financial crisis in Chapter Two of Book II of his *Wealth of Nations*.

commodity and money change hands simultaneously. However, Marx points out there may also be credit purchases. In Marx's terminology, money will serve as a means of purchase when the commodity changes hands. However, the money may not actually be paid until later, which Marx calls the means of payment, when the money is actually delivered. In the meantime, the seller becomes a creditor, the buyer a borrower. Thus, 'the role of creditor or of debtor results here from the simple circulation of commodities' (*Capital*: 233). Thus, there will arise interest rates, secondary markets in bills of exchange, and so on: 'Credit-money springs directly out of the function of money as a means of payment, in that certificates of debts owing for already purchased commodities themselves circulate for the purpose of transferring those debts to others' (*Capital*: 238).[46]

The exchange of commodities themselves will generate interest rates, as people buy on credit.[47] This further necessitates the need to accumulate a hoard of money, or a reserve fund, to pay for things previously bought (or purchased). So the splitting apart of the functions of money as a means of purchase from a means of payment not only generates interest rates; it can also generate credit crises. Thus, interest rates and financial crises do not necessarily come from the saving/lending nexus.[48] Also, in time, 'When the production of commodities has attained a certain level and extent, the function of money as means of payment begins to spread out beyond the sphere of the circulation of commodities. It becomes the universal material of contracts. Rent, taxes, and so on are transformed from payment in kind to payments in money' (*Capital*: 238). This further necessitates the need for people to acquire money.

With the monetization of society, it is not just misers who become concerned with the perceived desire and need to accumulate money. To some extent, everyone will be concerned with the goal to acquire money. They will need money to pay their bills, to pay their rent, to pay their taxes.

---

[46] For the historical development of private money based upon bills of exchange in 16th century Europe see Boyer-Xambeu, Deleplace and Gillard (1994).

[47] As Marx points out, historically credit buying was most important in the wholesale markets (*Capital*: 238, fn. 54).

[48] The mere exchange of commodities mediated by money can generate a monetary or financial crisis as: (a) people may be unable to pay for the things they have bought; thus (b) inducing the seller/creditors to call in their loans, that is demand immediate payment. See, for example, *Capital* 235–6. (Marx does not present his full analysis of money used as credit until Volume III of *Capital*.)

The fall 2008 credit crisis partly comes from this very fact that most purchases and sales are not spot. Almost all of them involve some degree of separation of time between delivery and payment of a good or service. Hence, there must be some minimal level of trust/faith that your trading partner will not more or less immediately go bankrupt between the delivery of a good or service and its payment. In the fall of 2008, this minimal trust was lacking, necessitating spectacular government interventions.

Here, then, is a major difference between ancient Greece and modern society. For Marx,

> money is itself a commodity, an external object capable of becoming the private property of any individual. Thus the social power becomes the private power of private persons. Ancient society therefore denounced it as tending to destroy the economic and moral order. Modern society . . . greets gold as its Holy Grail, as the glittering incarnation of its innermost principle of life. (*Capital*: 229–30)

Marx is essentially protesting against too much social power becoming the private power of individual people. I think this is why basically Marx sides with Aristotle and the ancients, and against Smith and the powerful privatizing moderns. Yet, things will of course become more complicated (and nasty) when we leave the exchange of commodities and the development of money and turn to the realm of production, capital and the creation of surplus value.

9.   Karl Marx on capital and character

9.1   INTRODUCTORY COMMENTS

For Marx, capitalism, or rather the capitalist mode of production, has its own laws of motion. From an Aristotelian point of view, it has a nature. That is, it actualizes itself, and develops its potentialities. Then it becomes more or less unnatural, or corrupted. It is overthrown, it dies. Marx assumes that he can understand capitalism's nature, and grasp its inner essence and working. Hence, he believes he can see not only where it is, but where it is going, where it is developing, how it is actualizing itself and will eventually supersede itself.[1] Just as one who knows a kitten knows, barring an unfortunate accident to the kitty, that it will develop into a cat, Marx thinks he can foresee the future development of the capitalist mode of production.[2]

So the subject matter of Marx's work is capitalism. This is pretty much the same as Smith and modern economic thought (Smith, of course, terming his society as commercial society). However, Marx wants to help overthrow capitalism, or at least hasten its demise, since that will, of course, happen anyway. According to Marx, he is dealing with 'the natural laws of capitalist production. It is a question of these laws themselves, of these tendencies winning their way through and working themselves out with iron necessity' ('Preface to the 1st Edition': 91). Nonetheless,

> Even when a society has begun to track down the natural laws of its move-
> ment – and it is the ultimate aim of this work to reveal the economic laws of
> motion of modern society – it can neither leap over the natural phases of its

---

[1]   For a vehement argument that Marx is indeed an ontological and epistemological Aristotelian who does get to the bottom of things and hence correctly grasps the inner essence of the capitalist mode of production, see Meikle (1985).

[2]   This I think is the Aristotelian source of Marx's belief in his own prophetic abilities. On the prophetic side to Marx, see Schumpeter, *Capitalism, Socialism and Democracy*, Chapter 1, 'Marx the Prophet' (1950: 5–8); for a generally unsympathetic reading of Marx, yet that does stress the prophetic side of his work, see Tucker (1972). Of course, one who knows a kitty will generally develop into a cat, already is familiar with cats. One who knows the capitalist mode of production in the 19th century does not already known nor is familiar with what it will grow into: a big difference. On this point, even Hegel was more humble than Marx since, according to Hegel, 'the owl of Minerva spreads its wings only with the falling of the dusk' (1952: 13); that is, you can philosophically explain the past, but you cannot predict the future.

development nor remove them by decree. But it can shorten and lessen the birth-pangs. (ibid.: 92)

So Marx presents himself as a sort of midwife to the revolution, helping along, easing the pain involved in the birth of a new society, one which will replace the capitalist mode of production.

The capitalist system can be viewed as based upon the production of surplus value.[3] The physiocratic theory attributed the economic surplus to land. The neoclassical theory largely attributes the surplus, or profit, to the marginal productivity of physical capital, to machinery and equipment. Marx, partly following Smith's lead,[4] attributes the surplus to the workers themselves. When paying wages to the workers, it appears as if the capitalists are paying for the work itself, or for the output produced by the workers. Instead, claims Marx, the capitalist is paying for the potential for work, where the value of what is actually produced is greater than the value the worker gets paid. Hence, claims Marx, 'all the mystifications of the capitalist mode of production, all capitalism's illusions about freedom, all the apologetic tricks of *vulgar economics*, have as their basis the form of appearance discussed above, which makes the actual relation invisible, and indeed presents to the eye the precise opposite of that relation' (*Capital*: 680, emphasis added).[5]

In the capitalist mode of production, it appears as if the workers are being paid for the value of their output. Yet, they are not; they are being exploited. The surplus they produce is being creamed off by the property owning classes. Yet, we are getting ahead of ourselves, jumping towards the climax to Marx's work. Let us step back and work through Marx's own presentation of his theoretical system.[6]

9.2   MARX ON CAPITAL

As Marx notes in the *Critique*, he is following Aristotle in the analysis of the form of capital: 'In Chapter 9, Book I of his *Politics* Aristotle sets forth

---

[3]   Indeed, I think Marx would argue this is its essential characteristic.

[4]   And certainly Ricardo's.

[5]   On Marx's conception of vulgar economics, and his distinction between vulgar and classical political economy, see *Capital*: 174–5, fn. 34; and *Theories of Surplus Value Part III*: 500–502. At the risk of being overly obvious, I will point out that to characterize an opponent's position as vulgar has the tendency to break down all discourse, dialogue and conversation with that opponent. While that may have been the end desired by Marx himself, I think contemporary Marxists should be quite chary in employing that epithet.

[6]   Marx, of course, with his self-confidence and Aristotelian epistemology, considers it not merely a presentation of a theoretical system, but the scientific appropriation and presentation of the underlying reality itself.

the two circuits of circulation C–M–C and M–C–M, which he calls 'economics' and 'Chrematistics' and their differences' (137 fn.).[7] Following Aristotle, Marx argues that in C–M–C, the selling of a commodity for money, and then the purchasing of another commodity with that money, 'consumption, the satisfaction of needs, in short use-value, is therefore its final goal' (*Capital*: 250). In explicitly Aristotelian terms, the final cause of this exchange of commodities mediated by money is the satisfaction of needs.

The circuit M–C–M, the use of money to buy a commodity and then sell that commodity, is really M–C–M′, where M′ is greater than M. In Marx's terminology, 'this increment or excess over the original value I call "surplus-value"' (*Capital*: 251). This movement is capital. So for Marx, capital is not just money, not just stocks.[8] It is the use of both money and commodities to acquire more money. Furthermore, 'the circulation of money as capital is an end in itself . . . The movement of capital is therefore limitless' (*Capital*: 253). Thus, in explicitly Aristotelian terms, the final cause of this circuit is completely different from the final cause of the previous circuit. The goal of M–C–M′ is simply to acquire more money; a goal that can never be fully satisfied. Indeed, here Marx once again footnotes Aristotle's *Politics*, quoting extensively from both chapters 8 and 9 of Book I, and giving his interpretation of the text (*Capital*: 253–4, fn. 6).[9]

So, 'capital is money, capital is commodities . . . a process in which, while constantly assuming the form in turn of money and commodities, it changes its own magnitude, throws off surplus-value from itself considered as original value, and thus valorizes itself independently' (255). Capital, for Marx, is a process, 'a self-moving substance' (256). Do not freeze the process and then just look at one part of it (as physical stock, as financial capital, and so on). Rather, capital is the process of self-expanding value. It is money used to acquire more money, but it goes through various forms in this growth, as both money and machines, and so on. Or, as Sraffa (1960) would later put it, it is the 'production of commodities by means of commodities'.[10]

Marx now here makes another significant leap. He asserts that 'the

---

[7] Marx adds that 'the two forms . . . are contrasted with each other by the Greek tragedians, especially Euripides' (ibid.).

[8] As it basically is in neoclassical economic theory.

[9] Marx makes his own translation of the Greek into German. Marx, of course, had a PhD in philosophy and wrote his dissertation on ancient Greek philosophy ('The Difference Between the Democritean and Epicurean Philosophy of Nature').

[10] Assuming money and labor power are commodities.

exchange of commodities creates no value' (266).[11] Even less does the lending out of money at interest *create* value. Here, Marx again quotes Aristotle, this time that acquiring more money through lending is the most unnatural form of chrematistics, or way to use money (267). Note there is now a significant change from Aristotle to Marx.[12] Aristotle spoke of using money to acquire more money. This is in line with his general argument that there are various ways to *acquire* property. Marx is in a sense concerned with the use of money to acquire more money, but he is also concerned with *production*, how can more value be produced? This, of course, is in line with Marx's general emphasis that humans are productive animals, and his division of history into different eras based upon various modes of *production*.

Marx finds the ability to produce more value, surplus value, in the sale and purchase of labor-power.[13] Marx means by 'labour-power, or labour-capacity, the aggregate of those mental and physical capabilities existing in the physical form, of the living personality, of a human being, capabilities which he sets in motion whenever he produces a use-value of any kind' (270). This, of course, is a very Aristotelian way to view workers: 'Labour-power exists only as a *capacity* of the living individual' (274, emphasis added); and 'labour-power becomes a reality only by being expressed; it is activated only through labour' (ibid.). So labor power is potential, which gets actualized by laboring.[14]

The worker, the owner of labor power, must be free. The worker is not a slave, is not a commodity, but the owner of a commodity. That commodity is the capacity to work. The worker is free in a double sense, in that the worker can sell his capacity to work to anyone, yet the worker must basically have no other commodity for sale, and so be free from access to the means of production.

According to Marx, 'the value of labour-power is the value of the means of subsistence necessary for the maintenance of its owner' (274). Granted, 'the determination of the value of labour-power contains a historical and moral element. Nevertheless, in a given country at a given period, the

---

[11] Neoclassical economics, with its focus on utility, would of course, dispute this. The idea that people, in terms of utility, may gain from trade goes at least as far back as Xenophon (for example Lowry, 1987: 78–9).

[12] As there was also from Aristotle to Smith, although the clarity was somewhat obscured by ambiguities in Smith's usage of the terms value and wealth.

[13] I am tempted to write that Marx finds this ability in the labor market; but Marx, of course, argues that the labor market does not really exist. Instead, there is a market for labor-power. For Marx, workers really sell their labor-power; it only seems or appears that they sell their labor.

[14] Also, 'By working, the latter [the seller of labour-power] becomes in *actuality* what previously he only was *potentially*, namely labour-power in action, a worker' (283).

average amount of the means of subsistence necessary for the worker is a
known datum' (275). Thus, the value of labor-power, of the worker, 'like
that of all other commodities, is determined by the labour-time necessary
to produce it' (340). Since the system, the economy, must reproduce itself
through time, 'the value of labour-power includes the value of the commodities necessary for the *reproduction*, for continuing the existence of the
working class' (377, emphasis added). Thus, 'given the value of these means
of subsistence, the value of his labour-power can be calculated' (430).[15]

The existence of a generalized market for labor-power arises only at
a specific time in history. Hence, according to Marx, capital itself, as a
generalized system of production, will also only arise at a specific time in
history:

> capital. The historical conditions of its existence are by no means given with
> the mere circulation of money and commodities. It arises only when the owner
> of the means of production and subsistence finds the free worker available, on
> the market, as the seller of his own labour-power. And this one historical pre-
> condition comprises a world's history. Capital, therefore, announces from the
> outset a new epoch in the process of social production. (274)[16]

Once this general market for labor power exists, capital, where
M–C–M', will come into its own. This is because the hired worker makes
more than it costs to reproduce himself (and his family). Hence, 'the value
of labour-power, and the value which that labour-power valorizes in the
labour-process, are two entirely different magnitudes; and this difference
was what the capitalist had in mind when he was purchasing the labour-
power' (300). The worker hired by the capitalist creates for the capitalist
more value than it costs to hire that worker. Hence, the creation of surplus
value, hence the exploitation of the worker, hence, for Marx, the true
source of all property (non-wage) income.

---

[15] Notice that here Marx is casually assuming that the worker is a male. Later in the
text Marx discusses the entrance of women into the labor-power market. Also, what needs
to be reproduced is not the individual worker, but the worker and the family of the worker,
so that the class of workers may be reproduced. This reproduction is largely done within the
family unit, with non-wage labor, often using non-purchased means of subsistence, and so
on. Problems with Marx's casual sexism, his privileging of the male point of view, his relative
neglect of the family and the role of women in society, and so on, have given rise to a whole
school (or arguably schools) of Marxist feminists.
[16] So note, capital for Marx is not the mere means of production, or factories, or plant
and equipment. It is a social relation which is historically specific. Marx describes the
origins of a generalized market for labor power, which is the result of the separation of the
workers from the land, hence from the means of production, in Part Eight of *Capital*, 'So-
Called Primitive Accumulation' (871–940). The classic 20th century text on this topic is E.P.
Thompson's *The Making of the English Working Class* (1963).

Remember, the workers are hired by money, which according to Marx represents objectified, abstract, homogeneous labor. It represents past labor, or dead labor. And now comes one of Marx's more colorful metaphors: the vampire motif.[17]

> incorporating living labour into their lifeless objectivity, the capitalist simultaneously transforms value, i.e. past labour in its objectified and lifeless form, into capital, value which can perform its own valorization process, an animated monster. (302)

So capital can be envisioned as dead labor, systematically sucking up living labor: 'Capital is dead labour which, vampire-like, lives only by sucking living labour, and lives the more, the more labour it sucks' (342). Note that this is actually pretty close to Smith's position, where stock, created by past labor, hires the workers and in the long run actually regulates the physical supply of workers.[18] Yet, Marx's terminology is much more colorful and graphic. For Marx, the human-produced means of production, which he calls constant capital, has a 'vampire thirst for the living blood of labour' (367).

According to Marx, this means of production, the machinery, plant and equipment, or constant capital, does not produce value or surplus value. Only the special commodity labor power does that.[19] So, 'the values of the means of production used up in the process are preserved' (307); but, the 'means of production never transfer more value to the product than they themselves lose during the labour process by the destruction of their own use-value' (312).[20] Thus, 'the value of the constant capital re-appears in the value of the product, but does not enter into the newly produced value, the newly created value-product' (421). Therefore, 'machinery, like every other component of constant capital, creates no new value, but yields up its own value to the product it serves to beget. In so far as the machine has value and, as a result, transfers value to the product, it forms an element in the value of the latter' (509).[21]

---

[17] Although he does have many. His entertaining, colorful rhetoric is, I believe, (just) one of the reasons for his awesome influence.

[18] Basically through changes in the infant mortality rate of the children of the working class; which, admittedly, is a pretty harsh mechanism.

[19] Labor power is also quite unique as a commodity in that, generally speaking, it is not produced with the goal of exchanging it in the market. (Although right-wing critics have argued that with overly generous family allowances in some 20th and 21st century welfare states, it is produced with the goal of acquiring money for the producer.)

[20] That is, through depreciation. As Sraffa points out, the remaining constant (or what loosely speaking may be termed fixed) capital may be considered a joint product (1960: 95).

[21] See also *Capital*: 512, fn. 26: 'a machine no more creates new value than any other part of constant capital'.

Capital then is really itself surplus labor:

> It is just as important for a correct understanding of surplus-value to conceive
> it as merely a congealed quantity of surplus labour-time, as nothing but objec-
> tified surplus labour, as it is for a proper comprehension of value in general
> to conceive it as merely a congealed quantity of so many hours of labour, as
> nothing but objectified labour. What distinguishes the various economic forma-
> tions of society – the distinction between for example a society based on slave-
> labour and a society based on wage-labour – is the form in which this surplus
> labour is in each case extorted from the immediate producer, the worker. (325)

So, for Marx, surplus labor itself will have different forms in different societies.[22] In all societies which have developed since primitive hunting and gathering communist societies, one class of people will appropriate the labor of another social class. In a capitalist society, capital, 'as an agent in producing the activity of others, as an extractor of surplus labour and an exploiter of labour-power . . . surpasses all earlier systems of produc-tion, which were based on directly compulsory labour, in its energy and its quality of unbounded and ruthless activity' (425). Hence, the means of production, employ the worker and 'they consume him as the ferment necessary to their own life-process, and the life-process of capital consists solely in its own motion as self-valorizing value' (ibid.). Note again, there is the vampire motif, where the dead are sucking the life blood of the living: 'this inversion, indeed this distortion, which is peculiar to and characteris-tic of capitalist production, of the relation *between dead and living labour*, between value and the force that creates value' (ibid., emphasis added).[23]

Once capital creates machinery, and the production process becomes more mechanized, then capital can employ more workers in the family, including women and children. With more workers hired by capital, each individual worker can be paid lower wages:

> The value of labour power was determined, not only by the labour-time nec-
> essary to maintain the individual adult worker, but also by that necessary to
> maintain his family. Machinery, by throwing every member of that family onto
> the labour-market, spreads the value of the man's labour-power over his whole
> family. It thus depreciates it. (518)

---

[22] See also *Capital*: 713.
[23] See also *Capital*: 548, where value is stored up or dead or past labor in the form of machines: 'the instrument of labour confronts the worker during the labour process in the shape of capital, dead labour, which dominates and soaks up living labour-power'. And later in the text, 'the worker's product is not only constantly converted into commodities, but also into capital, i.e. into value that sucks up the worker's value-creating power, means of subsist-ence that actually purchase human beings . . . the worker himself constantly produces objec-tive wealth, in the form of capital, an alien power that dominates and exploits him' (716).

This, of course, increases the exploitation of the working class.

Hence, in declared opposition to Adam Smith, Marx claims that capital is command over unpaid labor:

> Capital, therefore, is not only the command over labour, as Adam Smith thought. It is *essentially* the command over unpaid labour. All surplus-value ... is in *substance* the materialization of unpaid labour-time. The secret of the self-valorization of capital resolves itself into the fact that it has at its disposal a definite quantity of the unpaid labour of other people. (672, emphases added)

So, in an Aristotelian sense, Marx feels that he has gotten to the underlying truth, the underlying reality of the situation. Beneath the surface appearance of things, all income derived from property, that is profits, interest and rent, is in substance a form of theft. It is someone else's labor time that is not paid for. The Aristotelian material cause of surplus value is unpaid labor time.[24]

Capital, then, turns out to be a form of theft:

> surplus product, parts of the tribute annually exacted from the working class by the capitalist class. Even if the latter uses a portion of that tribute to purchase the additional labour-power at its full price, so that equivalent is exchanged for equivalent, the whole thing still remains the age-old activity of the conqueror, who buys commodities from the conquered with the money he has *stolen* from them. (728, emphasis added)

So, on the one hand, the relation between capital and the working class *appears* not to be theft, because it is the exchange in the market of equivalent for equivalent. On the other hand, Marx holds that beneath the level of appearances, it really is a form of theft, for example: 'The greater part of the yearly accruing surplus product, which is *embezzled* from the English workers without any equivalent being given in return, is thus used as capital' (761, emphasis added). Explains Marx, 'the constant sale and purchase of labour-power is the form; the content is the constant appropriation by the capitalist without equivalent, or a portion of the labour of others'. Hence, 'property turns out to be the right, on the part of the capitalist, to appropriate the unpaid labour of others' (730).

Note several points. On the one hand, by claiming that property income is really theft (or embezzlement, or appropriation, or tribute), there is

---

[24] See also *Capital*: 715 where Marx argues that capital 'sooner or later becomes value appropriated without an equivalent, the unpaid labour of others'. In *Capital*, Vol. III, Marx writes that 'capital obtains this surplus-labour without an equivalent, and in essence it always remains forced labour – no matter how much it may seem to result from free contractual agreement' (819).

a broadening of the idea of theft which may, and will indeed, be put to dangerous, deadly effect. In a sense, it is similar to the broadening of the term racist or mental illness. If the terms racist or mental illness are defined too broadly, then we will most all be racist, or mentally ill. In a sense, that may arguably be true, but then the broadening of the terms hides or obscures crucial differences in the degree of racism and mental illness.[25] Nonetheless, if capital, and property income in general are really a form of theft, then that is a wonderful reason why capital and the resulting property income should be taken back from the capitalists and large property owners.[26] It is a wonderful, indeed powerful, theoretical justification for a communist revolution. That, of course, was most likely the goal, the purpose, the Aristotelian final cause of writing *Capital: A Critique of Political Economy* in the first place: to provide a theoretical justification (or theoretical foundation) for communist revolution.

In Marx's younger writings, he was concerned with the concept of alienation, and critiquing religion.[27] While not major explicit themes in *Capital*, he does occasionally bring them up. So, for example, Marx writes, 'Since past labour always disguises itself as capital . . . it is *alienated*, as unpaid labour, from the worker himself, i.e. it is attributed to its form as capital' (757, emphasis added). Capital, then, may be pictured as alienated labor, and the worker is ruled by his product. Marx, devout atheist that he was, argued that this was similar to the field of religion. That is, we currently live:

> in a mode of production in which the worker exists to satisfy the need of the existing values for valorization, as opposed to the inverse situation, in which objective wealth is there to satisfy the worker's own need for development. Just as man is governed in religion, by the products of his own brain, so in capitalist production, he is governed by the products of his own hand. (772)

---

[25] In a sense we are back to the old Aristotelian issue that racism and mental illness should most likely be considered contraries, not contradictions. Yet our language tends to induce us to think in terms of contradictions: For example we either are or are not racist; are or are not mentally ill.

[26] Just as slaves should be taken away from or set free from their slave-masters/ owners. This, of course, is what happened in the US South during the course of the Civil War, which occurred while Marx was writing *Capital*. It is pertinent here that sometimes Marx called wage-laborers wage-slaves (for example *Capital*: 575, 925; *Capital* Vol. III: 595). William A. Williams calls the goal of emancipating US slaves, the taking away of the slave-owners' private property, the 'lid of Karl Marx's box' since 'the trap was apparent: if it was permissible to take private property in order to establish or maintain laissez faire, then no sophistry could deny the equal right to take it in order to construct socialism' (1961: 302).

[27] See the writings collected by Easton and Guddat in Marx (1967c), especially the well known 'Economic and Philosophic Manuscripts' of 1844 (283–337).

For Marx, in the religious sphere, people need to overcome the power of religion and religious authorities which, in reality, are merely alienated ideas, and alienated powers. Similarly, in the economic and social spheres, workers need to overcome the power of capital and the capitalists, and reclaim their alienated labor.

Hence, on the issue of capital, Marx reaches basically the opposite conclusions of Adam Smith. Smith felt he was studying commercial society. This is a society based upon trade, and persuasion and reason. The driving force in the society is an innately human one, to make a deal, to truck, to barter.[28] This, for Smith, was one of the reasons commercial society was so good and so natural.

Marx disagreed vehemently. For him, it was a capitalist society, one based upon the capitalist mode of *production*. As with Aristotle (and Smith), money could indeed be used to acquire more money.[29] Yet, it was really only done with the exploitation of labor power and the theft of their labor. It should be superseded; overthrown. Moreover, as with Aristotle (and to some extent, as seen above, with Smith), there are some major character issues which need to be addressed.

9.3   MARX ON CHARACTER

9.3.1   On Character in General in Capitalist Society

There is a certain tension in Marx's presentation of the character of the capitalists and workers in these mature economic texts.[30] On the one

---

[28]   *Wealth of Nations* (I.ii.1). And the best way to make a good deal, to make good exchanges, is to sympathize or empathize with the needs of your potential trading partner. This idea of sympathizing (or really empathy, but that was not a word available to Smith in the 18th century English language) is one of the key concepts linking up Smith's *Wealth of Nations* with his only other published book, *The Theory of Moral Sentiments*. A clever, good deal-maker will sympathize with the needs of others – the better to meet those needs and conclude a deal.

[29]   Again note that for Aristotle, there are various types of societies based upon *acquiring* things provided by nature. For Marx, there are various ways and types of society based upon people *producing* things. For the most part this was also true for Smith, with his four stage theory of socioeconomic development. The notable exception for Smith was his contemporary society, which by calling it commercial society, suggested that it was based upon trade, rather than production. What to call our own contemporary society, or how to characterize it, is contentious (for example Galbraith, 2004, Chapter II: 3–9).

[30]   Focusing on the *Critique* and *Capital Volume I*. These, of course, are the only two mature economic works by Marx published in his lifetime. The other two volumes of *Capital* were edited by Engels from notes left by Marx. The English edition of the three volumes of *Theories of Surplus Value* were posthumously prepared by the Institute of Marxism–Leninism in Moscow; they were first published in German by Kautsky 1905–1910.

hand, Marx presents their characters as how he thinks they really are in capitalist society. This is particularly evident in the *Critique* where he writes that 'The commodity-owners entered the sphere of circulation merely as guardians of commodities' (94). Thus,

> These distinctive social characters are, therefore, by no means due to individual human nature as such, but to the exchange relations of persons who produce their goods in the specific form of commodities. It is therefore as absurd to regard buyer and seller, these bourgeois economic types, as eternal social forms of human individuality, as it is preposterous to weep over them as signifying the abolition of individuality. They are an essential expression of individuality arising at a particular stage in the social process of production. (95)

Hence, for example, both the capitalists and the workers[31] will become very cosmopolitan and international in outlook. This is because, according to Marx, 'Commodities as such are indifferent to all religious, political, national and linguistic barriers . . . there develops the commodity-owner's cosmopolitanism, a cult of practical reason, in opposition to the traditional religious, national and other prejudices which impeded the metabolic process of mankind' (152).

On the other hand, particularly in *Capital*, there is a consciously *dramatic* element to the presentation. Indeed, in the preface to the first edition, Marx writes that 'individuals are dealt with here only in so far as they are the *personifications* of economic categories, the bearers of particular class-relations and interests' (92, emphasis added). In the main text he writes that 'the persons exist for one another merely as representatives and hence owners of commodities. As we proceed to develop our investigation, we shall find, in general, that the characters who appear *on the economic stage* are merely personifications of economic relations; it is as the bearers of these economic relations that they come into contact with each other' (178–9, emphasis added).

So, to some extent the characters of the capitalists and workers presented by Marx will be a caricature. Hence, for example, at the end of Part II, 'The Transformation of Money into Capital', where we are leaving the domain of circulation, in the buying and selling of labor power, an important change takes place.

> When we leave this sphere of simple circulation or the exchange of commodities . . . a certain change takes place, or so it appears, in the physiognomy of our *dramatis personae*. He who was previously the money-owner now strides out in

---

[31]   Recall that the workers are also commodity-owners; they own and are forced to sell their labor power, their capacity to labor.

front as a capitalist; the possessor of labour-power follows as his worker. The one smirks self-importantly and is intent on business; the other is timid and holds back, like someone who has brought his own hide to market and now has nothing else to expect but – a tanning. (280, emphasis in original)

So, there is a consciously dramatic element in Marx's presentation of people's characters. Also, note Marx does have a certain mordant sense of humor which has not been without its charms for generations of readers.[32] In any case, let us now turn to what Marx himself refers to as 'the protagonist of the *drama*, the capitalist' (441, fn. 2, emphasis added).

9.3.2   On the Capitalists' Character

When the holder of money uses it with the goal to acquire more money, Marx basically becomes pure Aristotle. Thus,

as the conscious bearer of this movement, the possessor of money becomes a capitalist . . . it is only in so far as the appropriation of ever more wealth in the abstract is the sole driving force behind his operations that he functions as a capitalist, i.e. as capital personified and endowed with consciousness and a will. Use-value must therefore never be treated as the immediate aim of the capitalist. (254)

The goal of acquiring more money takes over his soul. The capitalist becomes a caricature:

But, in so far as he is capital personified, his motivating force is not the acquisition and enjoyment of use-values, but the acquisition and augmentation of exchange-value. He is fanatically intent on the valorization of value; consequently he ruthlessly forces the human race to produce for production's sake. In this way he spurs on . . . the creation of those material conditions of production which alone can form the real basis of a higher form of society, a society in which the full and free development of every individual forms the ruling principle. (739)

Note two Aristotelian points. One, the chrematistic use of money to acquire more money wrecks (or overwhelms, takes over) the character of

---

[32]   One gets the feeling from reading Smith that he truly enjoyed thinking about economics, money, and so on. Not so for Marx who compared studying his work to going into hell ('Preface' to *Critique*: 23). This general attitude, I think, is also to some extent reflected in their personal lives, their home economics. Smith prudently increased his income and material economic security throughout his entire life. Marx had monetary problems all his life and was frequently financially supported by his great friend Engels. (Of course, it also made a huge difference that Smith basically supported the fundamentals of commercial society; whereas Marx was a declared revolutionary.)

the capitalist. Secondly, here is also Marx's vision, hope and prediction for a future where humans will indeed be able to develop/realize/actualize their full human potential. Marx is basically historicizing Aristotle, using an Aristotelian framework of humans developing their potentials. Yet, this happens through time, through the working out of the historical process. What develops is not so much the individual person in a lifetime, but the human species through the progress of history.[33]

Meanwhile, in the here and now, the capitalist, 'as a capitalist, he is only capital personified. *His soul is the soul of capital.* But capital has one sole driving force, the drive to valorize itself, to create surplus-value' (342, emphasis added). Competition drives, or rather forces the capitalist to work the workers hard, to pay them low wages, and to grow in order to survive economically. Hence, 'what appears in the miser as the mania of an individual is in the capitalist the effect of a social mechanism in which he is merely a cog' (739). Thus, the capitalist himself is subservient to the social forces unleashed by capital, by dead labor trying to absorb living labor so as to accumulate more dead labor. In Marx's colorful, heated, presentation: 'Accumulate, accumulate! That is Moses and the prophets! Therefore save, save, i.e. reconvert the greatest possible portion of surplus-value or surplus product into capital! Accumulation for the sake of accumulation, production for the sake of production' (742, exclamation points in original).

Note an important point here. If Marx is correct that the goal of the capitalist is to accumulate, then in the long run there should be no problem with savings limiting economic growth. This is because the capitalist himself will acquire the savings, or value, or surplus value, when (and if) he is able to sell his output. The value of the output will contain the surplus value appropriated from the worker which will enable the capitalist to 'save', accumulate and reproduce on an expanded scale. Hence, if Marx is correct, then there need be no policies to directly try to increase savings to increase economic growth. Economic growth will generate the 'savings' by the capitalists who will then use it to accumulate, and increasingly expand total output.

The drive or goal for more surplus value, for more profits, for more accumulation, does urge the capitalist on. The result, in a way, is much worse than pre-capitalist consumers of others' labor. In Marx's reading of history:

---

[33] Popper is quite right when he argues that 'it may be shown here how his [Aristotle's] theory of change lends itself to historicist interpretations, and that it contains all the elements needed for elaborating a grandiose historicist philosophy. (This opportunity was not fully exploited before Hegel)' (1945: 7). The same applies, mutatis mutandis, to Marx.

Capital did not invent surplus labour. Whenever a part of society possesses the monopoly of the means of production, the worker, free or unfree, must add to the labour-time necessary for his own maintenance an extra quantity of labour-time in order to produce the means of subsistence for the owner of the means of production . . . It is however clear that in any economic formation of society where the use-value rather than the exchange-value of the product predominates, surplus labour will be restricted by a more or less confined set of needs, and that no boundless thirst for surplus labour will arise from the character of production itself. Hence in antiquity over-work becomes frightful only when the aim is to obtain exchange-value in its independent shape, i.e. in the production of gold and silver. (344–5)

So overwork is worse in capitalism than in pre-existing social formations, with the significant exception in the gold and silver mines. This suggests that the problems Marx associates with capitalism – excessive greed, overworking of the laborers, and so on – are to some extent also rooted in money, the universal equivalent itself.

In commenting on a controversy whether night labor for children was bad for their health, Marx remarks, 'that such a question could provide the material for a serious controversy is the best demonstration of the way capitalist production acts on the mental functions of the capitalists and their retainers' (368, fn. 62). So, being a capitalist, essentially a spokesperson for capital, really does wreck their brains, wrecks their character. For capital:

the worker is nothing other than labour-power for the duration of his whole life . . . Time for education, for intellectual development, for the fulfillment of social functions, for social intercourse, for the free play of the vital forces of his body and his mind, even the rest time of Sunday . . . what foolishness! But in its blind and measureless drive, its insatiable appetite for surplus labour . . . (375)

Consumed by greed, capitalists, if not prevented by society, will overwork and wreck the lives of their workers. At the same time, this also happens not because they necessarily want to, but because they are coerced by competition. Thus, 'capital therefore takes no account of the health and length of life of the worker, unless society forces it to do so' (381). So, 'under free competition, the immanent laws of capitalist production confront the individual capitalist as a coercive force external to him' (ibid.). So, according to the capitalists,

competition with other capitalists . . . did not allow them to limit the hours worked by children voluntarily, etc. 'Much as we deplore the evils before mentioned, it would not be possible to prevent them by any scheme of agreement between the manufacturers'. . . taking all these points into consideration, we have come to the conviction that some legislative enactment is wanted. (ibid, fn. 82)

That is to say, here for Marx, the capitalists themselves may occasionally want legislation to curb the competition, to prevent themselves from overworking and killing children.[34]

Yet, generally, the capitalists cannot help treating the workers the way they do. If they were to give better conditions for their workers, they would most likely be driven out of business. Thus, unless checked by legislation, there will be a certain amount of 'brutality natural to a man who is merely an embodiment of capital' (416, fn. 68). And, of course, as with Smith, there will also be a natural tendency for the capitalists to lie and try to mislead the public (609).

On the other hand, when the capitalist gets rich, 'there develops in the breast of the capitalist a Faustian conflict between the passion for accumulation and the desire for enjoyment' (741). Thus, over time, the more that capital increases, 'the capitalist can therefore live a more pleasant life, and at the same time "renounce" more' (757). It may be noted that this apparently Faustian dilemma is rather neatly handled by the modern corporation. It generally distributes part of its profits in the form of dividends to the owner, who may spend or reinvest the money at his/her discretion. The corporation keeps the rest of the profits as retained earnings, to reinvest and accumulate. Hence, in contemporary society, much savings are accumulated by the corporation for their owners (and possibly managers).

If the character of the capitalists is necessarily warped by this use of money to acquire more money, the character of the worker is even more, to use Harry Braverman's term, 'degraded' (1974).

9.3.3 On the Workers' Character

For Marx, in general, the worker 'acts upon external nature and changes it, and in this way simultaneously changes his own nature' (283). This is key. As with Aristotle, you are, or become, what you do. Your character is largely the result of your habits, your life experiences, although there is more emphasis in Marx than Aristotle on the effects of actual production, of working.[35]

---

[34] With so-called globalization, this process is repeating itself. There are calls for raising the minimum standards throughout the world so that there will not be a 'race to the bottom'. Of course, most of these calls do not come from the capitalists themselves.

[35] This is clearly expressed by Marx in *The German Ideology*: 'As individuals express their life, so they are. What they are, therefore, coincides with what they produce, with *what* they produce and *how* they produce. The nature of individuals thus depends on the material conditions which determine their production' (1967c: 409, emphasis in original). See also *Capital*: 647.

Also, as with Aristotle, Marx stresses the importance of telos, or the goal in work. So, for example,

> the architect builds the cell in his mind before he constructs it in wax. At the end of every labour process, a result emerges which had already been conceived by the worker at the beginning, hence already existed ideally. Man not only effects a change of form in the materials of nature; he also realizes his own purpose in those materials. (284)

Thus, as with Aristotle, the final cause, the goal to build something, in a sense is also a first cause, or happens first in time.

However, in the specifically capitalist production process, things are not so good for the worker:

> It must be acknowledged that our worker emerges from the process of production looking different from when he entered it . . . when the transaction was concluded, it was discovered that he was no 'free agent', that the period of time for which he is free to sell his labour-pwer is the period of time for which he is forced to sell it, that the *vampire* will not let go. (415, emphasis added)

So, in one sense the worker is indeed free, free to sell to any capitalist his capacity to work. The worker is free at the level of the market where he exists as the owner of a commodity: his own potential to work. Yet, the worker is really forced to sell his labor capacity, since the worker is separated from the means of production, which are monopolized by the capitalist class. So there exists freedom for the worker to make the contract, the deal with a capitalist. Once the labor power is sold, Marx assumes that the worker must do as he is told. The worker is under the control of the capitalist (or the agent of the capitalist). During this time period, that is much or most of the worker's life, the worker is not at all free.

Marx acknowledges that there will be supervisory workers, a special kind of wage-laborer (450). Also, according to Marx, there will be workers to look after the whole of the machinery in the factories. To repair the machinery there will be engineers, mechanics, and so on. Thus, there will be a superior class of workers, part scientifically educated and partly trained in a handicraft (545). Nonetheless, for Marx, this is not where the emphasis is. Here, as most always with Marx, the emphasis is not on the middle, the mean, or Aristotelian contraries. Rather, the emphasis is on the extremes: the capitalist on the one side, the more or less common, unskilled worker on the other. We are generally dealing with contradictions, not contraries.

Hence, with manufacture, specialization and the division of labor, the particular workers will get molded by the work they do. Thus, 'the one-sidedness and even the deficiencies of the specialized individual worker become perfections when he is part of the collective worker' (469). That is, there is the 'development in a man of one single faculty at the expense of all others' (474). At this point in his analysis, Marx is quite Smithian. Thus, manufacturing 'converts the worker into a crippled monstrosity' (481); he is 'transformed into the automatic motor of a detail operation' (ibid.). The worker becomes an appendage of the workshop which 'mutilates the worker, turning him into a fragment of himself' (482). Marx quotes Smith on this issue, and in a footnote mistakenly says that Smith was a pupil of Adam Ferguson (483, fn. 47).[36] With manufacturing enterprise there is a 'crippling of the individual worker. It produces new conditions for the domination of capital over labour' (486). Things get even worse for the workers with the development of machinery and the further deskilling of the worker.

So Marx is concerned with the deleterious effect of work on the laborer. This is in contradistinction to Aristotle who was quite unconcerned with most human labor in general and certainly with slave labor.[37] Marx shares this concern with Smith, although Marx goes in much more detail and at greater length than Smith does in *The Wealth of Nations*. Looking to the future, Marx holds

> That monstrosity, the disposable working population held in reserve, in misery, for the changing requirements of capitalist exploitation, must be replaced by the individual man who is absolutely available for the different kinds of labour required of him; the partially developed individual . . . must be replaced by the totally developed individual for whom the different social functions are different modes of activity he takes up in turn.
> One aspect of this process of transformation, which has developed spontane-ously . . . is the establishment of technical and agricultural schools. (618)

Again, note the Aristotelian ideal of 'the totally developed individual'. Unfortunately, in the meantime, 'the dispersal of the rural workers over large areas breaks their power of resistance, while concentration increases

---

[36] Because of the relatively long gestation between the presentation of Smith's ideas in his courses and other public places (particularly various 'clubs'), and their formal appearance in *The Wealth of Nations*, it sometimes appears that people who learned from Smith actually taught Smith. This is clearly the case with John Millar, who was Smith's student but whose *Observations Concerning the Distinction of Ranks in Society* appeared in 1771, before Smith's own *Wealth of Nations*, and owed much to Smith's teachings in his jurisprudence course. See, for example, Pack (1996b: 262–4).

[37] Says Aristotle: 'The science of the slave would be such as the man of Syracuse taught, who made money by instructing slaves in their ordinary duties. And such a knowledge may be carried further, so as to include cookery and similar menial arts . . . But all such branches of knowledge are *servile*' (*Politics*: 1255b, emphasis added). Aristotle was more concerned with plants and animals than with slaves.

that of the urban workers. In modern agriculture, as in urban industry, the increase in the productivity and the mobility of labour is purchased at the cost of laying waste and debilitating labour-power itself' (638). With agricultural production, Marx wants 'its systematic restoration as a regulative law of social production, and in a form adequate to the full development of the human race' (ibid.). Again, there is the Aristotelian desire for the development of human potentialities. Note, however, for Marx, much more so than for Aristotle, this human development is accomplished through the development of meaningful work experiences, rather than freedom or extrication from work itself.

With industrial, mechanical production in the growing capitalist factories, the increases in capital accumulation

> distort the worker into a fragment of a man, they degrade him to the level of an appendage of a machine, they destroy the actual content of his labour by turning it into a torment; they alienate from him the intellectual potentialities of the labour process . . . they deform the conditions under which he works, subject him during the labour process to a despotism the more hateful for its meanness . . . it follows therefore that in proportion as capital accumulates, the situation of the worker, be his payment high or low, must grow worse. (799)

So Marx's complaint, his criticism, his critique, is not just based upon exploitation, income distribution and the taking (or stealing) of surplus labor in the form of surplus value from the workers. It is also what the system does to the workers themselves and to their characters. So, 'accumulation of wealth at one pole is, therefore, at the same time accumulation of misery, the torment of labour, slavery, ignorance, brutalization and *moral degradation* at the opposite pole' (799, emphasis added).[38]

Unfortunately, 'the advance of capitalist production develops a working class which by education, tradition and habit looks upon the requirements of that mode of production as self-evident natural laws. The organization of the capitalist process of production, once it is fully developed, breaks down all resistance' (899). It follows that, 'the silent compulsion of economic relations sets the seal on the domination of the capitalist over the worker. Direct extra-economic force is still of course used, but only in exceptional cases' (899). This suggests the need for a working class awakening, a revolution, the overthrow of the capitalist state and the capitalist mode of production.

---

[38] See also *Capital*: 615 where Marx writes of workers' 'mental and bodily degradation'.

10. Karl Marx on the state and change

10.1 MARX ON THE STATE

10.1.1 On the State in *Capital*

It is surprising and a bit remarkable that for a work which is a critique of *political* economy, the state very rarely appears in *Capital*.[1] Marx does write that in England the state is 'ruled by capitalist and landlord' (348) and England is 'the classic representative of capitalist production' (349, fn. 15). Almost his only discussion of the state in the text occurs in his various comments on the Factory Acts in England. On the one hand, the conflict over the length of the working day, working conditions, and so on, is a result of intense class struggles between the capitalists and the workers. On the other hand, there necessarily arises the absolute need for regulation by the state to prevent the total ruination of the workers. By Marx's reading of history,

> While the modern Factory Acts compulsorily shorten the working day, the earlier statutes tried forcibly to lengthen it. . . . Centuries are required before the 'free' worker, owing to the greater development of the capitalist mode of production, makes a voluntary agreement, i.e. is compelled by social conditions, to sell the whole of his active life, his very capacity for labour, in return for the price of his customary means of subsistence, to sell his birthright for a mess of pottage. (382)[2]

So in the fight for the modern Factory Acts to limit the length of the working day, 'their formulation, official recognition and proclamation by the state were the result of a long class struggle' (395). Repeating a theme found in Smith concerning the truthfulness of the capitalists, Marx writes that in this struggle 'no method of deceit, seduction, or intimidation was

---

[1] I think it is for this reason, and the fact that his characters, particularly those of the capitalists, are often caricatures, that some readers only of Marx's mature economic works mistakenly read him as a strict economic determinist.

[2] Recall that in our earlier discussion of Smith's views on regulations, Smith was against regulations on wages because all these previous attempts to regulate wages were laws concerning *maximum*, not *minimum* wage rates (see above, Chapter 7, subsection 7.1.2). Basically, both Smith and Marx saw these earlier regulations as attempts to lower wages and/ or lengthen the workday.

left unused' (396).[3] For Marx, 'the history of the regulation of the working day . . . prove[s] conclusively that the isolated worker, the worker as "free" seller of his labour-power, succumbs without resistance once capitalist production has reached a certain stage of maturity' (412). In the United States, the workers' ability to wage this class struggle was further weakened by slavery. There, 'every independent workers' movement was paralysed as long as slavery disfigured a part of the republic. Labour in a white skin cannot emancipate itself where it is branded in a black skin. However, a new life immediately arose from the death of slavery' (414).[4] Thus, the end of slave labor in the US improved the position of wage laborers.

Therefore, 'for "protection" against the serpent of their agonies, the workers have to put their heads together and, as a class, compel the passing of a law, an all-powerful social barrier by which they can be prevented from selling themselves and their families into slavery and death by voluntary contract with capital' (416). So, according to Marx, workers to some extent must be against their own freedom. That is, against their freedom to compete against each other for longer hours, lower wages, and worse working conditions; laws are needed to prevent them from doing this. Note then, that Marx assumes that generally workers, unless they put pressure on the state to pass laws protecting them, will compete against each other worsening their class position. So, Marx's basic assumption (or rather, reading of history) is that there will almost always be a surplus population of unemployed or underemployed workers generating this downward pressure on the working class standards of life and work.[5] As Marx sarcastically writes, 'The great beauty of capitalist production consists in this . . . [that it] always produces a relative surplus population of wage-labourers in proportion to the accumulation of capital' (935).[6]

---

[3] Later, when discussing the silk manufacturers' successful attempt to acquire special rights to hire child laborers, Marx writes that 'subsequent investigation showed that the pretext was a *deliberate lie*' (406, emphasis added). I think what frequently happens for capitalists (and others) is that lying is not a moral issue, it is an economic issue. They do a cost/benefit analysis: if the expected economic benefits exceed the expected economic costs of lying, then lie.

[4] Levy and Peart, who frequently work together, are very good in stressing that in general classical economists took a firm stand against slavery. See, for example, Peart's Presidential Address to the 35th Annual Meeting of the History of Economics Society (2008).

[5] This is similar to 1979 Nobel Laureate winner Sir Arthur Lewis' argument (1954) that in third world countries there is basically an infinitely elastic supply of labor. With increased 'globalization' and international mobility of capital (and to a lesser extent labor power), is this not the situation in the 21st century? More on this below in Part IV.

[6] See also Chapter 25, 'The General Law of Capitalist Accumulation', Section 3, 'The Progressive Production of a Relative Surplus Population or Industrial Reserve Army': 781–94. It of course makes a huge difference (or rather all the difference in the world) if one assumes that generally under capitalism we are at full employment (some variant of Say's law); or that generally we are at much less than full employment (Marx's position).

Thus, 'the immoderate lengthening of the working day produced by machinery in the hands of capital leads later on to a reaction on the part of the society, which is threatened in the very sources of its life; and from there, to a normal working day whose length is fixed by law' (533). So, according to Marx, particularly with the advent of the machine age of capitalism and large factories, workers are deskilled and degraded, thus severely weakening their power in the class struggle.[7] Hence, state legislation to protect the workers becomes absolutely necessary for the preservation of society, for the mere reproduction of the working class. Therefore, 'factory legislation, that first *conscious* and methodical reaction of society against the *spontaneously* developed form of its production process, is, as we have seen, just as much the *necessary* product of large-scale industry as cotton yarn, self-actors and the electric telegraph' (610, emphases added).[8] With the passage of the Factory Acts, the state can be seen as to some extent acting in the interests of *all* society, to protect and preserve the basic humanity of the working class.[9] On the other hand, the actions of the state, and the laws passed by the state, can also be interpreted as part of the class struggle, a struggle over the state itself.

10.1.2 Reflections on the Marxist Theory of the State In General

The most famous statement of Marx's view of the state probably comes in *The Communist Manifesto* (jointly written with Engels): 'The executive of the modern state is but a committee for managing the common affairs of the whole bourgeoisie' (Chapter I, paragraph 12; 2005: 43). Now, there are several reasonable ways to interpret Marx's position concerning the state. On the one hand, one can take a largely functional viewpoint, as taken by people such as Poulanztas (1973).[10] Here, the capitalist state has various functions which it needs to fulfill in order to help in the reproduction of the capitalist socio-economic system. This is actually similar to

---

[7] The classic Marxist work in the 20th century on the deskilling and degradation of workers is Braverman (1974). Murphy argues that Braverman is really following Ruskin, not Marx on this issue (1993: 175–6). But I think it is clear that the degradation of work in the capitalist mode of production is indeed a major theme of Marx.

[8] Note the difference between what is conscious, or social, and what is spontaneous, hence, in a sense, natural for Marx. I will discuss this ambiguity and tension between the natural and the social in Marx below in subsection 10.2.2.

[9] 'What could be more characteristic of the capitalist mode of production than the fact that it is necessary, by Act of Parliament, to force upon the capitalists the simplest appliances for maintaining cleanliness and health?' (611).

[10] For a critical Hegelian–Marxist investigation into what determines economic policy in capitalist societies which largely follows a functional approach see Reuten and Williams (1989).

Smith's position as written in *The Wealth of Nations*. Recall that Smith never wrote his book on 'the general principles of law and government' (*TMS*: 342). Rather, what we have in *The Wealth of Nations*, particularly in the very long Chapter 1 of Book V ('Of the Expences of the Sovereign or Commonwealth'), yet also scattered throughout the treatise, is an enumeration of various things or functions which the government ought to perform in his commercial society. So, in this sense, Marx and Smith are quite similar; the state has certain functions to fulfill.

One can also adopt a more straightforward interpretation of Marx's position, that the state is a tool or instrument largely used by the ruling class to further its own interests. Marx seems to adopt this position when he writes in *The German Ideology* that 'the state is nothing more than the form of organization which the bourgeois by necessity adopts for both internal and external purposes as a mutual guarantee of their property and interests' (1967c: 470). Here, with the state as a tool or instrument, the state itself clearly becomes an object of class struggle, where the various social classes attempt to use or grasp control of the state.[11] This is the position taken by people such as Ralph Miliband (1969) and his followers.[12] Note two things about this approach.

One, as seen above, this is also a key part of Smith's own position. Although Smith does not stress it, he does write in *The Wealth of Nations* that 'Civil government, so far as it is instituted for the security of property, is in reality instituted for the defence of the rich against the poor, or of those who have some property against those who have none at all' (V.i.b.11). Hence, government may be viewed to be a tool or institution which arises with the growth of private property, at a particular time in the evolution of history.[13] Again, Marx and Smith are not too far apart on this issue. The main difference is really one of attitude. Smith thinks the state is largely necessary and good for the development of class society. He compares his society to previous societies and largely approves of the difference. Marx is against his capitalist state and wants it overthrown. Furthermore, Marx largely compares his society to what he thinks the future can (and will) bring, and finds his society sadly wanting. Or to use

---

[11]   Or to destroy it entirely. Accordingly to Marx, this is what the workers of the Paris Commune were doing ('Civil War in France', 1971a: 349–52).

[12]   I think the fascinating work by Domhoff (for example, 1967, 1970, 1972, 1974) largely falls within this tradition of the state as instrument or tool either used by the ruling class or to be contested.

[13]   See the discussion above, Chapter 7, subsection 7.1.4. This historical viewpoint of the state changing with the evolution of society throughout various stages is most evident in his 'Lecture Notes on Jurisprudence' particularly 'Report of 1762–3', first published in 1978. On the similarities in the ideas in these lectures and Marx's, see Meek (1977, 'Part One': 1–94).

economic jargon, for Marx the opportunity cost of the status quo, the maintenance of his current society, is staggeringly high.

Secondly, note that in his quickly written political and journalistic writings commenting on contemporary events, Marx wrote of the state largely as a tool or institution which was fought over. In these writings, there is no evidence of strict economic determinism.[14] Rather there is a deep complexity of political analyses in these writings. This complexity is particularly evident in his writings on major political events in France: 'The Class Struggles in France, 1848–50'; 'The Eighteenth Brumaire of Louis Napoleon' and 'The Civil War in France'.[15] So, for example, in 'The Eighteenth Brumaire' Marx goes into great detail trying to 'demonstrate how the *class struggle* in France created circumstances and relationships that made it possible for a grotesque mediocrity to play a hero's part' (1971a: 244, emphasis in original). It is also here where Marx made his famous statement that 'Men make their own history, but they do not make it as they please; they do not make it under self-selected circumstance, but under circumstance existing already, given and transmitted from the past' (245). Marx gives a detailed, complicated account of Louis Napoleon's surprising rise to power; a person characterized as 'an adventurer dropped in from abroad, raised on the shoulders of a drunken soldiery which he bought with whisky and sausages and to which he has to keep throwing more sausages' (320). There was nothing pre-ordained or deterministic in Louis Napoleon's acquisition of state power.

Finally, particularly in Marx's younger writings, there was a third view-point on the state, where the state was alienated power.[16] Here, as noted above, just as religious ideas and religious authorities were really alienated ideas and alienated powers,[17] the state for the young Marx was essentially alienated political and social power. So, for example, in 'On the Jewish Question', Marx wrote that 'Political emancipation is also the *dissolution* of the old society on which rests the sovereign power, the character of the state as alienated from the people' (1967c: 238, emphasis in original). This vague notion of the state as another form of alienated power needing to be reacquired animated his call for radical actions so that:

> Only when the actual, individual man has taken back into himself the abstract citizen and in his everyday life, his individual work, and his individual relation-ships has become a *species-being*, only when he has recognized and organized his own powers as *social* powers so that social force is no longer separated from

---

14 Or at least not in the short (or 'immediate') run.
15 These writings are collected in Padover's *Marx on Revolution* (Marx, 1971a).
16 See, for example, Tucker (1969: 56–60).
17 See above, Chapter 9, section 9.2.

him as *political* power, only then is human emancipation complete. (1967c: 241, emphases in original)

Hence, there are Marxist functional, instrumental, and the state as alienated power theories of the state which find support in Marx's work.

At this point, I should address a terminological issue. As John Henry (2008) stresses, Marx made a distinction between the government and the state. The government for Marx is merely administration; the state is (at least in part) a tool for class oppression. So, returning to *The Communist Manifesto*, we find that Marx predicts that after the communist revolution, 'When, in the course of development, class distinctions have disappeared, and all production has been concentrated in the hands of a vast association of the whole nation, the public power will lose it political character. Political power, properly so called, is merely the organized power of one class for oppressing another' (2005, Chapter II, Paragraph 73: 71). Thus, after the communist revolution, the state will wither away, basically by definition.[18] If the state is an instrument for domination of one class by another, and after the completed revolution there is only one class, then the state can no longer exist. Instead, there will be mere government, and there will be 'the conversion of the functions of the state into a mere superintendence of production' (2005, Chapter III, Paragraph 54: 85). Marx, of course, badly underestimated the challenges involved in 'the mere superintendence of production'.[19]

Marx, as with Smith, never wrote his planned book on the state.[20] Hence, for both of them, we must keep in mind that we do not have their full thoughts on the matter: whether we call it the state, the government, jurisprudence, or politics. When it comes to encyclopedic completeness, Aristotle has both Smith and Marx beat, hands down. We have Aristotle's book on *The Politics*; and so much, much more. Had Marx written a book on the state, we may have had a full Aristotelian analysis, with a discussion of the four causes of the state. Then we would have been treated to a detailed analysis of the final cause or goal of the state; the various forms a state will take; the material basis of the state, that is, what it is made of; and the efficient cause of the state, how the state is actually run. As with Smith, the state would also no doubt be historically specific. The state would vary depending upon a variant of Smith's 'stage of society', Marx's own theory of various modes of production. Yet, that book was never written. Moreover, as far as I am aware, no Marxist has yet tried to write

---

[18]   Although in the transition period between capitalism and communism (that is, socialism), the state will temporarily still exist as an apparatus of the working class defending that class against other social classes and strata. See Henry (2008).

[19]   The classic text on these challenges is probably Hayek, *The Road to Serfdom* (1944).

[20]   See, for example, *Grundrisse*: 264. Also, Nicolaus (1973: 53–4).

such an Aristotelian–Marxist analysis of the state; it would, of course, be a massive undertaking.

10.2 MARX ON CHANGE

10.2.1 General Reflections

As with Smith, with Marx we are in the modern world: a world of evolution and real change. History does not go in circles; it is definitely going somewhere. Hopefully it is progressing (whatever that means; and how do we measure 'progress'?). And yet, progress is not a sure thing.

Also, for Marx, history is largely the working out of contradictions, not contraries. Recall that for Aristotle there were various types of changes, most of them being contraries. There were changes in quantity (growth and diminution), changes in place (locomotion) and changes in quality (alteration). However, coming-to-be and passing-away, generation and destruction, life and death, according to Aristotle, are not contraries; they are contradictions. They have no middle term.[21]

Historical change for Marx moves basically by contradictions, where there is no middle, rather than by contraries. One of the reasons Marx stresses contradictions over contraries in history is precisely because history does go somewhere. Among other things, it involves the life, development and death of various modes of production. For Marx, as opposed to Aristotle, history does not generally go in circles. Hence the need for an account based upon contradictions, for a story of life and death. So, for example, in most of *Capital*, there is a two-class model or story. Basically, for most of the text, there are the capitalists, and the wage earners. There is little emphasis on middle classes or strata. These two major classes, the capitalists and the wage earners, conflict and fight with each other. This relative absence of a middle class is the opposite of Aristotle who stressed the importance of the middle class for social stability. Of course, social stability was just about the last thing Marx, a committed revolutionist, wanted.

10.2.2 Natural versus Social in Marx's View of Historical Change

As with Aristotle and Smith, the 21st century reader of Marx will have some problem with the use of the term 'natural'. Recall that for Aristotle,

---

[21] See above, Chapter 3, section 3.1.

natural meant the best, or a perfection. So, for example, when water (or really grapes) turns into wine then it is natural; when it becomes vinegar, then it is unnatural. Money used to facilitate the circulation of goods is natural; money used to acquire more money is unnatural.[22]

Smith, in rebelling against this use of the term 'natural' in general, and in particular that the use of money to acquire more money is in any way unnatural or corrupt, generally uses the word natural to mean normal.[23] For Smith it was perfectly natural to use money to try to acquire more money. Moreover, a society largely based upon this goal, what Smith termed a commercial society, was also perfectly natural.

Marx, for the most part, rebelled against Smith's use of the word natural. Marx insisted that the world we live in is a social, not natural world. Hence, political economy deals with social issues, not natural issues, and its categories and concepts refer to social not natural things. So, for Marx, 'Nature no more produces money than it does bankers or a rate of exchange' (*Critique*: 155). Also, the commodity form is a 'definite social relation' (*Capital*: 165). Capital itself is not the mere physical means of production, but a social relation, self-expanding value, old dead labor vampire-like sucking up the lifeblood of living labor, and so on.[24]

Nonetheless, as we saw above,[25] in the 'Preface to the 1st Edition' of *Capital*, Marx also wrote that there are '*natural* laws of capitalist production' (91, emphasis added). Further in this preface Marx characterized his 'standpoint, from which the development of the economic formation of society is viewed as a process of *natural* history' (92, emphasis added). So, there is a bit of a problem or ambiguity with Marx's use of the terms nature and natural. On the one hand, everything with humans is social; we are a social species. Yet, this sociality arises 'naturally'.[26] Thus, for Marx, 'within a family and, after further development, within a tribe, there springs up *naturally* a division of labour caused by differences of sex and age' (471, emphasis added). In discussing the factory regulations in England to regulate the length of the working day, Marx claimed they 'developed gradually out of circumstances as *natural* laws of the modern mode of production' (394–5, emphasis added). There is a 'natural law of capitalist production' (793).

---

[22]   See above, Chapter 2, section 2.2.
[23]   Although Smith is not totally consistent in his use of the word natural; see above, Chapter 5, section 5.2.
[24]   See also *Capital*: 273 where Marx argues that nature does not produce the capitalist/labor power relation; rather it is a social relation and a product of historical development.
[25]   Chapter 9, section 9.1
[26]   For a work stressing the natural side of Marx with regards to value theory, see Lippi (1979).

According to Marx:

> The veil [of commodity fetishism] is not removed from the countenance of the social life-process, i.e. the process of material production, until it becomes production by freely associated men, and stands under their conscious and planned control. This, however, requires that society possess a material foundation, or a series of material conditions of existence, which in their turn are the *natural and spontaneous* product of a long and tormented historical development. (173, emphasis added)

So the natural for Marx is correlated with spontaneous; it is pre-planned. It is before the Communist Revolution. In Marx's dream or prophecy for the future, and comparing that future with the miserable present:

> the fact that the collective working group is composed of individuals of both sexes and all ages must under the appropriate conditions turn into a source of humane development, although in its *spontaneously* developed, brutal, capitalist form, the system works in the opposite direction, and becomes a pestiferous source of corruption and slavery, since the worker exists for the process of production, and not the process of production for the worker. (621, emphasis added)

So, for Marx, history up until his day was basically spontaneous, in a way natural (though at the same time social). This history would be succeeded by human reason, conscious democratic control of society and human development. So Marx is giving an account of human history. He wants conscious, rational change as opposed to unconscious change or spontaneous evolution. Marx wants to replace Hegel's putative cunning of reason, which happens behind people's backs, or Smith's theory of unintended results, or any Smithian invisible hands, with explicit, attempted human reason.

Hence, reason is important for Marx, and in a sense we are back to Aristotle. Yet, note again, Marx is historicizing Aristotle. For Marx, reason does not yet really exist in the current world. It will come to exist in the future, after the Communist Revolution. Hence, of the three authors in this study, for Smith there is the least emphasis upon reason.[27] This is because so often for Smith, changes – the evolutionary working out of human history (such as the growth in the division of labor and the

---

[27] As is only fitting for someone whose closest friend was no doubt David Hume. On the importance of instincts or 'hard-wiring' in Smith's views on the human species, see Wight (2009). That for Hume, rationality may (of course) be a possible consequence or result of human choices largely guided by passions, see Diaye and Lapidus (2005a, 2005b). See also Pack (1993).

development of human speech itself) – are unintended, decidedly not the result of conscious planning or human reason.[28]

Note also, it is the very idea of being subsumed to the dictates of economic markets which Smith appreciates as an improvement upon previous forms of personal servitude,[29] and which Marx vehemently opposes. Marx does not want humans bound, dictated to, or subservient to economic markets.[30] He thinks humans can get to a post-market, vastly improved society. This was not really an option considered by Smith.[31] Smith was more looking backwards in history at feudal relations of production and personal servants, and felt that was generally grossly inferior to commercial market relations. Smith tried to figure out ways to improve commercial market relations. Marx looked more to the future, thinking we could get past the anarchic dictates of the market. Was he being utopian?[32]

10.2.3 The Birth, Development and Death of Capitalism

In a sense, it is fruitless to have a separate section on Marx and change, since his entire analysis is based upon change and dynamics.[33] Moreover, to some extent, his entire work seeks to explain the rise, development and necessary fall of capitalism. Indeed, Paul Sweezy perceptively entitled his classic textbook on Marx's economics, *The Theory of Capitalist Development* (1942). So this section will give just a thumbnail sketch of his story. First, a brief look at his basic method. Good Aristotelian that he was, Marx was always concerned with the final cause or goal; various forms

---

[28]   Hayek and the Hayekians are keenly aware of this and stress this side of Smith's thought. For them, humans need economic markets precisely because the markets provide necessary information which humans cannot otherwise acquire. See, for example, 'Dr Bernard Mandeville' and 'Competition as a Discovery Procedure' in Hayek (1984). See also Hamowy (1987)

[29]   See Perelman (1989).

[30]   See, for example, *Grundrisse*: 158, 162, 196–7.

[31]   Recall, of course, that Smith wrote the *Wealth of Nations* in the decade before 1776, when it would have been very difficult for him to envision a stage beyond capitalism (or commercial society).

[32]   Of course, even to ask this question risks the posthumous wrath of Marx. Both Marx and Engels insisted they were scientific socialists, not utopian socialists (see, for example, *Communist Manifesto*, Chapter 3, Section 3, 'Critical-utopian Socialism and Communism', 2005: 82–6). But Marx was well aware that this was an issue for him too, for example: 'if we did not find concealed in society as it is the material conditions of production and the corresponding relations of exchange prerequisite for a classless society, then all attempts to explode it would be quixotic' (*Grundrisse*: 159).

[33]   As seen above (Chapter 9), even his concept of capital is value in motion, self-expanding value, dead labor sucking the life-blood of living labor, and so on.

or the formal cause;[34] and efficient causes, how things actually occurred. Yet, he was also keenly concerned with the *material* cause. Thus,

> Technology reveals the active relation of man to nature, the direct process of the production of his life, and thereby it also lays bare the process of the production of the social relations of his life, and of the mental conceptions that flow from those relations. Even a history of religion that is written in abstraction from this material basis is uncritical. It is, in reality, much easier to discover by analysis the earthly kernel of the misty creations of religion than to do the opposite, i.e. to develop from the actual, given relations of life the forms in which these have been apotheosized. The latter method is the only materialist, and therefore the only scientific one. (403–4, fn. 4)[35]

Thus, Marx insists upon getting to the material basis of human societies, and tracing the change in this basis throughout history. Yet, according to Marx, this is rarely done by the historian:

> The writers of history have so far paid very little attention to the development of material production, which is the basis of all social life, and therefore of all real history. But prehistoric times at any rate have been classified . . . according to the materials used to make tools and weapons, into the Stone Age, the Bronze Age and the Iron Age. (286, fn. 6)

This sort of material classification needs to be made for historic times as well. Thus, Marx wants to root his analysis as much as possible in technology, and the material basis of society. It must be historically specific.[36]

As we have frequently seen, the goal or telos or reason why something is done is also important for Marx. So for example, *vis-à-vis* machinery, 'the aim of the application of machinery under capitalism. Like every other instrument for increasing the productivity of labour, machinery is intended to cheapen commodities and, by shortening the part of the working day in which the worker works for himself, to lengthen the other part, the part he gives to the capitalist for nothing' (492).

In any case, the modern history of capital dates only from the 16th

---

[34]   For example, as we saw above, commodities, money and capital are, in a sense, all just various forms of value.

[35]   Actually, perhaps somewhat surprisingly, Smith did do this sort of analysis in his posthumously published essay 'The Principles which Lead and Direct Philosophical Enquiries' illustrated by the history of astronomy, history of ancient physics, and history of ancient logics and metaphysics. See Pack (1995b).

[36]   This, of course, was how Marx believed he was correcting Hegel's system; by grounding historical change in changes in the material world, rather than change being caused by the ideal, or the unfolding of the world spirit. Smith's analysis in *The Wealth of Nations* was also historically specific, actually being basically confined to his commercial stage of society. However, Smith's rhetoric tends to hide or mask this historical specificity.

century (when it 'starts to unfold') with world trade and markets (247). For the capitalist system to get off the ground, it needed to encounter free workers; people free from access to the means of production who are free (or forced) to sell their potential to labor. This history, the separation of the workers from the means of production, 'is written in the annals of mankind in letters of blood and fire' (875). Thus, a revolution occurs when 'great masses of men are suddenly and forcibly torn from their means of subsistence, and hurled onto the labour-market as free, unprotected and rightless proletarians' (876). In England, the peasants were forcibly driven from the land. By Marx's reading of history, originally they 'had the same feudal title as the lords themselves'; yet they were thrown off the land and, additionally, the great feudal lords usurped 'the common lands' (878). This process, which began in the late 15th and early 16th centuries, this ruthless theft of communal property, was so complete that 'by the 19th century, the very memory of the connection between the agricultural labourer and communal property had, of course, vanished' (889).

Marx's concluding paragraph to Chapter 27, 'The Expropriation of the Agricultural Population from the Land' is a damning one:

> The spoliation of the Church's property, the fraudulent alienation of the state domains, the theft of the common lands, the usurpation of feudal and clan property and its transformation into modern private property under circum- stances of ruthless *terrorism*, all these things were just so many idyllic methods of primitive accumulation. They conquered the field for capitalist agriculture, incorporated the soil into capital, and created for the urban industries the nec- essary supplies of free and rightless proletarians. (895, emphasis added for the 21st century reader)

Once the capitalist mode of production is in place, then there will be change induced by capital itself, by self-expanding value, by the drive for profit. On the one side, this drive is fueled by the incessant desire for profit, for more, by the owners of capital.[37] On the other side the drive is also fueled by competition. If one capitalist does not adopt the newest, cheapest technology, or does not extract the maximum amount of labor from labor power, then the competitor will do it. The reward for failing to adopt the latest technologies, or working the labor force to the utmost, of actualizing the potential from labor power, will be bankruptcy.

Thus, in the capitalist era, we now have a 'social formation in which the process of production has mastery over man, instead of the opposite' (175). Furthermore, once the capitalist mode of production exists, it repro- duces itself: 'We have seen how money is transformed into capital; how

---

[37] This side was, of course, discussed by Aristotle in dealing with chrematistics.

surplus-value is made through capital, and how more capital is made from surplus-value' (873).[38] Capital dictatorially rules labor power, allocating it throughout the production processes in society, and controlling it in the individual factories: 'where the capitalist mode of production prevails, anarchy in the social division of labour and despotism in the manufacturing division of labour mutually condition each other' (477).

Once capitalism enters the historical stage, there is a change in the labor process from relatively simple co-operation, where workers are first brought together by capital; to manufacturing.[39] In manufacturing plants, the extent of the division of labor is increased, productivity goes up, the value of labor power falls, and more surplus value is created for the capitalists. In Marx's critical estimation, 'Adam Smith said nothing at all new about the division of labour. What characterizes him as the quintessential political economist of the period of manufacture is rather the stress he lays on it' (468, fn.19). Tools are simplified, and workers get divided into skilled and unskilled laborers; both classes of workers are separated from their means of production, forcing them to work in the capitalist-owned factories.

Marx emphasizes that 'modern industry never views or treats the existing form of a production process as the definitive one. Its technical basis is therefore revolutionary, whereas all earlier modes of production were essentially conservative' (617).[40] In a footnote, Marx then quotes himself and Engels in a now famous and eloquent passage from the *Communist Manifesto:*

> Constant revolutionizing of production, uninterrupted disturbance of all social conditions, everlasting uncertainty and agitation distinguish the bourgeois epoch from all earlier ones. All fixed frozen relations, with their train of ancient and venerable prejudices are swept away. All new-formed ones become antiquated before they can ossify. All that is solid melts into air, all that is holy is profaned and man is at last compelled to face with sober senses, his real conditions of life and his relations with his kind. (617, fn. 29)

The workers' insecurity is enormous. The turbulence of the socioeconomic system 'constantly threatens . . . to snatch from his hands the means of subsistence, and, by suppressing his specialized function, to make him superfluous' (618).

---

[38] This suggests that the system does not need the savings of non-capitalist individuals. The savings are done by the capitalist class or their legal fiction, the modern corporation. More on this below in Part IV.

[39] See Chapters 13, 'Cooperation': 439–54 and 14, 'The Division of Labour and Manufacture': 455–91.

[40] Schumpeter of course picked up and developed this side of Marx's thought. See, for example, Schumpeter (1950, Chapter VII, 'The Process of Creative Destruction': 81–6).

With the development of the machine age of capitalism, 'Capital now sets the worker to work, not with a manual tool, but with a machine which itself handles the tool' (509). Things worsen for the workers. Thus, 'we nowhere find a more shameless squandering of human labour-power for despicable purposes than in England, the land of machinery' (517). The machines largely dispense with the need for muscular power, so capital can employ women and children, in addition to adult men. The introduction of machines leads to the lengthening, not the shortening, of the working day. Over time, the machines are speeded up, creating harder work for the labourer (536 ff.). The machines do facilitate what we would now call globalization:

> the cheapness of the articles produced by machinery and the revolution in the means of transport and communication provide the weapons for the conquest of foreign markets. By ruining handicraft production of finished articles in other countries machinery forcibly converts them into fields for the production of its raw material. . . . A new and international division of labour springs up, one suited to the requirements of the main industrial countries, and it converts one part of the globe into a chiefly agricultural field of production for supplying the other part. (579–80)[41]

As we saw earlier in this chapter, the rise of machinery and large-scale industry eventually and necessarily called forth regulation by the state to protect the workers. Two things happen once there are regulations on some of capital. One, there is a drive to avoid the regulations, for some capital to go to those sectors of the economy which are not regulated (605–9). Two, there is also the drive to make these regulations universal so that they cover all capital. Thus, there is 'the cry of the capitalists for equality in the conditions of competition, i.e. for equality of restraint on the exploitation of labour' (621).[42]

Marx predicts the rise of big businesses. Due to competition individual capitals are forced to grow, through internal accumulation and reinvestments (what he calls concentration of capital); and/or taking over other less successful parts of capital (Marx calls this centralization of capital).

---

[41] Following up and expanding on this train of thought, the second half of the 20th century saw the rise of radical Marxist-inspired dependency theorists; see, for example, Baran (1957), Frank (1967) and Amin (1976). Actually, in the 21st century, under the North America Free Trade Act, it was US farm goods which were exported to Mexico, displacing Mexican peasants from the land, who then emigrated from Mexico to the US. The US exported cheap food; Mexico exported cheap labor power.

[42] This process was played out on a national scale in the US in the late 19th and early 20th centuries, where there was the need to have national rather than state regulations to create a relatively level national playing field for capital. In the 21st century, with even more 'globalization' due to decreased communication and transportation expenses, there is an intense need for this process to be played out on an international scale. More below in Part IV.

Marx also expects there to be increasing differences in the standard of living between the working class and the capitalist class:

> it is possible, given increasing productivity of labour, for the price of labour-power to fall constantly and for this fall to be accompanied by a constant growth in the mass of the workers' means of subsistence. But in relative terms, i.e. in comparison with surplus-value, the value of labour-power would keep falling, and thus the abyss between the life-situation of the worker and that of the capitalist would keep widening. (659)

So, for Marx, real wages may go up in the future.[43] However, he does not think that wages will go up in proportion to increased worker productivity: 'the increasing productivity of labour is accompanied by a cheapening of the worker, as we have seen, and it is therefore accompanied by a higher rate of surplus-value, even when real wages are rising. The latter never rise in proportion to the productivity of labour' (753). Hence, the disparity of income between property-owning and property-less people, between the capitalist class and the working class, increases over time.

As we discussed above, eventually the capitalist mode of production must be replaced. Thus, 'the development of the *contradictions* of a given historical form of production is the only historical way in which it can be dissolved and then reconstructed on a new basis' (619, emphasis added). Note again the stress on Aristotelian contradictions, not contraries. Marx is dealing with the coming-to-be and the passing-away, the birth, life and eagerly anticipated death of the capitalist mode of production.

Marx believes he sees a wonderfully bright future embedded in the filthy, degrading bowels of the present. So, for example, he wants and anticipates, in the future, Aristotelian moderation, in the combining of factory work and physical and mental education for children. Thus, 'the germ of the education of the future is present in the factory system; this education will, in the case of every child over a given age, combine productive labour with instruction and gymnastics, not only as one of the methods of adding to the efficiency of production, but as the only method of producing fully developed human beings' (614). Note again the Aristotelian emphasis on the development, the actualization of the potential in human beings. Where Marx does sharply depart from Aristotle, however, is in his belief that people actually develop themselves through working; not only through the use of leisure based upon slave labor.[44] For Marx, labor is not

---

[43] See also *Capital*: 763.
[44] And possibly Athenian imperialism. The possible parallels between the imperialism of classical Athens' admittedly flawed direct democracy and the 21st century imperialism of the United States' admittedly flawed representative democracy are disturbing; scary really.

contemptible, fit only for slaves. Rather, labor itself is a necessary component for the full development of humans' potential.

Marx also foresees a fundamental change in the family form. He thinks that 'large-scale industry, in overturning the economic foundation of the old family system, and the family labour corresponding to it, had also dissolved the old family relationships' (620). Nevertheless, it simultaneously creates 'a new economic foundation for a higher form of the family and of the relations between the sexes. It is of course just as absurd to regard the Christian-Germanic form of the family as absolute and final as it would have been in the case of the ancient Roman' (621). For Marx the family form, as most all other forms in human society, is historically specific. The family will necessarily change throughout the course of history.

Marx's hope and prediction for the future is that, just as at the dawn of the capitalist era there had been 'the expropriation of the direct producers . . . accomplished by means of the most merciless barbarism, and under the stimulus of the most infamous, the most sordid, the most petty and the most odious of passions' (928). So in the very near future, 'What is now to be expropriated is not the self-employed worker, but the capitalist who exploits a large number of workers' (928).[45] Marx looks forward to and wants 'the revolt of the working class, a class constantly increasing in numbers, and trained, united and organized by the very mechanism of the capitalist process of production. . . This integument is burst asunder. The knell of capitalist private property sounds. The expropriators are expropriated' (929). Marx dreams on, claiming that 'capitalist production begets, *with the inexorability of a natural process*, its own negation. This is the negation of the negation' which will 'establish individual property on the basis of the achievements of the capitalist era; namely co-operation and the possession in common of the land and the means of production produced by labour itself' (929, emphasis added). So the post-capitalist system will have some form of common property in land and the means of production; of that Marx seems certain. Moreover, this revolution, according to Marx, is inevitable. So, in one sense, since the coming revolution is inevitable, then it is not social; it is natural. It will occur as a force of nature.

Marx concludes, in the last phrase of the next to last chapter of *Capital*, that we will have 'the expropriation of a few usurpers by the mass of people' (930). At the very end of that phrase is a footnote quoting himself and Engels in *The Communist Manifesto*. The quote in part reads:

---

[45]   In a twisted variant of this prophecy, in the 20th century in Nazi Germany, under *national* socialism, what was appropriated was not the property of the capitalists, but of the Jews; their lives were taken too.

The development of large-scale industry, therefore, cuts from under its feet the very foundation on which the bourgeoisie produces and appropriates products for itself. What the bourgeoisie, therefore, produces, above all, are its own grave-diggers. Its fall and the victory of the proletariat are equally *inevitable* . . . Of all the classes which confront the bourgeoisie today, the proletariat alone is a really revolutionary class. The other classes decay and disappear in the face of large-scale industry, the proletariat is its most characteristic product. (930, fn. 2, emphasis added; ellipsis in the original)

Thus, if we exclude the short final Chapter 33, 'The Modern Theory of Colonization',[46] then Marx begins *Capital* by quoting himself in the first paragraph of the *Critique*. That paragraph itself footnotes and quotes Aristotle that 'Of everything which we possess there are two uses', that is, a use value and an exchange value (*Politics*: 1257a). Over 800 pages later, after working through the various contradictions which he thinks necessarily, in a sense naturally, develop from this apparently simple commodity form, which has both a use and exchange value, Marx closes the work by again quoting himself (and Engels) from *The Communist Manifesto*. The workers will inevitably revolt against the capitalist system. They will take over the capitalists' property, which was really produced by the workers themselves,[47] but appropriated by the capitalist class. The Communist Revolution will necessarily, in one sense naturally and in another sense socially, come. It will no doubt not be too pretty, since: 'Force is the midwife of every old society which is pregnant with a new one. It is itself an economic power' (916). Expect some violence.

10.2.4   The Role of Religion versus Science and Historical Progress

Meanwhile, let us consider the consciousness of the worker in pre-communist society.

Steven Smith, in his perceptive study of *Spinoza, Liberalism, and the Question of Jewish Identity*, writes of a

radical idea of secularization, which was viewed not as the heir but as the replacement of the Bible. Thinkers of the radical Enlightenment, of whom Spinoza was a preeminent example, saw history as a progressive process of secularization, by which they meant the gradual and steady *substitution* of *reason* for *superstition* and *science* for *religion*, along with the moral and intellectual emancipation of the individual from 'self-incurred tutelage'. (1997: 87, emphases added)

---

[46]   Which to me feels as a bit of an addendum. It basically critiques Edward Gibbon Wakefield's two volume *England and America*, published in 1833. Although see Roberts' (2006: 51) creative Dantean reading of the place of this last chapter of *Capital*.

[47]   Or in the case of land, that should really be the joint heritage of all people.

So, by this formulation, reason and science are on one side; they are substitutes or replacements for the other side, superstition and religion. We saw above that Adam Smith was at least to some extent sympathetic to, or influenced by, this viewpoint. In discussing difficulties posed by the overly severe religious sects favored by the poor, Smith wrote that 'Science is the great antidote to the poison of enthusiasm and superstition' (V.i.g.15).[48] We also see this competition between science and religion in the mid-20th century when, for example, Karl Popper writes that science is 'one of the most important *spiritual* movements of our day'; indeed, a student who does not know science lacks an 'understanding of the greatest *spiritual* movement of his own day' (1945: 283, fn. 6, emphases added). So for Popper, science is associated not only with calm, dispassionate reason, but with a type of spiritualism as well. Moreover, for Popper, science is on one side and charlatans are on the other:

> science can be taught as a fascinating part of human history – as a quickly developing growth of bold hypotheses, controlled by experiment, and by *criticism*. Taught in this way, as a part of the history of 'natural philosophy' . . . it could become the basis of a new liberal University education; of one whose aim, where it cannot produce experts, will be to produce at least *men who can distinguish between a charlatan and an expert*. (1945: 284, fn. 6, emphasis in original)[49]

Marx himself[50] was in the radical tradition of secularization.[51] Religion was caused by material causes and

> For a society of commodity producers, whose general social relations of production consists in the fact that they treat their products as commodities, hence as value, and in this material form bring their individual, private labours into relation with each other as homogeneous human labour, Christianity with its religious cult of man in the abstract, more particularly in its bourgeois development, i.e. in Protestantism, Deism, etc., is the most fitting form of religion. (172)

---

[48]   See above, Chapter 6, section 6.6. Recall that for Smith 'enthusiasts' refers to members of overly austere religions.

[49]   Popper of course had his own understanding of what constitutes science, the details of which do not concern us here. The point is he equates science as a spiritual movement which is needed to expose charlatans.

[50]   If not Smith and Popper. As noted previously, Smith's views on religion are quite complex and difficult to decipher, particularly given his prudence and the power of the religious authorities in his day. For my own views, stressing Hume's influence on Smith's thought, see Pack (1995b). On the other hand, Anthony Waterman, who is certainly an expert in this field, thinks that Smith was most likely an orthodox Presbyterian (personal communication, HES meetings, Toronto, 2008). Kennedy (2009) agrees more with my views.

[51]   Early in his career he was a follower of Ludwig Feuerbach. See, for example, Marx's 'Luther as Arbiter Between Strauss and Feuerbach' (1967c: 93–5).

In a footnote which probably inspired Max Weber, Marx wrote that 'Protestantism, by changing almost all the traditional holidays into working days, played an important part in the genesis of capital' (387, fn. 92).[52] Marx's most famous statement concerning religion comes from an early work of his, 'Toward the Critique of Hegel's Philosophy of Law: Introduction'. There he wrote that

> *Religious* suffering is the *expression* of real suffering and at the same time the *protest* against real suffering. Religion is the sigh of the oppressed creature, the heart of a heartless world, as it is the spirit of spiritless conditions. It is the *opium* of the people. (1967c: 250, emphases in original)

Marx is using opium in (at least) two senses.[53] On the one hand, it can get you high,[54] give you a 'buzz'. On the other hand, opium is a narcotic. It can ease your pain, but also put you to sleep, dull your senses and your brain.

Marx wants to replace religion, this opiate of the people, with science. Religion itself will only completely vanish after the communist revolution.[55] However, as much as possible on this side of the revolution, Marx wants to substitute science, his science, his critique of political economy, for religion and superstition. Again, recall that the subtitle to *Capital* is *A Critique of Political Economy*. Moreover, Marx does consider political economy to be the science of the capitalist mode of production. It is a *bourgeois* science 'in so far as it views the capitalist order as the absolute and ultimate form of social production, instead of as a historically transient stage of development' ('Postface to the Second Edition': 96). So, for Marx, 'the categories of bourgeois economics . . . are forms of thought which are socially valid, and therefore objective, for the relations of production belonging to this historically determined mode of social production, i.e. commodity production' (169).

As for Marx's critique of this veritable science, 'In so far as such a critique represents a class, it can only represent the class whose historical task is the overthrow of the capitalist mode of production and the final abolition of all classes – the proletariat' ('Postface to the Second Edition':

---

[52] Weber would seize on this idea and develop it in *The Protestant Ethic and the Spirit of Capitalism* (1992). Note also Marx's statement clearly argues against any simple form of economic determinism, where efficient causality runs only from some sort of 'economic base' to some sort of 'superstructure'. See also fn. 9, pp. 882–3 where Marx describes the '"spirit" of Protestantism' in appropriately caustic terms.

[53] On how religion is an opiate of the masses in several senses see Hoch (1972: 19–25).

[54] Think back to Smith's 'enthusiasts'. For a history of narcotics see Davenport-Hines (2002).

[55] See *Capital*: 173.

98). So, in a sense, Marx's work can be seen as worker/proletariat political economy. In this view, there would be two sciences of political economy: bourgeois political economy, and its critique, Marxist or proletarian political economy. On the other hand, Marx seems to think that he is providing a 'scientific analysis of value and surplus value' (326, fn. 6).[56] So there is a certain tension here. Is Marx's work scientific in general? Or does it only represent the working class? Or can only workers and/or their representatives now do scientific analysis in the field of political economy?[57] Anyway, Marx does consider his work to be in some way scientific. He believes he has gotten to the bottom of the capitalist mode of production, he has used his reason to uncover and grasp a hold of the truth.[58] His work is intended to help the workers in the transition to a post-capitalist society. In that sense, for Marx, his scientific explanation of the way the world operates competes not only with bourgeois political economy, but with all forms of religious explanations as well.[59] Marx wants to substitute reason for superstition, and (his) science for religion. In this sense, Marx is definitely a child of the radical Enlightenment.

Moreover, in his 'Postface to the Second Edition' of *Capital*, Marx wrote that 'I therefore openly avowed myself the pupil of that mighty thinker [Hegel]' (102–3). Note, then, if Hegel was a pupil of Aristotle (Popper, 1945; Ferrarin, 2001; Marcuse, 1960 [1941]: 42) then so was Marx. Yet, Hegel historicized Aristotle in an idealized manner,[60] and Marx wanted

---

56   I am assuming that Marx is serious here. Of course, the whole discourse, the presentation of his work as a science, could be a joke, a dodge, to escape the Prussian censors as well as to secure the trust of the potential reader (Roberts: 2006); but I doubt it.

57   One way out would be to assume that all sciences (or at least the social sciences) are ideological. See, for example, Mannheim (1936: 125–31) that knowledge, especially in the social sciences, is largely, or perhaps entirely, historically and socially determined; including Marxism.

58   See, for example, *Capital*: 682: 'The forms of appearance are reproduced directly and spontaneously, as current and usual modes of thought; the essential relation must first be discovered *by science*. Classical political economy stumbles approximately onto the true state of affairs, but without consciously formulating it. It is unable to do this as long as it stays within its bourgeois skin' (emphasis added). Classical political economy almost grasps the truth; according to Marx, Marx does. See also *Capital*, Volume III where Marx notes that 'the reader will have realized to his great dismay, the analysis of the actual intrinsic relations of the capitalist process of production is a very complicated matter and very extensive' and that 'it is a work of *science* to resolve the visible, merely external movement into the true intrinsic movement' (312–13, emphasis added).

59   Some actual ramifications of this tension between Marx's attempted scientific explanation, particularly as a science of the working class, and religious explanations of the world, particularly those adopted by the poor, will be discussed below in Chapter 13.

60   Or to be more specific, in a Platonic manner. I think Hegel was largely attempting to synthesize both Aristotle and Plato in a historicist fashion where the Platonic ideal manifests or expresses itself through history. By Hegel's estimation, 'The development of philosophic

to ground his own dialectical history in the material world. In grounding Hegel's dialectic, Marx claims his own dialectic

> includes in its positive understanding of what exists a simultaneous recognition of its negation, its inevitable destruction; because it regards every historically developed form as being in a fluid state, in motion, and therefore grasps its transient aspect as well; and because it does not let itself be impressed by anything, being in its very essence critical and revolutionary. (103)

So Marx viewed his approach as critical and revolutionary. Yet, I think there is a broader aspect to this story, and that is the double-edged sword of the notion of historical progress itself. If one believes in historical progress, then there are two distinct ways to look at contemporary society. One is to look backwards, and to compare contemporary society to all previous societies. In that sense, one may be rather comfortable, satisfied, smug even with the given state of affairs; conservative even. After all, things have never been better!

On the other hand, one may look forward, as Marx did, and compare contemporary society to what it could and will be in the future. In that case, present society will look awful in comparison with what can come to be. So I think a grand, majestic philosophy such as Hegel's, which believed in historical progress, will naturally break down into a conservative side, which looks backward and is relatively satisfied with the current situation. It will also harbor a radical, forward, potentially revolutionary side, which is impatient with the status quo and wants to urgently move on with the historical dialectic; which, of course, was Marx's position.

10.3 CONCLUDING THOUGHTS ON MARX ON THE STATE AND CHANGE

It is my position that one major, crucial aspect of Marx's mature economic work was Aristotelian; indeed his work may be interpreted as a modern attempt to largely return to Aristotle. Yet, as with Adam Smith and most all moderns, Marx has a non-Aristotelian, modern conception of history, with history as real change which is going somewhere, not merely in circles.

Marx was not able to give us an Aristotelian analysis of the state, and he really does not have too much to say about the state in these

---

science as science . . . begins with Plato and is completed by Aristotle. They of all others deserve to be called teachers of the human race' (1995, Vol. 2:1).

mature economistic writings. However, he does give us a fairly complete Aristotelian analysis of what he views as the capitalist mode of production. Since Aristotle had four types of causality, Marx covers the four types of causality in *Capital*. This Aristotelian concern with all four causes is one of the things which makes Marx's work so long and complex.

Marx was concerned with the final goal of the capitalist mode of production: to create and appropriate surplus value, using value to expand into more value. Marx was concerned with the various forms of value, such as the commodity form, money, or capital. Marx was also concerned with the material cause of value, which he reasoned to be actualized living labor which becomes embodied, dead labor. This was what made all commodities commensurable. History itself since post-primitive communism has been the appropriation of labor by one class over another. In capitalist society this appropriation takes on the form of the appropriation of value, of surplus value created by the workers. And of course, Marx was concerned with the efficient causes, with how things actually happen in historical time.[61] Hence, the complexity of his analysis. Marx presents the birth, development and prophetic death of capitalism. This is an Aristotelian story of coming-to-be and passing-away; thus, his concern with Aristotelian contradictions, not contraries. Marx thinks he has grasped the inner essence, the scientific truth of the capitalist mode of production and presents it in *Capital*. His scientific work competes with religion in presenting an explanation of the world, particularly why there is so much pain and suffering in the world. Marx is especially competing against what Smith called the austere, severe religions; the religious systems favored by the poor. Marx believes he is on the side of reason and science; combating religion and superstition. Marx's work aims to aid in the change to a post-capitalist world.

Let us now pause, and look back at this mighty structure, and consider Kierkegaard's criticism of Hegel's work, which I think might well also apply to Marx's *Capital*: 'If Hegel had written the whole of his *Logic*, and had written in the Foreword that it was only a thought experiment, in which he had avoided various things at many points, then he would certainly have been the greatest thinker who ever lived. As it is, he is merely comical' (1968: entry A29). Of course, Hegel and Marx, both following Aristotle, did not think they were doing thought experiments; they both

---

[61] The Japanese and Canadian Unoites believe that Marx jumbles up various levels of analysis, a pure theory of the capitalist mode of production with historical analysis; and that these different levels of analysis ought to be mediated by a third-stage level of capitalist development (see Albritton, 1991). I am not sure these theoretical difficulties can be overcome if one wants to do a complete Aristotelian analysis of the capitalist mode of production dealing with all four types of causality – which is what I think Marx largely did.

thought they had grasped the truth. Nonetheless, when an influential philosopher goes seriously astray, one may call that person comical; not so for an influential economist.[62] From a 21st century perspective, it may seem to many that Hegel and Marx, brilliant as they were, could have used a little less self-confidence; although then, of course, they might never have produced their theoretical masterpieces.

---

[62] Although it is interesting that Keynes closed his *General Theory* by asserting 'the ideas of economists *and political philosophers*, both when they are right and when they are wrong, are more powerful than is commonly understood. Indeed the world is ruled by little else' (1964 [1936]: 383, emphasis added).

PART IV

Lessons for the 21st century

Introduction to Part IV

This part brings forth the ideas of Aristotle, Smith and Marx on the concepts of exchange value, money, capital, character, government and change into the 21st century. It considers key areas where these theorists do indeed offer us keen insight concerning contemporary issues around these concepts.

Bringing forward the question of what is exchange value to the 21st century, Chapter 11 introduces the controversial and enigmatic work of Piero Sraffa. I argue that in Sraffa's theoretical framework, it is not the commodity labor power which uniquely creates value or exchange value. Rather, it is any commodity, or actually all commodities, when they produce other commodities, which create or produce value. That is, commodities are commensurate simply because they are produced commodities created with the goal to be exchanged. This suggests that Sraffa is using a different theory of value from Marx and/or that Marx's labor theory of value is wrong.

Nonetheless, if in spite of the technical Sraffian criticisms on the determinants of value theory, Smith and Marx (and Aristotle) are correct concerning the genesis and functions of money, then the generalized exchange of commodities will generate a universal equivalent, that is, money. Thus, in a globalized economy, there will also be a tendency for there to be a world money. I argue that since the end of the Bretton Woods System, and the severing of the formal link between gold and most national fiat currencies, there is evidence that the US dollar is in the process of becoming world money. I discuss some of the theoretical and practical implications of this process.

Chapter 12 argues, again using Sraffa's work, that the source of property income and surplus value is not the supposed unique role and capability of labor power in the production process. It is rather the use of commodities in general to create more output than the amount used up in the production process. This conclusion is dramatized using a model of a fully automated society, of the sort first developed by Vladimir Dmitriev at the end of the 19th century. There, in spite of no workers, there still appears to be what may be termed surplus value as well as property income.

The chapter also argues that confusions over capital, and what is often considered the source of new capital, saving, are also a major source of sophistical controversies. If Smith and especially Marx are correct, then in normal times firms should be able to finance their own economic expansion and accumulate wealth, capital and savings. That is their goal; that is what they generally do. Limits on saving are not inhibiting economic growth; a lack of saving is not a cause of the current problems in the advanced capitalist countries. However, on another hand, Smith's work suggests that lying, thieving, incompetent managers are likely a major cause of current economic difficulties. The chapter approaches the issue of managers and their character from the context of the 20th century literature on the likely convergence of communist and capitalist systems due to technological and managerial challenges common to both systems. This convergence has led to critical problems with our managers in many of the major countries in the world.

Chapter 13 emphasizes Aristotle's concern that governments will have a tendency to become corrupt and rule in the interests of the governing, rather than in the interest of society at large; and discusses the applicability of this concern to the recent administration of George W. Bush. It also considers the concern of Smith (and Marx) that governments will rule in the interest of the rich and powerful, especially in the unduly narrow, short-run interests of the quite untrustworthy businessmen/capitalists. It also argues that over time, in the absence of general worldwide regulations on capital, there will be a tendency for wage, regulatory and tax arbitrage. As Marx stressed, regulations on capital need to cover the entire economic domain. Otherwise, capital will move or threaten to move to where wages and taxes on property income are lower, and regulations on capital are fewer or not enforced. This movement (and/or threatened movement) is currently weakening the tax basis of the modern liberal welfare state, and the middle class in all the advanced capitalist countries.

Finally, I argue that the decline of putatively communist societies at the end of the 20th century may[1] to some extent be viewed as a decline or failure of reason itself. One result of this is that protest movements in the 21st century now tend to take the form of enthusiastic, revealed, supernatural religious movements, as described and feared by Smith. Thus, to some extent we in the 21st century are back to the concerns of Smith, where overly rigorous religious movements were often the vehicle for social protest, rather than secular Marxist movements putatively based upon human reason. In some ways, our contemporary, possibly post-modern world seems to be recycling back to the pre-modern world. How strange; rather unexpected too.

---

[1]   And in practice has.

11. Exchange value and money in the 21st century

11.1 GENERAL COMMENTS

I have argued that Adam Smith basically begins his economic analysis with Aristotle, the distinction between use value and exchange value, and how money necessarily develops out of the exchange of goods. However, Smith then largely rejects Aristotle, particularly with regard to the desirability of using money to acquire more money. Nonetheless, the rejection is not complete. Not surprisingly, there are still plenty of residues of Aristotelian thinking and analysis in Smith's work.

A similar, though largely opposite story has been told with Marx. Marx explicitly begins his analysis with Aristotle, the distinction between use value and exchange value, how this necessarily generates money, and how money may be used to acquire more money. Indeed, I have argued that Marx's *Capital* can be viewed to be a largely Aristotelian account of the birth (coming-to-be), development and anticipated death (passing-away) of the capitalist mode of production, a system of production based upon the goal of using money to acquire more money. Marx stresses all four of Aristotle's causes: the final, formal, material and efficient causes of this historically specific capitalist mode of production. Marx also thoroughly knows his Smith, and sees his own account as a critique of modern political economy, which of course includes a critique of Smith's work, the most systematic, comprehensive account of capitalism.[1] Nonetheless, as with Smith and Aristotle, there are still many similarities and residues of Smith's modern work in Marx's modern work; most notably in their modern account of historical change, as well as the role of government in class societies.

---

[1] Marx's terminology. Smith, of course, would say he was dealing with commercial society. Aristotle would no doubt call it a chrematistic society.

11.2 THE DIALECTICAL DANCE OF ARISTOTLE, SMITH AND MARX ON VALUE AND EXCHANGE VALUE AND 21ST CENTURY IMPLICATIONS: SRAFFA'S INTERJECTION

For Aristotle, goods have a use value, they may be used; and an exchange value. Money will necessarily arise out of the general exchange of goods. Aristotle would like to know how these goods can be made commensurable. When they are exchanged in determinate ratios, or sold for money, what determines their just price? Moreover, what is common in them that enables equitable, just exchanges to take place? Aristotle suggests money, then need, and then basically gives up. It is not clear what enables goods to be exchanged in definite ratios. For example, knives and wine are incommensurable in terms of sharpness. One cannot say if a particular glass of wine is sharper than a particular knife. For things to be commensurable, there needs to be a common unit, some commonality by which they may be compared. Moreover, the measuring rod of this common unit must be homogeneous with the thing measured.

Following Aristotle, for Smith, an object can have a value in use or a value in exchange. Smith generally appears to have some kind of labor theory of value, and he generally emphasizes the labor factor in the creation of value and wealth.[2] However, it is not clear if Smith had a labor-commanded, a labor-disutility, or a labor-embodied theory of value. Indeed, there are also Physiocratic residues in Smith's work where sometimes it seems that he does not have any labor theory of value at all, where, for example, cows may be viewed to be productive laborers, where agricultural workers seem to be the most productive workers, and so on. Nonetheless, in spite of this ambiguity, for Smith, labor is clearly the real, the ultimate, the only universal and accurate measure of the exchangeable value of all commodities.

Marx in a sense combines Aristotle and Smith on the question of value and exchange value. Marx claims that abstract general labor is the material substance of value. All commodities are exchangeable because they are produced by human labor; that is, actual human labor is what makes commodities commensurable. Thus, capitalists purchase human labor power or capacity. This human labor capacity then actualizes itself by really laboring, and the human labor becomes embodied in the resulting product. Thus, on the one hand, Marx sees himself as finally answering Aristotle's two thousand-year-old question – what makes grossly different

---

[2]   Most notably in his emphasis on the division of labor in increasing output.

goods comparable, equal, commensurate? It is that they are the result of the human act of laboring. On the other hand, Marx is also following Smith in Smith's insistence that labor time is the measure of value. By accepting Smith's position that labor time is the true measure of value, combined with Aristotle's position that the measuring rod must be homogeneous with the thing measured, Marx must conclude that value itself is congealed labor time. However, the value in the commodity can only reveal or express itself when the commodity is actually exchanged for another commodity (or sold for money). That is, the intrinsic value of a commodity can only manifest itself as exchange value, in the exchange for another commodity (or sale for money).

In 1960 Sraffa published his *Production of Commodities by Means of Commodities*. This had important consequences, the full ramifications of which are still, perhaps, yet to be fully played out. Modestly subtitled 'Prelude to a Critique of Economic Theory', it was, of course, meant to be the basis of a critique of the neoclassical 'marginal theory of value and distribution' (1960: vi). In a sense, it is a peculiar, external critique since, as Sraffa himself points out, its 'standpoint' is 'that of the old classical economists from Adam Smith to Ricardo' (v). Indeed, as the Marxist Ronald Meek (1961) quickly pointed it, it could also be viewed as a magnificent 'rehabilitation of classical economics'. I think Sraffa's models are indeed reasonable ways to interpret and mathematize the works of economists such as Smith and particularly Ricardo;[3] and in a way Marx too. Nonetheless, within a few years, it was realized that Sraffa's work could be used not only to criticize the marginal productivity theory of prices and income distribution, but Marx's labor theory as well. This criticism perhaps culminated and was largely summarized in Ian Steedman's *Marx After Sraffa* (1977). A critique (or perhaps only a prelude to a critique) of neoclassical economics;

---

[3]   Mark Blaug writes that 'Sraffa's classic book, *Production of Commodities by Means of Commodities* (1960) may be justly described as Ricardo in modern dress' (1978: xiii). Yet, that over-focusing on Sraffa's slim book may also lead to an unduly narrow interpretation of the classical economists, and in contemporary theory to basically another sterile formalism depressingly similar to the 'dead alley' of neoclassical general equilibrium theory (see Blaug, (1999, 2001: 160; and most recently 2009)). For Blaug, there is a key trade-off between rigor and relevance, with Sraffian Economics, as a type of general equilibrium theory, leaning much too far to the rigorous, yet not relevant side of the spectrum. Blaug's general point, that there is indeed a trade-off between rigor (including mathematical rigor) and relevance (2003), is a highly subversive counterpoise to the general view of rigor, math and economic thought. It is particularly noteworthy coming from the author of the classic *Economic Theory in Retrospect*. The major 20th century mathematical economist John Hicks is another prominent example of an economist extremely proficient in formalizing economic theory, yet ultimately disappointed with the gross results. Compare his early work, for example, *Value and Capital* (1939), with his later work, for example his last book, published 50 years later, *A Market Theory of Money* (1989).

a rehabilitation of classical economics; and a critique of Marx's labor theory of value: pretty powerful elixirs from such a slight, 95-page book.

In any event, in his first chapter, Sraffa presents a mathematical model of separate industries using various commodities to produce commodities, where commodities are both the output and the inputs of the production process. He calls this 'Production for Subsistence', where the commodity outputs are in total quantitatively the same as the commodities used up as inputs. Hence, there is no surplus of commodities created by the commodities. For the economic system to reproduce itself in time, at the end of the production period the outputs of each industry must exchange in definite ratios (or 'values') so they can become inputs into the other industries. Following his notation, there are 'k' commodities produced by 'k' separate industries. A is the quantity annually produced of commodity a, B is the quantity annually produced of b, and so on. Let A_a, B_a, . . ., K_a be the quantities of a, b, . . ., k annually used in the industry producing A. Let A_b, B_b, . . ., K_b be the corresponding quantities used to produce B, and so on. These input and output quantities are assumed to be known. The unknowns are P_a, P_b, . . ., P_k which represent the prices (or values)[4] of the units of commodities a, b, . . ., k. It is assumed that the prices of the outputs are the same as the prices of the inputs; hence, the system can be assumed to be in some sort of general (or reproductive) equilibrium. Sraffa has a series of k equations:

$$A_a P_a + B_a P_b + \ldots + K_a P_k = A P_a$$

$$A_b P_a + B_b P_b + \ldots + K_b P_k = B P_b$$

$$\ldots$$

$$A_k P_a + B_k P_b + \ldots + K_k P_k = K P_k$$

Sraffa takes one commodity as a standard of value and makes its price one. He counts up the number of linearly independent equations, finds they are the same as the number of relative prices to be determined, and concludes that he can theoretically determine all relative prices in his mathematical world.[5]

Note that with this theoretical system, the commodity labor power does

---

⁴ Sraffa's system makes no distinction between prices and values; he uses the terms interchangeably (1960: 9).

⁵ In this chapter Sraffa also gives specific numerical two- and three-commodity system examples and explains the necessary exchanges and resulting equivalence of disparate commodities which must take place for the systems to reproduce themselves (1960: 3–4).

not necessarily appear. Hence, in Sraffa's theoretical world, it is not the commodity labor power which uniquely creates value or exchange value. It is rather any commodity, or all commodities when they produce other commodities, which create or produce value which then need to be exchanged for other commodities.[6] Now, there are several ways to look at this result. On the one hand, one may say that Sraffa is not using any kind of a labor theory of value. Rather he is using a completely different theory of value,[7] a commodity theory of value where commodities themselves create value. On the other hand, one can interpret Marx as being wrong when he claims that what makes commodities commensurate, that they may be exchanged with each other in definite ratios, is that they are produced by human labor power. Instead, they may be viewed to be commensurate simply because they are commodities. As commodities they are goods generally made with the goal to be exchanged. Moreover, as commodities they basically *must* be exchanged for the system to successfully reproduce itself: be that system a theoretical mathematical model, or the capitalist system itself.[8] There is nothing unique about the commodity labor power in creating value. This distinction between Marx's labor theory of value and Sraffa's approach will become more poignant when we consider capital and the creation of surplus value and surplus commodities in the next chapter.

11.3   MONEY AND THE GLOBAL ECONOMY IN THE 21ST CENTURY

Aristotle's monetary analysis suggests that to the extent everything may be exchanged, for a price, for money, this leads to a flattening of life. Life will lose much of its preciousness. Everything becomes commensurable, everything becomes just more or less of that one thing. Nothing is unique, nothing is priceless.[9]

---

[6]   That this is not an example of commodity fetishism (as charged by, for example, Roosevelt, 1975) see Pack (1985b: 81–4).

[7]   This is the position of, for example, Freeman, Kliman and Wells (2004, 'Introduction': ix–xx). See also Kliman (2007).

[8]   This was demonstrated dramatically in fall 2008 when the Bush administration hyperventilated that if the US Congress did not pass a 700 billion dollar bailout package for Wall Street, then there would be a 'financial Armageddon'. These scare tactics (which were previously so effective in cowering Congress to support the War Against Iraq), plus the incentive it gave for various firms and state governments to declare that they too needed bailout money, scared people from buying and hence exchanging commodities, leading to really major problems and dramatically deepening the recession.

[9]   This is a major reason why, I think, the sexual services industry is generally held in some disrepute in contemporary society; also, partly why the debate over what kind of marriages should be legally permissible is so passionate. People generally do not want to think

For Smith, following Aristotle, money develops out of the exchange of products. The flattening of life which results from relations between people taking the form of impersonal price relations does not really concern Smith. Indeed, for Smith, compared to personal dependent social relations in previous societies, such as feudalism, or even personal servants in his contemporary society, the anonymity or impersonal attributes offered by monetary relations is basically a good, not a bad thing.

Smith generally assumes that money is a produced commodity. For Smith, the value of money (and thus the general price level) is in some sense determined by its cost of production. Again, following Aristotle, money in practice becomes both a means of exchange and a measurer of value. Smith does not really go any farther than Aristotle in his account of money. As with Aristotle, Smith generally assumes spot markets, where money and a good exchange simultaneously. Hence, as opposed to, say, the giving of a gift, credit does not arise out of the mere exchange of commodities.[10]

For Marx, following both Aristotle and Smith, the exchange of goods will also necessarily generate money, or what Marx calls a universal equivalent. Marx, as opposed to Smith, returns to Aristotle's concern about what makes goods commensurable. Marx holds that it is not money, which he generally assumes to be gold, which makes commodities commensurable. Rather, it is because commodities are in essence materialized labor time that the exchange of commodities is able to generate a universal equivalent, thus converting the particular commodity gold into money.

Following Aristotle and Smith, money may be said to act as a medium of exchange between commodities (or rather, for Marx, value changes its form between the commodity form and the money form). Money also becomes a measurer of value. Money, because it can buy anything, becomes desired as an end in itself. Qualitatively, it has no limits. Money may also be used as a means of payment, where commodities are bought at one time period (what Marx calls the means of purchase) but the money is actually handed over or paid at a later date (money then acting as the means of payment). Thus, as opposed to Aristotle and Smith, credit, bills of exchange, interest rates, and so on can arise directly out of the exchange

---

that their loved ones, or their sexual partners, are seamlessly replaceable. Rather, they want to think of them as unique; as indeed they are.

[10] Classicists, sociologists and anthropologists generally argue that the giving of a gift creates a credit-type relationship because if I give you a gift, you, to some extent, owe me a gift in the future. This intensifies social relations and social bonds, which, depending upon your point of view (or the exact situation) will either be a good or a bad thing.

of commodities. Buyers and sellers may become debtors and creditors. Breaks in the credit chain may potentially disrupt the system.[11]

The analysis of Smith and Marx suggests that money will necessarily stay with society as long as there is the general exchange of various commodities. That is, generalized commodity production and exchange will necessarily generate a universal equivalent, that is, money. Early dreams or hopes of some communists in the 19th and 20th centuries that with the arrival of putatively communist revolutions money, a universal equivalent, could be abolished were just that: dreams. Moreover, the analysis of Smith and Marx suggests that there will most likely be a universal money or equivalent in *the world*, probably taking the form of a precious commodity (gold or silver). Since the end of the Bretton Woods agreement in the early 1970s, the formal link between gold and most national currencies has been completely severed. Since then, there is some evidence that the US currency, the US dollar, is in the process of becoming world money. I think this is one major reason why in recent years the US has always run a balance of trade and/or balance of current account deficit: if the world is dollarizing, to acquire those dollars people in other countries sell us their commodities.

Moreover, there is also evidence that parts of the US government realize this potentially incredible windfall. As Porter and Judson, two economists working for the Federal Reserve Board, argued: 'Today, foreigners hold US currency for the same reasons that people once held *gold coins*: as a unit of account, a medium of exchange, and a store of value when the purchasing power of the domestic currency is uncertain or when other assets lack sufficient anonymity, portability, divisibility, liquidity, or security' (1996: 883, emphasis added). They claim that 'US currency today provides many of the monetary services that *gold coins* once did' (1996: 884, emphasis added). Emphasizing how difficult it is to actually track down how much US currency is held outside the US, and thoughtfully informing us that a mere briefcase can hold a million dollars in $100 bills, they estimate that in 1995 between $200 and $250 billion in US currency was held outside the US (1996: 883).[12]

To the extent that the US currency becomes international money, then

---

[11]   Marx does not go into detail about credit crises until Volume III of *Capital*, after he has extensively discussed the various circuits of capital in Volume II.

[12]   Much of this currency is indeed held by out-and-out criminal elements. Yet, conducting business or simply moving assets in the form of US currency is frequently a useful way for both criminal and non-criminal elements anywhere on earth to discreetly shield their activities from various tax authorities, spouses, ex-spouses, lovers, friends, enemies, political opponents, and so on. This characteristic of currency should lead to an increase in its demand as we enter deeper into the information age; currency is not demanded simply for its liquidity.

Smith and Marx's position that the quantity of money in any particular country is basically determined by the needs of the economy comes into play again. On the one hand, the current position of the US is sort of equivalent to ancient Athens sitting on silver mines owned by the state. An issue becomes what should the government do with this money which they own?[13] Yet, actually, the US position is much better than sitting on a gold or silver mine. Since currency costs basically nothing to produce, the government does not need to hire slaves or wage laborers to dig it up. Hence, somewhat surprisingly, with the dollar becoming a world currency, some classical insights derived from the workings of the old gold standard come into play again. Furthermore, I think the dollar becoming a world currency probably also contributed to the demise of monetarist thought at the end of the 20th century in the US. By printing more money, that money does not necessarily stay in the US. Just as in Smith's time the government could not effectively control the amount of gold in a country, so now the US government has trouble controlling the supply of money which stays in the US. The link between the Federal Reserve Board changing the supply of money (and by any definition, of course, currency is part of the money supply) and changes in nominal US GDP is weakened.[14] If the worldwide demand for US currency is great enough, then until it is satiated, increases in the US money supply will not so much affect the value of the dollar or the general price level as they will simply increase the flows of dollars abroad. The result will necessarily be continuing US balance of trade and current account deficits as foreigners seek to acquire what is in some ways world money.[15]

The US government of course is concerned to protect this asset. They are against international counterfeiters. Just as on the gold standard there was always a problem with 'fool's gold' or fake gold, now there is a concern with fake US dollars. In a study initiated by the charmingly named 'Antiterrorism and Effective Death Penalty Act of 1996', the US Department of the Treasury reported on 'The Use and Counterfeiting of United States Currency Abroad' (2006). They recognize that 'US currency is thus a valuable *export* whose quality and integrity should be protected'

---

[13]   See Xenophon's intelligent discussion of this issue in 'Ways and Means' (1925).

[14]   Or at the very least complicated. Theoretically, it could indeed be argued that if a change in the money supply leads to a stable systematic split between money that remains in the domestic economy, and money that goes abroad, then the link between money supply and nominal GDP could be stable and knowable; but this seems rather doubtful in practice.

[15]   Sometimes it is argued that a US current account deficit and/or trade deficit *must* cause problems for the US economy in the form of a balance of payments constraint leading to some necessary combination of currency depreciation, high interest rates and slow economic growth (for example, the articles by Howes and Singh in Howes and Singh (eds), 2000). This will not occur if the worldwide demand for US dollars as money continues to grow as the dollar becomes world money.

(2006: 23, emphasis added). Here arises another opportunity for the long arm of the US law to grow even longer: use the Secret Service (which is in charge of combating counterfeit US currency) to go outside of the country to deploy 'task forces to target counterfeiters and to provide support to local authorities' (2006: x). The US Secret Service currently has permanent offices in 15 foreign countries (2006: 52); furthermore, it conducted an 'International Currency Authentication Training' program in 27 countries from 2004 to March 2006 (2006: 54–5). The report estimated that in December 2005 the amount of US currency held abroad had grown to $450 billion (out of $760 billion in total circulation) (2006: 35). Thus, if we compare this with the previous study by Porter and Judson, the amount of US currency held abroad had essentially doubled in a decade. The Treasury Report gathered the most data on $100 bills (and was most concerned with the counterfeiting of that denomination). It estimated that in 2005 there was $350 billion dollars of $100 bills held outside the US. In 1970, before the demise of the Bretton Woods system, there was only $5.7 billion of $100 bills held abroad; a major increase in 35 years (2006: 2).

Yet, of course, US currency held abroad is only the tip of an iceberg. Or, rather, it is the hard base upon which an enormous monetary and credit superstructure is built.[16] For example, resting above the currency are dollar-denominated bank deposits in foreign banks and in the foreign branches of US banks all around the world.[17] These dollar-denominated bank deposits can, of course, be converted into US currency if the banks (or their depositors) demand it. Then, of course, on top of these demand and time deposits there are abroad certificates of deposits; commercial paper; medium-term notes (one to five years in maturity); and so-called Eurobonds, all issued outside the US, nonetheless denominated in dollars.[18] As Smith and Walter point out, using these markets is an excellent

---

[16] Note that in contemporary society, most money is actually credit. For example, in the US even the most narrow definition of the money supply (M1), is both US currency outside of banks and demand accounts in domestic banks. Yet, demand accounts are in a sense a loan from the depositor to the bank. (Indeed, bank deposits are liabilities on a bank's balance sheet.) In a financial panic, the bank depositors could call in their loans, demand currency from the banks and, through the so-called money multiplier, reduce the supply of money (and in the process bankrupt the banks). This, of course, is what happened to the US banking system in the early years of the Great Depression. The Federal Reserve Board is quite concerned that a variant of this scenario will repeat itself – with similarly disastrous results.

[17] According to Meulendyke, writing for the Federal Reserve Bank of New York, the Bank for International Settlements estimated that US dollar deposits in banks outside the United States averaged $530 billion per year from 1991 to 1996 (1998: 210). So this would probably be more than twice the amount of US currency held abroad in those years.

[18] See, for example, the discussion in Smith and Walter (1997), especially Chapters 8 'International Money and Foreign Exchange Markets' (215–41) and 9 'Eurobonds and Other International Debt Issues' (242–73); and also their earlier book (1990).

way to avoid paying taxes (for example 1997: 225) and to avoid regulations (for example 1997: 243–4). Indeed, in their judgment, due in part to
the absence of regulation, 'many of the best ideas to influence the US bond
markets had their origin in the Eurobond market' (1997: 249). At the time
of their 1997 book, Smith and Walter estimated that bonds denominated
in dollars and issued outside the US were comparable in size to the entire
domestic US investment-grade corporate bond market (1997: 243).

Yet, I think the biggest question is to what extent do foreigners equate
the US government debt itself as a potential form of international money,
particularly as a store of value which is at the same time extremely liquid?
If, as asserted above, US currency is providing many of the services that
gold coin once did, then is not the government debt to some extent equivalent to gold itself? US currencies and US government debt are in fact close
substitutes. For many economic actors, holding US government debt will
be a bit better than holding currency, since almost always the debt pays
positive nominal interest rates. Yet note: here there is a tremendous difference between now and the time of the classical economists. Then, when
the government borrowed its own money, if they were on a gold or silver
standard, the government could not simply produce its own gold or silver
if the creditors demanded hard, species payment (unless of course, the government owned gold or silver mines). Yet, now, when the US borrows its
own money, if the creditor demands 'hard' payment in US currency, there
is basically no problem. The government can simply print more of its own
currency to back up its own debt; in essence, the government is currently
borrowing something that it has the ability to create at approximately zero
cost. Not a bad deal for the US government! Thus, to the extent that the
US government debt is becoming world money, or functioning as gold
used to under the international gold standard, then the US government
largely has a blank check to simply borrow money at low interest rates.[19]
Of course, at some point, the US could satisfy the entire world demand for
world money. In that case, the ideas of the monetarists and the quantity
theory should come back into play: printing more money would increase
prices; borrowing more money should drive up real interest rates. In the
meantime, though, the US federal government appears to be able to easily
fund its debt.[20]

---

[19] As of the end of September 2008, the Treasury Department estimated that foreigners
held about $2.86 trillion of the US debt (US Department of Treasury, 2008: 48); total US
federal government debt was about $10 trillion. Analogous to the stockpiling of gold under
the old international gold system, much of this debt is held as stockpiled reserves in foreign
central banks.

[20] Of course, if there was a sudden switch from a dollar world money to, say, a Euro
world money, then there would be major issues for the US economy, including a fall in the

Note another intriguing issue: to the extent that the world uses the dollar as a unit of account in international food and commodity markets, Smith's and Marx's explanations of the workings of the old gold standard may come into play, again though, in an altered way. As the Federal Reserve Bank of New York is well aware, 'The dollar acts as a unit of account. International commercial contracts are most commonly denominated in dollars, even when neither party to the contract is based in the United States. The practice is most common in raw material and commodity markets, which are unified globally and deal in standardized contracts' (Meulendyke, 1998: 210). Under the old gold standard, according to both Smith and Marx, a fall in the value of gold would lead to a worldwide rise in prices. For Smith and Marx, gold has some kind of real value, being somehow the cost of producing new gold (Smith) or the amount of labor embodied in that gold (Marx). Currently the US dollar, probably for Smith, and certainly for Marx, has no real intrinsic value. It is, however, a symbol of value. If the dollar is a worldwide money, used as a unit of account in trading some commodities, then to the extent the dollar falls in relative value to other currencies, this seems to be in some way equivalent to the value of gold falling under the old system. This suggests that a fall in the value of the dollar *vis-à-vis* other currencies may generate a worldwide increase in the price level, particularly in those standardized internationally traded commodities which use the dollar as a unit of account.

There is indeed some anecdotal evidence that this has in fact been happening recently. When the US economy appeared to be in trouble in 2007 and the first part of 2008, originally from credit problems spilling out of the subprime mortgage-backed securities market, the value of the dollar fell as international financial investors moved out of dollar-denominated assets. At the same time, the price of goods in the raw material and commodity markets went up, just as one might predict if the world were on a gold standard and the value of gold fell.[21] In the latter part of 2008, as the

---

international value of the dollar, rise in interest rates, and so on. For fears that foreigners, particularly foreign central banks, could stop funding the US deficit, or merely threaten to, and that would put constraints on US political power (as if that would necessarily be a bad thing!) see Setser (2008). I suspect these fears are probably overblown; see, for example, US Department of Treasury (2006: 26–7).

[21]   Wray (2008) argued that international commodity prices went up largely due to financial speculation. Note that these two explanations are not necessarily incompatible. Rather, they are mutually supporting and reinforcing, contributing to worldwide economic instability. Thus, to the extent that major economic players perceived there to be an inverse relationship between the international value of the dollar and worldwide commodity prices, they speculated on rising commodity prices when the dollar fell – thus contributing to the rise in prices. To the extent international commodity markets are opening up to financial speculation, we should expect to see the typical (yet exacerbated) booms and busts in these prices, due to overly optimistic and pessimistic oscillating waves of animal spirits.

financial troubles deepened and spread worldwide, the value of the dollar went *up*. The worldwide demand for the dollar went up, as people shifted out of their own currencies to the dollar-denominated assets. At the same time, as the value of the dollar increased *vis-à-vis* other currencies, the prices of key internationally traded commodities fell worldwide – just as might be predicted using an international gold standard.

As Aristotle, Smith and Marx all emphasized, the exchange of commodities creates money, or what Marx calls a universal equivalent. For centuries, this commodity tended to be a precious commodity, usually gold or silver. Since the world went off the international gold standard in the early 1970s, the world market seems to be searching for another world money, and to some extent may have found it in the dollar. The world could always go off a dollar standard to, say, a Euro standard, just as before there were shifts between a gold standard and a silver standard. Moreover, to the extent the world economy manifests great instability, there will no doubt be new calls for some kind of consciously managed new world money (for example Davidson, 2008). Whether the more or less private markets themselves choose a world money, or one is explicitly created and managed by governmental authorities, it seems that if Smith and Marx are correct, and as the world becomes more closely connected, a world money will necessarily continue to manifest itself through the course of the 21st century.

12.   Capital and character in the 21st century

12.1   CAPITAL CONTROVERSIES (AGAIN)

Recall that for Aristotle money can be used to acquire more money. For Aristotle, this is chrematistics and is unnatural. Chrematistics is a corruption or perversion of the proper use of money which should be used to facilitate the exchange of goods, the transfer of goods from excess to deficient owners. With, for example, moneylending and the retail trade, the proper use of money is corrupted.

For Aristotle, the emphasis is not on accumulating wealth. Rather, the society has a certain amount of wealth, and this wealth should be used to aid in the development of excellent citizens. So, for example, Aristotle writes that 'may our state be constituted in such a manner as to *be blessed with the goods of which fortune disposes (for we acknowledge her power)*: whereas excellence and goodness in the state are not a matter of chance but the result of knowledge and choice' (*Politics*: 1332a, emphasis added).

Compare this with Smith, where the emphasis is on increasing the *wealth* (and hence, also the power) of the nation.[1] For Smith, people own stock. Part of the stock is set aside to be consumed. Another part is used to generate revenue or income. This part of stock is capital. Much of this capital takes the form of money which is advanced as wages to workers. The capitalists then own the resulting produce of that labor. Thus, the workers originally create the stock, the capital, yet the capital itself then hires or demands the workers. That is, the capital employs the worker more than the worker employs the capital. Smith insists that this is all perfectly natural. Here Smith decisively parts company from Aristotle. Also, Smith changes the meaning of the word natural from the best, the excellent, the goal or end of a thing, to the normal or the ordinary.[2] Marx would later object to Smith's use of the word natural, generally insisting

---

[1]   And not necessarily the nation's excellence.

[2]   This I believe is the general rule; however, Smith's use of the word natural is quite multifaceted and complex. For a recent discussion of the various uses of 'natural' in Smith as well as earlier concepts of the natural see Aspromourgos (2009: 43–53).

that all these things (value, exchange value, money, capital, and so on) are social, not natural phenomena.

For Marx, capital is the production of surplus value, the use of both money and commodities to acquire or accumulate more money. As with Smith and opposed to Aristotle, capital does not merely acquire more money; it actually produces more wealth and value. For Marx, labor power, or labor potential, is the crucial commodity which is bought and sold. In agreement with Aristotle, the goal of capital (or chrematistics in Aristotle's terminology) is without limit. It can never be fully satisfied. Capital is self-expanding value, the creation and appropriation of surplus value. This surplus value is created by one class, the workers who own and sell their labor power; and it is appropriated by another class, the capitalists. In Aristotelian fashion, labor power or capacity is potential. This potential gets actualized by laboring. The worker creates more value than it costs to reproduce himself and his family. Hence, only the workers create value; they are the true source of all property (non-wage) income. Workers are hired by money which represents objectified abstract labor, or dead labor. Like a vampire, this dead labor sucks up the living labor. Marx's position is actually close to Smith's position in which stock, created by past labor, hires the workers. Marx is really following Smith but with his own colorful twist and definite change in emphasis: a true critique of Smith's work. Marx emphasizes that machines, plant and equipment do not produce value or surplus value. Only the workers do that. Hence, the workers produce the wealth, the capital, which then dominates and exploits them. Thus, capital for Marx in essence is not only command over paid labor, as explained by Smith. It is also command over unpaid labor. Hence, property income is really a form of theft. This is a major reason why the capitalist system should be superseded; overthrown. This, of course, is the opposite of Smith's defense of commercial society.

Marx's controversial claim that only the commodity labor power creates value and surplus value led to what has come to be known as the transformation problem.[3] Marx attempted to answer this problem in the

---

[3]   That is, the transformation from the asserted essential, fundamental embodied labor/value analysis of *Capital* Volume I, to the relatively more superficial prices of production/mark-up on total capital invested in *Capital* Volume III (around which quite superficial market prices would actually tend to gravitate). For a superb history of this continuing problem for Marxist economics up to the last decade of the 20th century, see the two volume Howard and King (1989: Chapter 2, 'Engels and the "Prize Essay Competition" in the Theory of Value': 21–41; Chapter 3, 'First Debates in Value Theory, 1895–1914': 42–64); (1992: Chapter 7, 'The Falling Rate of Profit': 128–48; and Chapters 12–15 in Part IV, 'Value and Exploitation': 227–310). On more recent history, see Kliman (2007; Chapter 3, 'A Brief History of the Controversy': 41–54). On current interpretations of the problem, see for example the various articles in Freeman, Kliman and Wells (2004).

posthumously published Volume III of *Capital*, edited by Engels.[4] For Marx, only money spent to hire labor power, which he called variable capital, creates surplus value. Money spent on other commodities in the production process did not create value or surplus value; Marx called this money constant capital. Thus, by Marx's reckoning, 'profit . . . is thus the same as surplus-value, only in a mystified form . . . because there is no apparent distinction between constant and variable capital in the assumed formation of the cost-price' (Vol. III: 36–7). Thus, 'the relationships of capital are obscured by the fact that all parts of capital appear equally as the source of excess value (profit)' (Vol. III: 45). For Marx, 'surplus value and profit are actually the same thing and numerically equal' (ibid.: 48). Even though, in reality, only the commodity labor power and the money used to hire labor power create surplus value, according to Marx it *appears* that all capital is productive of value and surplus value because competition will tend to generate an average rate of profit based on total capital invested in the production process (variable and constant capital using Marx's terminology). Thus, what Marx calls the prices of production will be the cost of production and a mark-up for the average rate of profit. Thus, 'these different rates of profits are equalized by competition to a single rate of profit' (158); although, 'under capitalist production, the general law acts as the prevailing tendency only in a very complicated and approximate manner' (161). Marx claims that 'the law of value regulates the prices of production' (180); therefore, 'the sum of the profits in all spheres of production must equal the sum of the surplus-value, and the sum of the prices of production of the total social product equal the sum of its value' (173). To some extent, we are once again back to Adam Smith: 'The price of production includes the average profit. We call it price of production. It is really what Adam Smith calls *natural price*' (198, emphasis in original).

These ideas concerning prices of production have been mathematized

---

[4]   Was Engels up to the job of editing Marx's notes into Volume II and especially Volume III of *Capital*? Maybe not. See the fascinating discussion in Howard and King (1989), Chapter 1, 'Friedrich Engels and the Marxian Legacy', 1883–95' (1989: 3–20). Schumpeter's comment is also germane: 'I observe that the few comments on Engels that are contained in this sketch are of a derogatory nature. This is unfortunate and not due to any intention to belittle the merits of that eminent man. I do think however that it should be frankly admitted that intellectually and especially as a theorist he stood far below Marx. We cannot even be sure that he always got the latter's meaning. His interpretations must therefore be used with care' (1950: 39, fn. 24). The editors of the new historical-critical edition of the works of Marx and Engels, the second Marx–Engels-Gesamtausgabe, are also quite critical of Engels' role as editor of Volumes II and III of *Capital*. See, for example, the articles by Bellofiore and Fineschi (2009b), Fineschi (2009), Hecker (2009), Reuten (2009) and Roth (2009) in Bellofiore and Fineschi (eds) (2009a).

by the enigmatic Sraffa.[5] Let us return to his mathematical models. Sraffa deals with truly capitalist production in his second chapter, which he calls 'Production with a Surplus' (1960: 6–11).[6] Recall that from the previous chapter, following Sraffa's notation, there are 'k' commodities produced by 'k' separate industries. A is the quantity annually produced of commodity a, B is the quantity annually produced of b, and so on. A_a, B_a, . . ., K_a are the quantities annually used in the industry producing A. A_b, B_b, . . ., K_b are the corresponding quantities used to produce B, and so on. Again, the input and output quantities are assumed to be known. Now, however, the system generates a profit, or surplus value, surplus commodities: more commodities are produced as output than are used up in the production process as inputs. The unknowns in Sraffa's theoretical system are the relative prices and the rate of profit. In computing the resulting prices of production, and in a sense following Marx,[7] Sraffa assumes an average rate of profit (r) based upon the monetary value of all the advanced capital. Assuming that all payments to commodity inputs are paid in advance:

$$(A_a P_a + B_a P_b + \ldots + K_a P_k)\,(1 + r) = A P_a$$

$$(A_b P_a + B_b P_b + \ldots + K_b P_k)\,(1 + r) = B P_b$$

$$\ldots$$

$$(A_k P_a + B_k P_b + \ldots + K_k P_k)\,(1 + r) = K P_k.$$

Moreover, $A_a + A_b + \ldots A_k$ is less than or equal to A; $B_a + B_b + \ldots + B_k$ is less than or equal to B; . . .; $K_a + K_b + \ldots + K_k$ is less than or equal to K. That is, the quantity produced of each commodity is at least equal to the quantity of it which is used up in all branches of production.[8] These equations basically state that the resulting prices of production of each good

---

[5] '[T]he elusive figure of Sraffa' (Marcuzzo, 2005: 445); 'Piero Sraffa is an enigma' (Pasinetti, 2005: 374).

[6] Sraffa himself, of course, does not use the term capitalist production; indeed, he insists on scarcely using the term 'capital'; see his terse explanation (1960: 9).

[7] As well as the other classical economists. Arguably the first person to successfully mathematize these theories was the obscure Russian mathematical economist Vladimir Dmitriev (1974 [1898]). See Nuti (1974a, 1974b). Sraffa had a copy of Dmitriev's book in his personal library.

[8] This assumes that the Hawkins–Simon's condition is met, and implies that the Frobenius root of what is in essence an input–output table is less than one. Hawkins himself developed his condition while mathematizing Volume III of Marx's work (personal communication). See his penetrating footnote six on Marx, judiciously placed at the end of his article (1948: 320–21). Hawkins' article contained a mathematical error which was corrected by the young Herbert Simon (Hawkins and Simon: 1949).

produced in each separate industry are equal to the prices paid for all of the inputs, plus a mark-up for the average rate of profit. Sraffa counts up his equations and theoretically unknown variables, and tersely concludes that his 'system contains a number of k of independent equations which determine the $k - 1$ prices and the rate of profits' (1960: 7).[9]

Sraffa thus gives us a theoretical system where commodities produce more as outputs than are used up as inputs, and where commodities need to be exchanged in definite proportions so that the production process can reproduce itself in time. He theoretically determines the relative prices or exchange values which must happen for this reproductive process to occur, as well as the rate of profit. Again, note: the commodity labor power does not necessarily appear. Hence, in Sraffa's theoretical world, it is not the commodity labor power which uniquely creates surplus value and profits. Instead, it is any commodity, or rather all commodities which produce more commodities as output than are used up as inputs into the productive process which create surplus value. Hence, in this world, it is not only the commodity labor power value which generates surplus value and profits. Marx's distinction between variable and constant capital appears specious.

Note the ironic symmetry here. Sraffa presented his theoretical models initially as the prelude to a critique of the neoclassical marginal productivity theory of prices and income distribution. Yet, in Sraffa's world, there generally are *no margins*. He generally assumes production of a given output and then generates equations so that the system can reproduce itself after the appropriate exchange of commodities in definite ratios. With no change in output, there are no marginal productivity curves, no marginal revenue curves, no marginal cost curves, and so on. Indeed, there are really not even any supply and demand curves.[10] Hence, in Sraffa's world, prices are not and cannot be determined by supply and demand: not a comforting solution for economists rigorously trained to believe that prices are determined by the workings of supply and demand curves.

Yet, similarly, in Sraffa's world, the commodity labor power does not necessarily appear;[11] nonetheless, his work was and has been used to criticize the labor theory of value. Just as Sraffa's work criticizes the marginal productivity theory of prices and income distribution even though it contains no margins, it also criticizes the labor theory of value even though it does not necessarily deal with labor. Again, not a comforting solution

---

[9] Sraffa also gives a numerical example of a two-commodity system with a surplus of output of commodities over the commodities used to produce them (1960: 7).

[10] Unless one wants to say that all supply and demand curves are vertical; but that does not seem to be a very helpful way to view the situation.

[11] Although it does generally appear in later versions of his model; see especially Chapter VI, 'Reduction to Dated Quantities of Labor' (1960: 34–40).

for those (relatively few) economists trained to believe that prices are fundamentally determined by the socially necessary labor time required to produce a commodity.

I think the implications of the Sraffian-based critique can be most clearly seen if we consider a numerical model of a fully automated society.[12] Let us suppose a theoretical world where robots make everything (they are the only inputs) and there are only three outputs: robots, gold[13] and wheat. Suppose in a year (or one production period) in the robot industry 28 robots can produce 56 more robots. So in that industry, basically one robot is producing 2 robots, and let us assume at the end of the year each old robot is 'used up', discarded, in some sense gone. Assume that in the gold industry 16 robots can produce 48 units of gold and that in the process all the robots are 'used up'. Assume that we are on a gold standard where one unit of gold = \$1. Assume that in the wheat industry 12 robots can produce eight units of wheat and are also then used up. In total, 56 robots are used up in the production of 56 robots, 48 units of gold and 8 units of wheat.[14]

Let P_r be the price of one robot; P_w the price of one unit of wheat; r the rate of profit (and the price of one unit of gold is by definition one). Using the above approach, we now have three equations and three unknowns:

1. $28P_r (1 + r) = 56P_r,$
2. $16P_r (1 + r) = 48,$
3. $12P_r (1 + r) = 8P_w.$

The system can be solved. The rate of profit is determined in the first equation and is 100 percent.[15] Note that the rate of profit is determined only in the equation or industry (or industries) which produces so-called basic outputs which are used back in the production process as inputs.[16] The rate of profit is not determined (as Marx is generally interpreted to have held) by all the industries. Through substitution, the price of one robot is \$1.50 and the price of a unit of wheat is \$4.50.

---

[12]   This is discussed in more detail in Pack (1985b, Chapter 4, 'A Model of a Fully Automated Society': 43–9).
[13]   Gold may be conceived as both money (see below) and a luxury good.
[14]   The model can be said to be one of simple reproduction (that is, it cannot grow) since the total number of robots produced (56) is the same as that used up in the production process. For the economy to expand or grow, resources (that is, robots) would have to be shifted from one of the other two industries and 'employed' in the robot-producing industry.
[15]   The equation also has a solution of $P_r = 0$; however, this solution is ruled out by the second equation.
[16]   See Sraffa (1960: 7–8).

In this mathematical/theoretical framework, a rate of profit emerges because the system as a whole produces more as outputs than are used up as inputs. Prices or exchange values emerge because the outputs are produced in different 'industries', and they must be exchanged with each other so the system can reproduce itself in time.

One would tend to believe, following Marx's theory, that in a fully automated society, there would be no workers, no surplus value, no profits.[17] Indeed, this is the conclusion explicitly reached by Ernest Mandel. He claimed 'capitalism is incompatible with fully automated production in the whole of industry and agriculture because this no longer allows the creation of surplus-value' (1975: 207). Yet, the above equations suggest that this is not so, and that Marx's labor theory of value is quite wrong. Indeed, this also was the conclusion originally reached at the end of the 19th century by the Russian mathematical economist Vladimir Dmitriev:

> Conceivably a state of technology could exist where the profit level is determined in a production process where *no 'living' power is involved at all* and 'reproduction' of goods (including machines) is effected by machines driven by free 'inanimate' natural forces. Therefore, we can imagine a state of society where *wage labor is not used* in production, but where *'surplus value' will nevertheless arise, and where*, consequently, *there will be profit on capital*. (1974 [1898]: 214, emphases in original)[18]

Granted, it is easy to make fun of and ridicule these types of models of a fully automated society, and to say they are equivalent to the hypothesis 'if chicken had teeth' (for example Denis, 1968: 265). Also, these types of mathematical models recently have been criticized because they assume some sort of equilibrium in general, and in particular they assume that the price of the outputs will be the same as the price of the inputs.[19]

Yet, I think these models do provide some powerful and interesting

---

[17] Although workers in the past would have created the original robots, workers are not used in the reproduction or current production of robots – or anything else. Hence, by Marx's labor theory of value, one would think that no value or surplus value is currently being created.

[18] See also Pack (1985b, Appendix C, 'Dmitriev's Model of a Fully Automated Society': 119–125) for a fuller discussion.

[19] See, for example, Kliman (2007). Kliman can solve models of a fully automated society by insisting that with no workers, profits must be zero, and then letting output prices differ from input prices (2007: 41–4; 178–9). Kliman is a member of the recent temporal single-system interpretation of Marx which claims to have finally solved Marx's transformation problem. However, with their interpretation of Marx, there is indeed no transformation problem because they basically change Marx's conception of value as commensurable abstract embodied labor, by immediately giving every unit of labor a *monetary* price. Thus, there is really no separate calculable value and price of production analysis, and therefore there is nothing to be 'transformed'. Moreover, by letting output prices vary from input

insights. For one thing, they demonstrate the importance of property relations and property rights. These models of a fully automated society assume that all the output is owned by the capitalists, or the people who own the various 'industries'. Those who do not own the industries, the former workers, have no access, claim, or right to the output of society. They would be in terrible straits. So those who do not own any of the means of production, and who have no access to the means of production, who are not allowed or wanted or needed in the production process, would likely suffer greatly in a fully automated society.[20]

These models also suggest that even in a fully automated society, we could still be in an era of 'scarcity'. One robot could only make so much in a given production period – be it other robots ('capital' goods), gold ('luxury goods') or wheat ('consumer goods'). So these outputs will not necessarily be free. They will still have prices or exchange values. Note also that it could be in the interests of the owners of the industries to restrict output. If the robots produced too much, if they indeed flooded the market, if they worked 24-hour days churning out more robots, gold and wheat, then the markets could indeed be flooded, driving down prices. Hence, it could be in the owners' economic interests to periodically constrict output. On the one hand, this is reminiscent of Veblen, where the 'businessman' periodically sabotages the production process.[21] On the other hand, this is indeed precisely what parts of the oligopolistic sectors of society do at the outset of every recession. If firms in these industries cannot produce and sell output at prices that will cover their costs of production, then they will temporarily close up shop. This is, of course, exactly what the automobile industry is doing or threatening to do worldwide as I write this on a naturally beautiful but economically dreary Christmas Day 2008. Output of automobiles is going down not because humans are exhausted from making them, or are forgetting or are unable to make them; but because in the current market they cannot be sold at sufficiently high prices to cover their costs of production. So, I believe these models suggest that even if we were in a fully automated society, with current property relations, we could still have variations in output and recessions.

Which brings us back to the criticisms that these are general equilibrium models. In a sense, they are indeed general equilibrium models.

---

prices, their models tend to be mathematically underdetermined, thus allowing them to set equal various equivalences. See Mongiovi's trenchant critique (2002).

20   And no doubt as society approaches such a state.

21   See, for example, (1975 [1904]); but this is a major theme which runs throughout his work.

Nonetheless, they may be used to demonstrate why the system will rarely (if ever) reach 'equilibrium'. As the philosopher David Hawkins claimed:

> Simple mechanical models, defined by linear differential equations, have been described repeatedly since the time of Marx's *Capital*, Vol. III. These are usually known as general equilibrium models, although the term 'equilibrium' is somewhat misleading. (1964: 337, fn.)

The term equilibrium is somewhat misleading because one may use a so-called general equilibrium model without arguing that the system will necessarily reach equilibrium. Indeed, this is what Marx himself did, especially in Volume II of *Capital*.[22]

Finally, these models of fully automated societies are interesting and becoming more relevant because as we proceed through the so-called information age,[23] more parts of the economy are essentially becoming automated. I will pursue implications of this fact more in the next chapter on change. First, I want to consider the issue of savings and capital.

12.2   SAVINGS AND CAPITAL

As with the controversies over how to measure, conceptualize and understand capital, there are ambiguities, controversies and, I believe, outright sophisms in how to understand capital's close counterpart saving, and saving's apparent plural, 'savings'. The sophism comes into play by using different definitions of saving and savings to confuse people.[24] This happens in the US most notably in sophistical arguments to reduce taxes on property income (paid, of course, disproportionately by the relatively rich) as well as efforts to privatize the social security program.

Saving in traditional contemporary economics textbooks is defined as a flow. It is that portion of the flow of personal income (in, say, a year) that is accumulated rather than spent or transferred. Its merely apparent

---

[22]   For more on the issue to what extent Marx can be considered a general equilibrium theorist, with some people (such as Hollander) insisting that Marx was one, and others (such as Aglietta) insisting the opposite, see Pack (1985: 134–6). See also Groenewegen (1982).

[23]   It may, perhaps, more accurately be called the disinformation age. On the difficulties governments especially seem to be having in 'telling the truth', see the articles in Panitch and Leys (eds) (2005). But, as we will see below, this issue of giving out misleading information is also a major problem with our managerial class in general. Moreover, corporations, particularly in their advertising, tend to be less than forthright (McChesney et al., 2009) and, to varying degrees, these fundamentally dishonest practices of our leaders tend to be emulated by the rest of society.

[24]   So, in a sense we are back to Aristotle. See, for example, his *Sophistical Refutations* (165b–166a).

plural, savings, has a different definition: it refers to an accumulated *stock* of saving, as in the term savings account.[25] Notice, in this definition, 'savings' is not really a plural; it is a singular.[26]

It is often held that the expansion of capitalist production is held back by the lack of saving, especially personal saving;[27] as if we were back in an 18th century Smithian world where the major constraint to increasing the wealth of the nation was inadequate supply of saving. Rather today, much saving (as well as investment) is done by corporations; and therefore much of people's saving is done by the corporations they own. In the US Bureau of Economic Analysis, personal saving does not include retained saving in the corporate sector, so focusing on this statistic alone will give a misleadingly low picture of the amount of savings by individuals, since individuals largely own the corporate sector.[28] Moreover, if Smith and Marx are correct, then in normal times, through the competitive process, capitalist firms will be able to set prices high enough through a price mark-up, so that they will be able to collect a more or less 'average rate of profit' based upon the value of their total invested capital.[29] Which is indeed what happens: US corporate firms then distribute some of this profit to shareholders in the form of dividends. They keep the rest as retained earnings which are available for reinvestment. So, for example, in the relatively prosperous, expansionary years at the end of the 20th century, from 1995 to 1999, undistributed corporate profits ranged from $133.6 to $220.0 billion per year, or $947.8 billion over the five-year period, about 2.3 percent of GDP.[30] These are savings ultimately owned by 'persons': the shareholders.

Moreover, the firms also have available to them funds exempt from taxes, depreciation allowances, which are available to be reinvested.[31]

---

[25]   See Sutch (2006) for an excellent discussion of various ways to conceptualize saving.

[26]   See, for example, the 'usage note' to the definition 'saving' in *American Heritage Dictionary of the English Language* (1992: 1607).

[27]   Or that inadequate personal saving is the primary cause of the US balance of trade deficit. See, for example, Feldstein (2008: 118–19). The speciousness of this line of argument on the cause of the US trade deficit was handled in the previous chapter. If the US dollar is in the process of becoming world money, then there will most likely be a trade deficit.

[28]   This ownership is both indirect (through pension funds and mutual funds) and direct.

[29]   The mark-up is over anticipated average costs; prices are not set according to marginal costs. The marginal cost curve in classical Smithian and Marxian theory is not necessarily upward sloping; indeed, it is not necessarily even known to the firm.

[30]   Carter et al. (eds) (2006: Table Ca9-19; Table Ce69-90). This data is from the Bureau of Economic Analysis. During this time period, yearly undistributed corporate profits as a percentage of GDP ranged from about 1.5 to 2.7 percent.

[31]   Actually, many investments in capital goods in the US may be totally 'expensed' and not depreciated; thus, increasing accounting expenses in the current year, decreasing taxable income and generating funds more quickly which may be invested.

These funds enable the firms to reproduce on basically the same scale, if they so desire, yet using the most recent investment goods and technology.[32] From 1995 to 1999, these depreciation allowances, or 'corporate consumption of fixed capital' as termed by the Bureau of Economic Analysis, ranged from $512.1 to $665.5 billion dollars per year, or $2922.8 billion over the five-year period; about 7.0 percent of GDP (ibid.).

Moreover, firms also make investments in so-called intangibles which are generally not treated as investments in the official statistics. These investments include expenditures on research and development, on personnel development and training or so-called human capital, as well as investments to purchase or create trademarks, patents, and so on.[33] One study tentatively estimated that in 1999, business investment in intangibles was approximately one trillion dollars, roughly the same as investment in tangible capital at that time (Corrado, Hulten and Sichel, 2006: 2).

Thus, the apparent lack of saving and investment in the US to a large extent is a result of very narrow definitions employed by the Bureau of Economic Analysis.[34] It has recently caused Richard N. Cooper to lament that:

> Much concern has been expressed also about the decline in personal savings in the United States . . . it is worth noting that national accounts view saving in physical terms appropriate for the industrial age: structures, equipment, and inventories. Software production was counted as investment only a few years ago. A measure of saving designed for the knowledge economy would include educational expenditures and purchases of consumer durables, all of which are currently reckoned as 'consumption' in the year in which the expenditure takes place. Moreover, American corporations have made extensive investments in intangible assets not counted as investment in the national accounts, including research and development, on-the-job training of personnel, and building brand value, which together in recent years have exceeded investment in plant and equipment . . . Properly measured, and allowing for the ultimate ownership of corporate saving Americans save nearly 40 percent of GDP. (2008: 95, fn. 1)[35]

Moreover, during normal times, funds are also available to the corporate sector via the Federal Reserve Board. With increasing output, to maintain the general price level, the Central Bank will expand the money supply, so that more credit is potentially available to the corporate sector. Moreover, when they target the federal funds rate (or any other particular

---

[32] Thus, in practice, assuming technological change, actually increasing production.

[33] These expenditures are also generally 'expensed', not depreciated; hence, they do not tend to show up in the official statistics as investments.

[34] For a defense of their unduly narrow definition of savings see Bureau of Economic Analysis (2008: 2–6).

[35] See Cooper (2006) for a more extensive elaboration of his position.

interest rate), they are essentially providing a horizontal supply of money (and potentially credit) at that rate. So in normal times, in the absence of excess banking reserves, the corporate sector as a whole can basically borrow as much money as it wants.[36] Thus, during normal times, through retained earnings, depreciation allowances, their own internal investments and the actions of the Federal Reserve Board, established firms which are able to sell their output at (or near) their projected mark-up prices should not have trouble accumulating and/or borrowing funds to expand production – if they so desire.[37]

The sophism comes in first claiming that there is an inadequate supply of saving, defined as a flow, which is in itself probably quite erroneous; second, in switching the concept to saving*s*, the stock or financial wealth of individuals, which is, of course, highly concentrated; and third, in arguing that to increase saving, the government needs to reduce taxes on saving*s*, that is on property and property income. Thus, the ceaseless proposals from the wealthy and/or their spokespeople to reduce taxes on estates, capital gains, dividends, the proposal of various tax shelters so that high income people can shelter property income, or income from saving*s*, without actually increasing their saving; and so on, and so forth. Currently, it is far from the case that the economy is not growing due to a lack of saving; indeed, lack of saving is approximately the least of the economy's current problems.[38]

Similar sophism comes in the various proposals to privatize the social security system. Contributions for government social insurance, basically social security taxes, accounted for 11 percent of earnings in 2006; employer contributions were 49 percent of this total, and employee and self-employed paid the other 51 percent (Bureau of Economic Aanalysis, 2007). These taxes are not counted as saving in the official government

---

[36] See Moore (1988). Individual firms will, of course, face an upward supply of credit due to increases in perceived risk as they borrow more money; thus increasing debt to equity ratios, increasing cash flow to service debt, and so on (see, for example, McKenna and Zannoni, 1990).

[37] Of course, as I write this in January 2009, these are not normal times: a credit crunch, financial panic, radically increased uncertainty, fear, extreme fall in aggregate demand, a liquidity trap, and so on. Yet, it is notable that the Fed is providing money to the private sector at basically zero percent interest rates – indicative that the absolute lack of adequate funds available for investment is far from the cause of the current difficulties. Rather, it is the extreme lack of confidence in the financial sector that borrowers will be able to pay back the loans. There is currently a lack of credit from the financial to the non-financial sector, not a lack of societal savings. See, for example, Minsky (1986).

[38] Of course, as Keynes emphasized, lack of growth, or a recession or depression will cause saving to go down; eventually physical capital too if the depression is severe enough. Moreover, in a recession, attempts to increase saving by individuals (as well as firms) will deepen the recession.

statistics. Yet, from the individual point of view, these are a form of saving, and this is not necessarily a bad way to 'save' for the future. Let the working generation pay taxes to the retired generation; then have the next generation pay when the current generation retires.[39] Certainly, as recent events have demonstrated, this may indeed be less risky than people investing themselves in the financial and real estate markets for their retirement. Moreover, there may be much less graft and corruption if the government handles the retirement accounts than if this is done by the private sector. After all, if enterprising entrepreneurs cannot mislead, take advantage of, and swindle frail elderly people, then who can they swindle? There will be administrative and managerial challenges whether retirement pensions are handled by either the public or the private sector. The problem of corrupt, thieving, or incompetent managers in general is an issue I will discuss in the next section. Yet, note another point: there is no economic reason why the social security program must be funded by payroll taxes, which are essentially regressive taxes on wage income. It can be funded by general income taxes, estate taxes, whatever. It is true, if social security were privatized, and people paid lower or no social security taxes, and invested that income in financial assets, statistically 'saving' would indeed go up.[40] So what? People would not necessarily be financially more secure in their retirement years; indeed, most likely, the opposite.[41] Moreover, this would not necessarily promote economic growth.

12.3 CHARACTER AND THE CRITICAL PROBLEM WITH OUR MANAGERS

Our current society has some critical problems with some of the characters it produces. Recall that Aristotle did not like chrematistics – money used to acquire more money – because of what it does to people's character.

---

[39] Of course, this assumes that the next generation will agree to pay taxes to support their parents' generation – which entails its own set of risks. There is certainly the potential here for intergenerational conflicts. The intergenerational nature of the social security system is based upon a dependency rate that makes the payment of benefits sustainable. Given the aging of the population in advanced capitalist countries, reforms such as modestly increasing the retirement age would allow the system to continue to operate under pay-as-you-go.

[40] As claimed by Mankiw in an address to the Council of Foreign Relations when he was Chairman of the Council of Economic Advisers to the Bush administration (2005). It is interesting that in this address, Mankiw accused people who disagree with him of being sophists (6–7). This was emblematic of the Bush administration's general rhetorical strategy: misleadingly accuse your opponents of doing what you in fact are doing.

[41] Since, as we should all too currently be aware, systemic financial crisis can completely evaporate people's retirement savings.

Aristotle did not use a Benthamite idea of people rather mindlessly pursuing pleasure and avoiding pain. That is what animals do. We humans use our reason to reflect, think, deliberate, bring back and reconsider memories from the past. We are also creatures formed by habit and habits; what we do, along with the choices we make, forms our character. To make wise, responsible choices we need adequate leisure. Humans should consume goods ultimately for the life of the mind, for reason, to develop human excellences and potentialities. We need to control our appetites, passions and desires.

For Aristotle, using money with the goal to acquire more money knows no limit, since one may buy most anything with money. This leads to greed and ruins our character. People are led to believe that their internal and external needs are infinite. They accumulate unneeded amounts of wealth, and consume unneeded goods. Society itself becomes corrupted as people's goal becomes to acquire money, rather than to be, say, an excellent doctor, or an excellent general. Passions dominate our reason.

With the formation of character, Smith again largely follows Aristotle. For Smith, character is largely a function of upbringing, habits, experience; character in turn will give rise to particular conduct and behavior. Again, for Smith, there is no neoclassical idea of people effortlessly weighing costs and benefits to make their decisions.

Yet, Smith dramatically parts from Aristotle in largely admiring the characters formed in commercial society, where people do use money to acquire more money (and in so doing generally do increase the wealth of the nation). For Smith, people in commercial societies will tend to be sober, hardworking, industrious, productive. Smith, for the most part, does not lament that the goal of using money to acquire more money will be without limit and promote greed.

Nonetheless, there are also major problems with the characters of most all the main actors in Smith's commercial society. The merchants and manufacturers will lie, dissimulate and mislead the public in pursuit of their profits. Moreover, if they make too much profit, they will become dissolute and disorderly. Their copious, profligate expenditures will set a bad example, and induce much of the rest of the country (particularly employees) to do the same.

Smith, in a sense, does follow Aristotle in that people of use to each other do form a kind of friendship. Thus, by Smith's reckoning, international trade and commerce should lead to international friendliness. According to Smith, this did not occur largely due to the impertinent jealousy, mean rapacity and monopolizing spirits of the merchants and manufacturers acting in their narrow economic self-interest. Nonetheless, now that in the 21st century many capitalist countries are ruled by their businesspersons and/or the hired representatives of businesspersons, this would seem to be quite a potential problem. How do we control our capitalist leaders?

Moreover, there are serious problems with managers of commercial enterprises, and Smith would be against managerial capitalism. Managers will tend to be abusive, wasteful, fraudulent; they will tend to rob the owners, to be negligent in performing their duties, and lavish in their expenses. This is a remarkably prescient point made by Smith which we shall shortly consider in more detail.

There will also be major character problems with Smith's leisure class, the landlords who live off the rent of their land. Aristotle emphasized the importance of leisure in promoting virtuous, thoughtful citizens in the participatory democracy of Athens. Yet, Smith's overly leisured landlords will tend to become lazy, intellectually slothful, indolent, ignorant and unable to properly even look out for their own economic interests. They will be tricked by the more clever merchants and manufacturers.

Of course, for Smith, the workers will also have character problems. In a sense, Smith again parts company from Aristotle; Aristotle was not really concerned with the everyday world of work and slave labor. Smith was concerned with the common workers. Due to long hard work, too little leisure, and the extreme division of labor limiting their experiences and outlook, workers will tend to have major character deficiencies. On the other hand, Smith's analysis is again basically Aristotelian, with his concern and emphasis on education, habits and actual experiences in the formation of workers' character.

Smith goes beyond anything in Aristotle in analyzing the different types of religions and character.[42] Common people will tend to adopt strict, austere forms of religion. Since they are so poor, on the edge of economic disaster, they fear too much gaiety, good humor, intemperance, breach of chastity, because they are easily ruined. They join religious sects which are excessively austere and unsocial. They become 'enthusiasts' and superstitious. These sects can become dangerous. I will discuss the implications of Smith's analysis further in the next chapter on change.

For Marx, the capitalist's character is pure Aristotle. Consumed by greed, driven by the desire to acquire more money, as well as the competition of the other capitalists, this chrematistic use of money to acquire more money wrecks the character of the capitalist. For Marx, the capitalist is internally and externally driven to accumulate, save, reinvest and work the employees to the utmost. As with Smith, the capitalists will also lie and try to mislead the public.

---

[42] In a sense anticipating Nietzsche's *On the Genealogy of Morality* (1994 [1887]).

As with Smith, yet even more so, and in contradistinction to Aristotle, Marx is concerned with the workers' character, and particularly with what the production process does to the workers. Similar to Aristotle (and Smith), habits and experience mold character. As with Smith, the workers' character is degraded and deformed by the minute division of labor in the production process; these problems are intensified with the introduction of machines in the factories.

Marx looks to the future, after the revolution, when there will be the actual development of human potentialities. Marx largely historicizes Aristotle: for Marx humans as a species basically develop their character through historical time.

Thus, both Smith and Marx are in a sense following Aristotle in stressing the importance of education, habits and experience on the formation of character; and the reciprocal nature of character in determining how humans actually behave. Marx is more Aristotelian, in stressing the deleterious effects upon a person's character which the pursuit of money will generate. This particular problem does not deeply concern Smith. Nevertheless, Smith's critical, indeed fundamentally pessimistic stance concerning people's character in general: the capitalists, the landlords (or rentiers in general), the workers, the poor *vis-à-vis* their choice of religion, and particularly the managers of commercial enterprises, resonates deeply with the concerns of contemporary 21st century society. The problem with our well-paid managers particularly merits further consideration; let us now consider this issue.

From the middle towards the end of the 20th century, there was a literature on the thesis that due to technological, organizational and managerial similarities there was a tendency for the advanced capitalist and communist systems to converge. Due largely to technological imperatives and the need for planning, to manage the chaotic vicissitudes of the market, capitalist countries would need to become more like the communist ones. Similarly, the communist societies, to increase their flexibility, would need to decrease their central planning, to some extent rely more on the market, and become more like capitalist societies.[43] Sometimes this convergence was welcomed. For example, John Kenneth Galbraith wrote that:

> Decentralization in the Soviet-type economies involves not a return to the market but a shift of some planning functions from the state to the firm. This reflects, in turn, the need of the technostructure of the Soviet firm to have more of the instruments for successful operation under its own authority. It thus contributes to its autonomy. There is no tendency for the Soviet and the Western systems to convergence by the return of the former to the market. Both have

---

[43]   On the literature as of the 1970s, see the references in Bell (1973: 113, fn. 91).

outgrown that. There is measurable convergence to the same form of planning. (1967: 108)[44]

With regards to the United States, there was a need for a large government public bureaucracy to police the powerful private bureaucracy of large corporations (Galbraith, 1970: 73). Galbraith himself in the mid-20th century was not too concerned that there was a tendency for corporate managers to be larcenous and/or incompetent. Rather, 'management does not go out ruthlessly to reward itself – a sound management is expected to exercise restraint' (1967: 115).[45]

Others were not so sanguine. Marcuse, for example, held that 'both systems show the common features of late industrial civilization: centralization and regimentation supersede individual enterprise and autonomy; competition is organized and "rationalized"; there is joint rule of economic and political bureaucracies; the people are coordinated through the "mass media" of communication, entertainment industry, education' (1961: 66). For Marcuse, in advanced capitalism 'the system thus tends toward both total administration and total dependence on administration by ruling public and private *managements*, strengthening the pre-established harmony between the interest of the big public and private corporations and that of their customers and servants' (1964: 35, emphasis added). Arguing against Galbraith's view of the benefits of the countervailing powers of big government versus big business (and to a lesser extent, big labor), Marcuse wrote that 'the countervailing powers do not include those which counter the whole' (ibid.: 51).

With the fall of the Soviet Union at the end of the 20th century, and its replacement by various byzantine forms of robber capitalism, this debate and literature about convergence between the two systems may appear moot, irrelevant, outdated. Yet it is not. For example, I think what is insufficiently appreciated in the West is the extent to which the fall of communism was brought about from above: from influential sectors of the Soviet *managers* and ruling class. As George Orwell (1946) predicted, the Soviet managers and administrators looked at the capitalist system, and decided they would be financially better off as managers in a capitalist system and as capitalists themselves.[46] Thus, there was a relatively

---

[44]   See also his conversation with the Russian economist Menshikov at the very end of the Soviet regime (Galbraith and Menshikov, 1988).

[45]   On Galbraith's general vision as expressed in *The New Industrial State*, and his two earlier influential books *American Capitalism* and *The Affluent Society*, see Pack (2009).

[46]   In this age of deliberate misinformation, Orwell's prescient writings on the deliberate impoverishment of language also bear rereading. See, for example, his 'Politics and the English Language' (1968 [1946]).

peaceful, rapid demise of the Soviet system, immediately followed by the looting of state property in the former USSR on a truly magnificent, awesome scale.[47] While the Russian GDP fell about 50 percent from 1990 to 1995 (Arbatov, 1997), by 2006 the total personal wealth of Russia's fifty wealthiest billionaires was estimated to be $192 billion, equivalent to the market capitalization of 32 percent of all Russian companies, both private and state-owned (Menshikov, 2007: xv). According to Menshikov,

> The wealthiest property owners emerged from the ranks of former shadow economy kingpins, who initially accumulated a certain amount of capital within the Soviet planned economy, and from among the managers of state-owned enterprises, who, as we have seen, were able to grab controlling stakes in those companies as they were privatized, thus becoming their owners. (2007: 189)

Menshikov asks (and answers) 'why did the "new class" ultimately prefer capitalism . . . Chiefly, it was because the socialist ideology . . . sets strict limits on income, personal fortunes, the ability to bequeath fortunes, and power' (ibid.: 16–17). This was a major cause of 'the destruction, by the communist elite, of the very system that had made them masters of society' (ibid.: 16).[48]

I think what then happened is that managers in the advanced capitalist countries[49] at the end of the 20th century and the beginning of the 21st century saw what was occurring in the former Soviet Union. They realized that they could also be much more aggressive in pursuing their narrow economic self-interest. That is, influenced by the audacity, mendaciousness and sheer wealth of the managers in the ex-Soviet Union, western managers realized they too were 'leaving money on the table'.[50]

In the first few years of the 21st century, the enormous increase in the income and wealth of our leading managers seemed to be merely a source of entertainment and amusement.[51] So, for example, people could read in the newspapers how a President of Disney received $140 million in severance pay after fourteen months on the job (Glater, 2005); or how a Co-President of Morgan Stanley for three months received $32 million

---

[47] See, for example, Braguinsky and Yavlinsky (1997) and Glinkina, Grigoriev and Yakobidze (2001); also Linz and Krueger (1996), although calling these managers 'pilferers' does a disservice to the grand enormity of their thefts.

[48] Menshikov has long been one of Russia's leading experts on capitalism; see, for example, his early work *Millionaires and Managers* (1969).

[49] Particularly in the US.

[50] I personally first heard this delightful expression at a committee meeting of technocrats; it was uttered by the organization's chief financial officer.

[51] This and the next paragraph are from Pack (2009).

(*New York Times*, 2005). Ben Stein, in an otherwise sympathetic newspaper article explaining that the people who really take risks in society are soldiers, not hedge fund managers, could still write in 2005 (and with no hint of irony) that hedge and commodity fund managers who are getting $250 to $500 million a year 'do something very useful, helping to allocate capital and to make money for the shareholders and for the people who invest with them'. If only that were true!

Yet, there are several major problems with our leading managers. For one thing, they are appropriating a significant amount of surplus value, property income.[52] In a study on executive pay, Bebchuk and Grinstein found that 'aggregate compensation paid by public firms to top-five executives during the period 1993–2003 added up to about $350 billion . . . aggregate compensation paid by public firms to their top-five executives was 9.8 percent of the aggregate earnings of these firms during 2001–2003, up from 5 percent during 1993–1995' (2005: 1).[53] That is, the amount of surplus value (or profit) being appropriated by the top managers is significant and was increasing from the final decade of the 20th century through the first decade of the 21st century. Moreover, according to the authors, the study if anything underestimated the value of executive compensation since, while including 'salary, bonuses, long-term incentive plans, the grant-date value of restricted stock awards and the (grant-date) Black–Scholes value of granted options' it did not include the value of executives' pension plans (2005: 2).

There are also serious problems with the general honesty and competence of our managers – as Smith predicted. Our managers in the financial services sector, the people managing other people's money, seem to be particularly ethically and administratively challenged. So, for example, we read in the newspaper that 'Merrill Lynch lost $27 billion last year, and still managed to rush through $14 billion worth of year-end bonuses in the days before it was taken over by Bank of America' (Krasne, 2009).[54] This calls into question not only the competence of the manager/chief executive of Bank of America for letting them do that, but also the honesty and character of the managers at Merrill Lynch. And of course, various out-and-out Ponzi schemes are now being exposed, the largest one in the US

---

[52]   In Stein's defense, from a neoclassical point of view, if managers are receiving massive amounts of income, then at the margin they must be very productive; hence, 'useful'. I think from a classical point of view, either Smithian or Marxian, it is pretty clear that these managers are basically appropriating other people's income, or indeed, wealth.

[53]   Page references are to the 06/2005 Olin Discussion paper, not to the 2005 *Oxford Review of Economic Policy* version.

[54]   See also the front page article in the *New York Times* by Ben White 'What Red Ink? Wall St. Paid Hefty Bonuses' (2009).

(as of this writing) being one by Bernard Madoff, who apparently lost $50 billion.[55] Moreover, with various governments lending money to various private corporations, to the extent that the managers in the West are using that money to further enrich themselves, we are really converging back to the Russian system: essentially the appropriation of state resources by our managers. From an Aristotelian perspective, this also to some extent is to be expected. If you give money to people who habitually enrich themselves with other people's resources, who have developed bad habits, then out of habit they will use that new money to further enrich themselves. They have developed bad characters. My guess is that the potentiality and actuality of time in prison for some of these managers could eventually change their habits. On the other hand, without some increase in the expected costs of doing 'business as usual' by our managers, then our managers will continue to conduct 'business as usual'. Larcenous behavior will continue.

From the example of the USSR (and to a somewhat lesser extent, capitalist) managers, it is all too clear that Marx was far too sanguine about potential difficulties in administering and managing enterprises. Smith's insights into the managers' character seem much more pertinent; indeed prescient. So, from a Smithian and 21st century perspective, a key problem in our society is how do we control our managers? Yet another extremely important question is how do we control our government?[56] We turn now to that question.

---

[55]   That was the original reported December 2008 estimate. By March 2009 the reported estimate had increased 30 percent to about $65 billion (Henriques 2009). Actually, these estimates are probably much too high, since they seem to include the phony 'earnings' capaciously credited to the Ponzi dupes, rather than just the value of their original investments.

[56]   From another point of view, these are two sides to the same question: how do we control our managers, be they corporate or governmental?

13. Government and change in the 21st century

13.1 THE PROBLEM OF GOVERNMENT

For Aristotle, different types of government will have different goals, hence governments themselves will have different characters. The government should most likely be ruled by people in the mean, the middle classes. Hence, there is a need for a stable government and society to have a large middle class. Moreover, just as one studies the choices made by individuals to know their goals or ends, one should study the choices made by various governments to come to know their goals or ends.

The emphasis for Aristotle is not on the historical development of the state. Rather, it is on the different types of states, their forms and their goals. Governments in their true or natural forms will rule in the interests of their citizens. In their defective, corrupted, unnatural forms, governments rule in the interests of the rulers themselves. Since history is basically circular, there is always the tendency for good, natural governments to degenerate, to become corrupt, to turn into their bad unnatural forms. This is a problem.

The good, natural state will help develop the capacities, the potentialities of its citizens. It will help citizens develop their excellences, so they can lead a good life, an excellent life, and not mere life or mere existence.

Smith's position, I argue,[1] was in many ways close to that of a modern 20th century US liberal democrat in terms of the role of the government; nonetheless, I do not think he would necessarily be in favor of a fully developed social welfare state.

Smith was against many or most of the governmental rules and regulations in his time because these mercantilist rules were basically made by and for the rich and powerful. Yet, Smith was not an advocate of strict laissez-fare. There is a positive role for active government policies. Indeed, whenever laws were passed in favor of the workers, they tended to be just and equitable. There are times, even, when the government can and should force people to be kind, charitable and beneficial.

---

[1]   Above, Chapter 7; and also most extensively in Pack (1991).

Nonetheless, people frequently misread Smith as being pro-laissez-faire partly because Smith simplifies his own position on this issue at the end of Book IV of his *Wealth of Nations*. Moreover, because Smith writes in such a smooth, engaging, comforting style, he shows how a commercial system can theoretically work as a largely self-regulating system; this theoretical demonstration calls forth admiration for the actual system itself. People following Smith studied how the commercial system worked. Smith helped change the subject matter of economics, or rather to some extent began the *modern* economics tradition, from an emphasis on economics as adminis-tration, to an emphasis on exchange in the monetized part of society;[2] or really to chrematistics itself.[3]

Yet, Smith was also suspicious of government in general. There are limits of knowledge on the part of the government, which hamper the gov-ernment from effective administration of individuals' detailed concerns. Moreover, the government is generally ruled by the rich and powerful. Indeed, for Smith, the government only arises at a specific stage of socio-economic development. For Smith, there is no government or state in the hunting stage of society (although this may not be so evident to the casual reader, since this assertion is buried deep within the text of his *Wealth of Nations*). Government's function is primarily to protect private property, the property of the rich from the poor. Hence, I think there is in Smith a deep distrust of government; this prevents him from being, as with Aristotle, a full theorist of the welfare state.

Government for Smith is largely a function of the stage of socioeco-nomic development. These stages for Smith tend to succeed each other and take place in historical time; a completely different conception of history (and change) from that of Aristotle (and the ancients in general).

For Marx, the state in capitalist society on the one hand needs to set limits on the length of the working day; minimum working conditions in the factories for maintaining cleanliness and health; and minimum wages to protect the working class, to insure the mere physical reproduction of the working class through time. Thus, to some very limited extent, the state (in *Capital*) can be seen as acting in the interests of all society; yet, for the most part, the state hardly appears in *Capital*.

From Marx's writings, there emerge several plausible interpretations of the role of the state. Firstly, as with Smith, the state can be viewed to have a functional role. The state has certain functions which it needs to fulfill

---

[2] This is basically how Boulding, for example, characterized the economy (1970: 17–18).
[3] As Tony Aspromourgos (2009) puts it in his recent study, Smith was successful in largely 'framing' modern political economy.

to assure the reproduction of the capitalist system. Secondly, the state may be viewed as a tool or instrument to protect the interests of the ruling class and/or to be fought over; contested by various classes. Again, this is similar to Smith's view of the state. Thirdly, the state may be viewed as an alienated power that needs to be reclaimed by the mass of people. This is quite different from anything to be found in Smith. Indeed, it is partly going back to Aristotle, or at least to the ideal of classical Athenian direct participatory democracy by its citizens.

Marx's vision is that after the revolution, the oppressive parts of the state serving the ruling class will no longer exist. Instead, what was the state would become a mere means of administration, and would help in the development of the capacities of its citizens. This is again a going back to Aristotle, but it is historicizing Aristotle: the state can really only fulfill its goal of developing the capacities of its citizens in history, after the communist revolution. Meanwhile, before the revolution, Marx's views on the state are very Smithian: the state has certain functions to fulfill in contemporary society, and it is a tool or instrument which is contested by various classes. Smith basically looks backward: compared to the past, things look quite good, and we can, if we try, reform things to make the world even better. Marx is focusing forward: we have the potential to do much, much better. Let us have a revolutionary break with our past so that we can proceed to truly fulfill our human potentialities.

Smith wanted a relatively small government in his time largely because the leaders would tend to use it to help the rich and powerful, not the bulk of society. I think partly due to the fear of communism, and the harshness of actually existing capitalism in the 19th century, the very end of the 19th century and the 20th century saw the rise of the welfare state in the West. As John Kenneth Galbraith argued,

> In an extraordinarily logical response to Marx, the later development of the welfare state, the support for mass education, the abolition of child labor and the Keynesian attack on the capitalist crisis would all address the points of capitalist vulnerability he identified. All of these steps against Marx, it might be added, would in their time be accorded a measure of condemnation as being themselves Marxist! (1987: 137–8)

In Germany,

> What was seen as the principal danger of the time was the active intelligence of the rapidly growing industrial working class and its well-perceived openness to revolutionary ideas, in particular to those emanating from their recently deceased countryman Karl Marx. In the clearest example of fear of revolution as an inducement to reform, Bismark pressed for the amelioration of the more stark cruelties of capitalism. (ibid.: 210)

William A. Williams has also argued that to some extent the rise of some planning in the US was led by some of the corporate leaders themselves:

> the corporation leaders feared social upheaval . . . In their way, therefore, the proponents of a system based on the large corporation were capitalists who accepted, on the evidence of their own experience as well as their casual and distorted knowledge of his ideas, the analysis made by Karl Marx, and set about to prevent his prophecy of socialism and communism being fulfilled. (1961: 351)

Smith was pro-worker and an advocate for the common laborer. Therefore, he would most likely have been in favor of many or most of the 20th century rules and regulations designed to curb the power of the rich and mighty. However, with the fall of communism in Eastern Europe and the former Soviet Union at the end of the 20th century, the fear of communism greatly receded. I think this led to increased tendencies for the wealthy to use the capitalist state to further their own narrow economic interests. Thus, in the 21st century, Smith's fears of the undue power of the wealthy on the policies of the state, particularly the capitalists, the businessmen, who cleverly seek to use the government as a tool to promote their own narrow interests at the expense of the rest of society, become quite pertinent, insightful and germane. The undue business influence on government is a real danger to society.[4] It has led to policies which increased the potential instabilities of capitalism – instabilities which we are currently experiencing.

Yet, this also brings us back to Aristotle's analysis and his concerns. For Aristotle, there is always a tendency for a government to become corrupt, and for the rulers to rule in their own interests rather than society at large. There is certainly ample evidence that this was the case in the US during the administration of George W. Bush.

This case has been strongly made by John Kenneth Galbraith's son, James, in *The Predator State* (2008). What the younger Galbraith calls the predator state is pretty close to what Aristotle would call a corrupt state: 'the systematic abuse of public institutions for private profit, or equivalently, the systematic undermining of public protections for the benefit of private clients' (Galbraith, 2008: xiii). Galbraith documents the turning of regulatory agencies over to business lobbies; the partial privatization of

---

[4] It is interesting in this regard that in the US the quite incompetent and corrupt (see below) President George W. Bush was the first President with an MBA degree. As Smith would have feared, Bush seems to have served some business interests well, though at the expense of society at large. It will also be interesting to see how much and for how long the current worldwide economic difficulties succeed in diminishing narrow corporate influence in various governments.

national security; the designing of initiatives in Medicare to benefit drug companies and the diverting of public resources to clients and friends. Galbraith views the Bush administration as 'an unapologetic government of businessmen and lobbyists' (8–9). It was 'an alliance of representatives from the regulated sectors – mining, oil, media, pharmaceutical, corporate agriculture – seeking to bring the regulatory system entirely to heel. And . . . those who saw the economic activities of the government . . . merely as opportunities for private profit on a continental scale' (131).[5]

Thus, 'the second Bush administration simply and systematically nominated the most aggressive antienvironment, antisafety, anti-consumer-protection advocates it could find – business lobbyists in most cases – to every regulatory position that it could not afford to leave unfilled' (143). So, for example, one could read in the newspaper that:

> The Interior Department's chief official responsible for investigating abuses and overseeing operations accused the top officials at the agency on Wednesday of tolerating widespread ethical failures, from cronyism to cover-ups of incompetence.
> Simply stated, short of a crime, anything goes at the highest levels of the Department of Interior . . . Mr. Griles resigned after allegations surfaced that he pushed policy decisions that favored some of his former oil and gas industry clients and that he tried to steer a \$2 million contract to a technology firm that had also been one of his clients . . . Mr. Griles is once again a lobbyist in Washington. (Andrews, 2006)[6]

By Galbraith's reckoning, 'nothing is done for the common good. Indeed, the men in charge do not recognize that public purposes exist' (147). The Bush administration did not cope with the problems of global warming; it bungled the preservation, evacuation, and rebuilding of New Orleans due to Hurricane Katrina; and so on. Indeed, the Bush administration did not mind being thought incompetent, since the charge of incompetence actually covered up their predations; indeed, their corruption.

Then there was, for many people, the rather shocking Bush war on civil liberties. There was basically spying on Americans at will and without judicial oversight. There was the wiretapping and monitoring of phone calls and emails without obtaining warrants. There was the demanding of personal records from libraries, universities and internet service providers, along with a thoughtful gag provision that prevented those served

---

[5] For a rather sensationalist account of the relatively petty corruption in government which Smith warned against, see Stone's book about 'superlobbyist' Jack Abramoff (2006).
[6] See also Broder (2007) for another, rather typical, newspaper account of regulators being taken over by the regulated to further the interests of the regulated.

with these demands from even telling anyone about it.[7] There was the monitoring of peaceful protests. There was the taking of people off the streets and delivering them to prisons around the world where they could be more conveniently tortured than in the US. There was the denial of the right of habeas corpus if the person was designated by Bush as an 'enemy combatant', and thus being subjected to unlimited detention. Hence, the President could indefinitely imprison people without charge, and put people on trial based on hearsay evidence. And of course there were the detention policies at Guantanamo Bay in Cuba and other locales, where prisoners were sometimes carefully, and at other times carelessly, tortured.[8] And there was even the outing of a covert CIA agent, Valerie Plame, by the Bush administration itself, in retaliation for her husband's criticisms of the administration's 'bogus claim that Niger provided uranium to Iraq' (Dean, 2004: 171).[9] How above-the-law; how 'un-American'; how un-Constitutional; how corrupt; how Aristotelian! Aristotle himself would not have been surprised by this behavior; of course, neither would Smith (nor Marx).

13.2 CHANGE

For Aristotle, the universe has always existed; it is permanent. The various living species on earth are also permanent. History basically goes in circles. Things get as good as they can. They realize their potential and actualize themselves, thus becoming more natural. Then corruption sets in; they become more unnatural: basically a cyclical story.[10]

For Smith, human history does go somewhere. Smith actually gets his four stage theory of socioeconomic development from Aristotle: the hunting, shepherding, farming and commercial stages of society. For Aristotle, these types of societies (or really people) basically co-exist in time: some people hunt, some are shepherds, some farm, some trade (*Politics*:

---

[7] Again, note the prescience of George Orwell (1949). In fact, Orwell has inadvertently donated his name to this sort of behavior: it is Orwellian.

[8] See, for example, Cassel (2004). The American Civil Liberties Union diligently kept up with (and eventually helped to expose) many of these nefarious practices; see their website, www.aclu.org.

[9] No saint himself, Dean is good at stressing that the function of the excess of secrecy in the Bush administration was to protect itself. As former counsel to President Richard Nixon, Dean is an expert in this field.

[10] This aspect of Aristotle's system is relatively difficult to reconcile with Judeo-Christian thought: no Aristotelian talk of creation, or of history going somewhere new. There is, though, a strain of weariness in this part of Aristotle's thought that is most reminiscent of *Eccleciastes*.

1256a–b).[11] Smith takes these different types of people, classifies them as societies, and historicizes them, thus arriving at an evolutionary or developmental conception of history. History evolves: a shepherding society may develop out of a hunting society; a farming society may develop out of a shepherding one; and finally a commercial society may arise from the agricultural society. Although there are still hints of circularity or at least stagnation in Smith's analysis, this is not the dominant strain in his work. For example, there is little likelihood that a modern commercial society will devolve to a complete farming society, let alone a hunting one.[12]

Human history is not guided by planning or reason. Rather, it is largely the unintended consequences of human action which drive human history. Hence, for Smith, there is less emphasis on the importance of reason than with Aristotle, and history is not going in circles. However, there are still some Aristotelian residues of a presumed natural growth or development of human history, particularly in Book III of *The Wealth of Nations*.[13]

Yet, and this is crucial, Aristotle assumed that species were permanent. I suspect Smith knew this was not so. In any event, the moderns would soon enough know it. If species could die out, then presumably they could also be born, develop, evolve. Moreover, history could not be circular: once a species is gone, it is gone! There is no coming back from extinction.[14]

With Marx, as with Smith, we are in the modern world of evolution and real change; history is not merely moving in circles. History for Marx is the working out of Aristotelian contradictions, not contraries. There is birth, life and death: coming-to-be and passing-away.

Marx generally insisted, particularly *vis-à-vis* Smith, that humans live in a social, not a natural world. Yet, also this social world in a sense arises naturally, spontaneously, pre-planned. So in a sense, for Marx, the current social world is natural. After the communist revolution, Marx anticipates and wants truly planned production, where the means and processes of production will exist for the workers. Then there will be conscious, rational social change. Then human society will clearly be post-natural. Reason then will replace the Smithian unintended consequences of human action. In another sense we will then be back to Aristotle, where change,

---

[11]   Aristotle also notes that some are fishermen and some brigands. I think fishing societies for Smith could be subsumed as a type of hunting society. For Smith there is no separate brigand stage of development.

[12]   Perhaps somewhat surprisingly, this devolution seems to be occurring in some societies at the end of the 20th and beginning of the 21st centuries. For example, Mongolia, thanks to post USSR western-advised deindustrialization strategies, has apparently largely reverted back to a shepherding society (Reinert, 2008: 173–9).

[13]   For a recent study of this book, see Kim (2009).

[14]   At least given current homo sapiens technology.

especially for the better, is a result of reason realizing itself in the world. Hence, Marx again historicizes Aristotle, where reason comes into its own through human history, through time.

Thus Smith basically looked back at the past, thought commercial society was generally better than previous societies, and sought ways to improve and reform his commercial society.[15] Marx looked more to the future, and thought his society was so much worse than what it could potentially be.

Marx sought to explain the rise, development and necessary fall of capitalism. His *Capital* can be seen as an Aristotelian project explaining capitalism, emphasizing all four types of Aristotelian causality: final, formal, efficient and material. This is what makes Marx's work so complex and difficult to grasp.

In detailing his story, Marx notes that with regulations on capital to protect society, there is a need to make these regulations universal, to cover all capital. Otherwise, capital will simply flee to the unregulated sectors of the economy. Currently, with the international mobility of capital, I think it is imperative that regulations also be completely spatial: if there are regulations in some geographic locales on capital, capital will tend to move to where these regulations do not exist, or are not enforced. I will return to this point presently.

Marx foresees that the capitalist mode of production will end in a revolution where the capitalist expropriators will be expropriated. In this coming revolution, there will be some violence, as always occurs in the transition from every old society to a new one.

As far as religion and change is concerned: with the radical idea of secularization and the radical Enlightenment, there was viewed the need to substitute reason and science for religion and superstition. Marx was in that tradition. Marx was hence fighting a war on two fronts: one, against classical political economy, whose most complete expression was in Smith. Hence, the subtitle of *Capital: A Critique of Political Economy*. At the same time, Marx was also fighting against what he saw as religious superstition.

The 20th century of course saw the rise of communist revolutions in various parts of the world. However, they did not take place in the most advanced capitalist countries, as predicted by Marx. Rather, they took place in relatively unindustrialized or non-industrialized countries such as Russia, China, Vietnam, Cuba, and so on. As noted in the previous section, partly in response to the threat of communism, economic reforms occurred in the leading western capitalist countries, taking the edge off the

---

[15]   Though of course his work in particular, and Enlightenment thought in general, did contribute to the French Revolution and so was, in practice, revolutionary.

harshness of the system as described by Marx. Moreover, living standards rose for the workers in these countries, particularly in the quarter century after World War II.

There was no communist revolution in Germany as anticipated by Marx. However, in the 20th century, partly in response to and as a reaction to the threat of Marxist international socialism, there arose in Germany so-called *national socialism*. What was appropriated was not the wealth of the capitalists. Rather, what was appropriated was the wealth of, among others, the Jews, by members of the 'German nation'. Of course, the lives of the Jews were also taken. Marx himself came from a Jewish back-ground, although his father converted to Christianity. Thus, one aspect of the furious reaction against communism, and against Karl Marx, the chief theoretical spokesperson for communism, was retribution against the people from whom Marx came. So, in the early to mid-20th century Germany, it was not the wealth of the capitalists that was appropriated, but that of the Jews. Although Jewish wealth and lives had been taken in Europe at various times for hundreds of years, the thoroughness and com-pleteness of the national socialists was unprecedented.[16]

After World War II, partly as a result of the competition with the com-munist system, workers wages went up in the advanced capitalist countries. For example, according to Edward Wolff, from 1947 to 1973, real wages in the US grew by 75 percent (2004: 7). However, in the US, the real wage, the median average hourly wages and salaries of production and non-supervisory workers in the total private sector, adjusted for inflation, has been stagnant or falling since 1973. Again, according to Wolff, 'Between 1973 and 1993, the real wage declined by 14 percent, though it has since risen by 7 percent from 1993 to 2000, for a net change of −8 percent (2004: 3). Thus, 'in 2000, the hourly wage was $14.08 per hour, about the same level as in 1968 (in real terms)' (2004: 7). Both the relative and the absolute share of income to the bottom half of the population fell in the last quarter of the 20th century (2004: 3–4).

Of course, incomes stagnated or fell in the 1970s due to the stagflation caused by the rise of energy prices and the resulting supply side shock; and they stagnated or fell in the early 1980s due to the monetarist 'cure' for inflation by throwing the economy into recession.[17] Yet, I think median

---

[16] I think Marx himself actually shared the anti-Semitism in his own age. See for example his essay 'On the Jewish Question' (in Marx 1967c) and the discussion in Ben-Sasson (1976: 728–9, 803–7). Anti-Semitic comments are scattered throughout *Capital*, although to be fair to Marx, he had quite critical comments to make against most all religions.

[17] See Baird (1973) for an excellent textbook argument why (for the monetarists) stagfla-tion in the short run is the monetarist solution to inflation (inflation for the monetarists, of course, being caused by an excess supply of money, rather than a supply side shock).

incomes have also stagnated since then at least in part due to the collapse of communism in Eastern Europe and the former Soviet Union. I think communism (or rather the threat of communism) is definitely good for the average workers in non-communist countries. It assists them in the class struggle to gain higher wages. As Adam Smith would have appreciated, the capitalist system seems to function better and is more equitable towards the common worker when it is in direct competition with another, alternative socioeconomic system.

Thus, we are currently witnessing increasing inequality in wealth and income. According to Wolff, in the US in 2004, the top 1 percent of households owned 34.3 percent of all wealth. The next 4 per cent owned 24.6 percent of wealth; so the top 5 per cent owned 58.9 percent of the wealth. The bottom 40 per cent of the households owned almost no wealth; the average wealth of this poorest 40 percent was $2200 (2007: 11). In terms of income, in 2000 the top 1 percent acquired 20 percent of all income. The next 4 percent acquired 15.2 percent; so the top 5 percent acquired 35.2 percent of all income (ibid.). Again, according to Wolff, 'In 2004, the richest 1 percent of households held about half of all outstanding stock, financial securities, trust equity, and business equity, and 37 percent of non-home real estate. The top 10 percent of families as a group accounted for about 80 to 85 percent of stock shares, bonds, trusts, business equity, and non-home real estate' (2007: 25).[18]

I think wages have also stagnated due to increased globalization. As Marx pointed out, if rules and regulations (or higher wages) are imposed upon capital in one part of society, then capital will tend to move to the unregulated or under-regulated sectors of society. This is what is now happening in the world at large. Capitalism, particularly with the end of communism in Eastern Europe and the former Soviet Union, is a worldwide, international system. Thus, capital will try to move to those parts of the world where costs are lower: be these costs regulations, taxes, or wages. This is what the finance textbooks call tax, regulatory and wage arbitrage. In an international world, with a tendency towards the law of one price, capital will more from countries with relatively high taxes and expensive (from their point of view) regulations and wage rates, to countries with lower taxes, fewer regulations and lower wages.[19] Thus, in the 21st century there is downward pressure on wage rates in all the relatively

---

[18]   On unequal wealth and income distribution in the US see also Reitz and Spartan (2005).

[19]   And workers, of course, will try to move from the poorer countries to the wealthier ones, further generating downward pressure on wages. This is one of the main reasons for the intense political controversies over immigration issues in nearly all advanced capitalist countries.

wealthy advanced capitalist countries. Moreover,[20] there is also systemic downward pressure on tax rates (particularly taxes on property income) and pressure to have fewer regulations on capital in general. The current financial troubles may temporarily reverse this trend; yet, I think the long-run tendency is evident. In the absence of worldwide rules, regulations on capital, taxation rates, minimum wage rates, and so on, there will be a tendency for capital to go to those parts of the world where taxes are lowest, regulations the fewest and wages the cheapest.[21] In the 21st century, regulations on capital will have to be on an international level. How to do this, particularly with governments so controlled by the mercantile interests, is a, or possibly *the*, key question of our times.

Hence, in the absence of new global rules and regulations on capital, in the advanced capitalist countries there will be continued systemic downward pressure on wage rates;[22] continued downward pressure on taxes upon property income; continued pressure to deregulate the economy and to have fewer regulations on capital. On the issue of the need for regulations on capital in all sectors of the economy, everywhere, Marx was right.[23]

13.3   RELIGION, CHANGE AND THE FUTURE

It is frequently argued that the entire modern age is over, and that we live in some sort of frenetic post-modern era. Post-modernism seems to be characterized by a certain disjointedness. Unlike the theorists considered in this study, in post-modernism there is a distinct aversion to big pictures or grand narratives which can get a firm hold of the truth, or at least the essence of any given situation or broad era.[24]

Furthermore, it may be true, as the great mid-20th century Canadian economic historian Harold Innis argued, that what is really important in human history is not changes in the mode of production as claimed by

---

[20]   Until the current worldwide financial and economic crisis.

[21]   For the realization that, in the early 20th century US, regulations on capital had to be at a national, not just a state or local level, see, for example, Weinstein (1968).

[22]   For a largely neoclassical approach which also essentially reaches this same conclusion, see Bivens (2008). See also Costello, Smith and Brecher (2007).

[23]   Here, the financial services industry, the banking sector, was adroitly adept at leading the way to deregulation, and to helping other industries avoid regulations and taxes. See, for example, Smith and Walter (1990, 1997, especially Chapter 6, 'Regulatory Issues': 153–84). For an informative insider look at some of the accounting scams creating and using complex derivatives to avoid paying taxes, see Partnoy (1997). May the US investment banking industry rest in peace.

[24]   See, for example, Eagleton (2005) and Sanbonmatsu (2005).

Marx (and Engels). Rather, what is crucially important is changes in our means of communication. This is because changes in the means of communication alter the very way we think and understand the world and therefore what we do (Innis, 1951, 1972 [1950]). If Innis is correct, then it may be that with the ushering in of the new means of communication by computers as well as the internet at the end of the 20th and beginning of the 21st centuries, we could conceivably be experiencing the ending of the modern era and beginning a new post-modern era. The new means of communication would be one marked by a dramatic 'lightness' and resulting incredible swiftness and spatial capacity, combined with extreme temporal ephemeralness.[25] It appears all too easy to lose information (and thoughts) in the computer age.[26]

Nonetheless, I think it was the end of the communist regimes in Eastern Europe and the former Soviet Union at the close of the 20th century which will ultimately, and most clearly, mark the end of an important era.[27] Moreover, the decline of Marxist-inspired governments at the close of the 20th century can also be interpreted at a certain level as a failure of reason. Therefore, that it has been followed by the rise of mystical and faith-based movements and government is no coincidence.

Recall that Marx anticipated and called for a revolution in the name of science. In many ways the ultimate secular scholar (and social scientist), Marx and his followers felt they were promoting 'scientific socialism'. They wanted to replace the anarchy of the market, Smith's theory of unanticipated consequences from human action, or any possibly semi-mystical invisible hands, with conscious, rational, human planning. So, for example, Herbert Marcuse, in an influential study of Hegel and the rise of social theory, significantly titled his book *Reason and Revolution* (1960 [1941]). According to Marcuse, reason itself is revolutionary for Hegel (properly understood) and, by extension, for Marx (and everyone else) too. Thus,

---

[25]   On hard media versus light media in Innis's thought, see, for example, Godfrey (1986: ix-xiii). Marshall McLuhan (1964; 1969), with his motto, 'the medium is the message' was a popularizer of Innis's work in this field in the latter part of the 20th century.

[26]   Who has not experienced the joys of a crash of a computer hard drive without a 'back-up'? On the other hand, with current and future technology, there is also the opportunity for discrete bits of information to circulate in cyberspace more or less forever; another disconcerting thought.

[27]   If indeed it is the end of the *entire* modern era. Note, by the way, these two theses are not necessarily incompatible. An Innisian interpretation of the decline of the Soviet centralized system would be that it was simply incapable of dealing with the spatial and temporal necessities associated with computer technology and the internet. China itself is currently experiencing difficulties with these technologies as it seeks to reform (while largely maintaining) its system.

> Dialectical logic . . . rejects any claim of sanctity for the given . . . It holds that 'external existence' is never the sole criterion of the truth of a content, but that every form of existence must justify before a higher tribunal whether it is adequate to its content or not . . . Progress from one logical category to another is stimulated by an inherent tendency in every type of being to overcome its negative conditions of existence and pass into a new mode of being where it attains it true form and content. (131)

The higher tribunal before which every form of existence must justify itself is human reason itself. Therefore, 'when, for instance, we speak of the determination of man, and say that that determination is reason, we imply that the external conditions in which man lives do not agree with what man properly is, that his state of existence is not reasonable and that it is man's task to make it so' (135).

So, reason is revolutionary. Therefore, the failure of the communist revolution, the collapse of those societies in Eastern Europe and the former Soviet Union, is thus also in a sense a failure of reason. This somewhat ironically brings us back to Adam Smith. For recall, Marx was not just arguing against Smith and critiquing political economy; he was also arguing and competing against the claims of religion. And recall that for Smith, poorer people, because of the economic uncertainties of their position, are most likely to gravitate to the more mystical, fundamental, disagreeably rigorous forms of religion. Marxism and fundamental religious movements thus are to some extent substitutes, that is competitors for the hearts and minds of the poorer people in society.

We see this to some extent in the US. So, for example, Frank, in his deservedly popular and perceptive book, *What's the Matter With Kansas? How Conservatives Won the Heart of America* (2004)[28] explains how the Republican Party successfully combined conservative religious and social issues with pro-business economic policies. He writes, 'nearly everyone has a conversion story they can tell: how their dad had been a union steelworker and a stalwart Democrat but how all their brothers and sisters started voting Republican; or how their cousin gave up on Methodism and started going to the Pentecostal church on the edge of town' (3). Thus, workers vote Republican with economic policies that help the affluent, because the Republican Party claims to support conservative, fundamentalist religious values. Hence, Kansas is 'a state . . . spectacularly ill served by the Reagan–Bush stampede of deregulation, privatization, and laissez-faire. It sees its countryside depopulated, its towns disintegrate, its cities stagnate' (76). And, 'this is not just the mystery of Kansas; this is

---

[28] Published in Great Britain under the title *What's the Matter with America?*

the mystery of America' (ibid.). That is, in the absence of (or replacing) a secular left protest against the economic policies and results of contemporary society, there is a religious right protest against the social and cultural policies and results of contemporary society. Relatively poor people join strict religious movements. As Smith argued, these people become concerned with the vices associated with too much gaiety and mirth: too much drinking; recreational use of drugs; sex outside of religiously approved marriage; the possible results of sex outside of religiously approved marriage (abortion); non-religiously approved marriage (gay marriage); pornography produced in Hollywood, seen in movies, on television, on the internet, and so on. According to Frank, this focusing on social and cultural issues clearly hurts the economic interests of Middle America and helps the wealthy: 'The trick never ages; the illusion never wears off. Vote to stop abortion; receive a rollback in capital gains taxes. Vote to make our country strong again; receive deindustrialization' (7).

Thus, the Republican Party since the Reagan years has relatively successfully wed traditional economic policies which favor the wealthy, with proclaimed traditional social and cultural values favored by the religious right.[29] To the extent they are able to successfully argue the primacy of religious, social and cultural concerns over economic concerns, they are able to garner widespread support from relatively poor people, and win elections. One unanticipated result of the contemporary financial difficulties and the abrupt fall in the stock market in autumn 2008 was the reintroduction of the primacy of economic concerns, and the consequent election of the liberal Democrat Barack Obama.

So, with the fall of Marxist-inspired communism in Eastern Europe and the former Soviet Union at the end of the 20th century, class conflicts between the rich and poor tend to now manifest themselves not so much as economic conflicts but as social, cultural and religious conflicts. We are back to the concerns (and insights) of Smith about the disagreeable problems caused by overly rigorous enthusiastic religions.[30] This change, of course, is most notable in the Middle East and in the Islamic world. Hence, for example, we see the relative shift in power from the secular,

---

[29]   I think this is particularly noteworthy with their concern with gender issues and the changing economic, social and sexual relations between the sexes, which they tend to view with fear and acute anxiety. See, for example, Pack (1987: 472, 476). See also Pack's novella about the socioeconomic theories of the clever, popular buffoon Rush Limbaugh (2008b).

[30]   Note that if we date Smith at the beginning of the modern era and assume that he was most concerned with the religious conflicts in a slightly earlier pre-modern era, and if we are now indeed in a post-modern era, then the conflicts and concerns of the post-modern era are recycling back to the same (or strikingly similar) conflicts and concerns of the pre-modern era. To some extent, world history is starting to look cyclical again.

vaguely left wing Palestinian Liberation Organization, to the Hamas. The secularist Saddam Hussein and his statist Baath Party in Iraq represented more the 20th century; Osama bin Laden, Al-Qaeda and other radical fundamentalist Islamic movements, the 21st century. The despair of people who considered themselves unduly poor and/or oppressed frequently manifested itself in Marxist-inspired movements throughout the later part of the 19th and most of the 20th centuries;[31] movements ultimately claiming to be based upon science and reason. Today, that despair is much more likely to be channeled into fundamentalist religious movements, based upon various revealed theologies. Moreover, recall that Smith wrote that 'Science is the great antidote to the poison of enthusiasm and superstition' (V.i.g.15); the great antidote to fundamentalist, overly rigorous religious views. With the discrediting of Marxian socialism, and the resulting rise of social protest in the form of fundamentalist religious movements, I expect to see continued, fierce competition between various putative sciences (human reason) and various putative revealed religions (God's 'Will'). Do not expect these multifaceted controversies to go away anytime soon.[32] The decline of reason-based Marxist movements and societies has been partially replaced by the rise of faith-based religious movements and societies.

Yet, I do not want to overstate these tendencies. There are still Marxist-inspired movements and governments in Latin America and Asia.[33] Moreover, the Marxist ideal that we can get to a post-exchange, post-capitalist society certainly seems feasible and possibly correct if we take a long enough view. If we recall the model of a fully automated society discussed in the last chapter, there are reasons for thinking that there could still be prices in that society, if the output is produced in limited quantities. Yet, if the output was continuously produced, so that it exceeded demand, then I would think the goods would eventually be free; there would be no need to ration them through a market. Moreover, here neoclassical price theory merges with classical price theory. If the marginal cost of producing something is zero, in neoclassical theory there are strong efficiency and welfare arguments that its price should probably also be zero: free. Moreover, as the economy becomes more of an information economy, parts of it are already in a sense fully automated. With the internet and current technology, the marginal cost

---

[31] See, for example, Dunn (1972).

[32] That there are substitutions between secular union-based political action and religious groups see Straub (2006). That there is indeed also a religious essence to Marx, see Tucker (1972: 21–7).

[33] See, for example, Amin (2009).

of producing (and especially reproducing) information is basically zero. This, of course, is why the US government and firms in the information business place so much stress on so-called intellectual property rights.[34] They want to constrict output of information (songs, books, movies, and so on) and be able to charge a price for something that costs essentially zero to reproduce.

Here, in a weird way, we are also back to Aristotle. Recall that Aristotle wanted to restrict, or rather control and limit, the needs of the body for the sake of the human soul, human reason. In the advanced capitalist countries, due to tremendous increases in productivity, a relatively small amount of labor is actually used to produce material goods for our bodies. For example, in the US in 2007, out of about 146 million in the labor force, only around 2 million worked in agriculture, forestry and fishing; only about 28 million were in the construction and manufacturing sector.[35] Most of the rest were in various 'service sectors' providing services to other people. So the proportion of the work force actually producing material goods in the advanced capitalist countries is rather low and is declining.

This also brings us back to the importance of property relations. In the model of a fully automated society discussed in the last chapter, it was originally assumed that only some people owned the output, or had the property rights to what was produced in that society. The others – the workers who at some point in the past had worked and created the material base for that society – were not needed, had no income and had no property rights to the output; clearly, not a stable situation. Yet, is this the direction our society is heading: a society of potential plenty yet with mass privation, because large sectors of society have no legal claim to any of the potential or actual output?[36]

The Marxist vision is one of communism: lost in the past, and to be recovered in the future. This is perhaps most clearly seen in Engels' account of *The Origin of the Family, Private Property, and the State* (1972 [1884]).[37] Quoting the American anthropologist Lewis H. Morgan, discussing the native American family or gens, Engels believed that

---

[34]   See, for example, Chang (2002) and Shadlen (2009).

[35]   Source: *Statistical Abstract of the United States*, 2009, United States Department of Commerce, Bureau of the Census, Table No. 600. Note, this to some extent underestimates the number of workers in the manufacturing sector providing for US consumption since the US that year imported so many manufactured products – yet I think the general trend is clear enough.

[36]   See Macpherson's discussion of some of the implications of a fully automated society (1978: 199–207).

[37]   I think Samuel Hollander is quite correct on the pivotal influence of the young Engels on the young Marx concerning economic issues, as well as Marx's overall general vision

All the members of an Iroquois gens were personally free, and they were bound to defend each other's freedom; they were equal in privileges and in personal rights . . . and they were a brotherhood bound together by the ties of kin. Liberty, equality, and fraternity, though never formulated, were cardinal principles of the gens . . . It serves to explain that sense of independence and personal dignity universally an attribute of Indian character. (120)

It is, I think, remarkable the hold the native American society had on radical social thought in Europe.[38] Continuing in this vein, Engels writes:

Everything runs smoothly without soldiers, gendarmes, or police; without nobles, kings, governors, prefects or judges; without prisons; without trials . . . the household is run in common and communistically by a number of families, the land is tribal property, only the small gardens being temporarily assigned to the house-hold . . . There can be no poor and needy – the communistic household and the gens know their obligations toward the aged, the sick, and those disabled in war. All are free and equal – including the women. (128)

Looking to the future, Engels concludes that 'Democracy in government, brotherhood in society, equality in rights and privileges, and universal education foreshadow the next higher plane of society to which experience, intelligence, and knowledge are steadily tending. It will be a revival, in a higher form, of the liberty, equality and fraternity of the ancient gentes' (217). This dream, or goal, or ideal of a better world in the future, a communist world modeled on Native American society but at a higher level of material, socioeconomic development, has been partly shattered and destroyed by the developments in the 20th century. Yet, I doubt this dream will ever entirely go away. There is too much trouble and instability with our current socioeconomic system; and there are indeed economic trends which suggest that one day the era of economic scarcity could indeed be over.

---

when he writes, 'The range of Marxian theoretical issues touched on by Engels in his *Outlines of a Critique* published in 1844 but composed in 1843 – the *Umrisse* – is impressive; and it can be shown that Marx owed a largely unacknowledged debt to Engels . . . Beyond this, all the Marxian predictions regarding a revolution emerging from the processes of capitalist development – processes generating untenable conditions for labor including essentially increasing instability and secular depression of living standards – are to be found in Engel's writings during the 1840s before Marx devised his technical notions of "surplus value" and "exploitation". Engels in fact provided the *vision*' (2008: 488, emphasis in original). Also, on the importance of Engels' *The Condition of the Working Class in England* (1999 [1845]) for Marx's thought, Hollander (2008: 489–90).

[38] Consider also Rousseau's work, for example his *Discourse on the Origin of Inequality* (1992 [1755]). I think this broad connection between Native American societies and general radical European social thought is underappreciated in the literature.

In the meantime, there are some crucial, nasty administrative problems which need to be urgently addressed. Recall that before Smith, before the modern era, economics was largely the study of administration (Lowry, 1987, 1991, 1995).[39] Whether or not we are now in an entirely new post-modern era, which is recycling back to the pre-modern era, there are indeed grounds to think that economic theory itself is returning, and must to some extent return, to its pre-modern concern with administrative issues.

On the one hand, certain aspects of the dominant 20th century neoclassical paradigm are falling into disrepute.[40] Certainly, a theory which generally assumes that people have perfect information is uniquely ill-suited to deal with economic issues in an information age. Moreover, assuming that humans have perfect information in a sense makes humans into gods, not mortals: only gods could have perfect information. With the widespread resuscitation of God as well as the growing popularity of sundry revealed religions in the 21st century,[41] this idea that humans are little gods, this peculiar form of idolatry, will probably become more distasteful to many people; including economists. Similarly, the rise of behavioral economics, with its emphasis that, contrary to general neoclassical assumptions, in fact people are not perfectly rational, would seem to be both long overdue and a correcting reaction to absurd, unearthly assumptions concerning the human soul. Behavioral economics, criticizing this aspect of neoclassical economics, fits in with the current world geist.[42]

Also, there are administrative challenges that need to be met. The rise of feminist economics can be seen to be a form of institutionalism and a revival of emphasis on administrative concerns. Its emphasis on the crucial role of the family, the distribution and organization of power and work in the household, that is home economics and economics as provisioning, is in a sense a return to pre-Smithian, administrative views of the proper

---

[39]   That the definition of the subject matter of economics is indeed contested terrain, see Backhouse and Medema (2009).

[40]   See, however, Davis, who argues that neoclassicism 'is not so much a failed programme as a finished one' (2006:16).

[41]   It is, I think, an indicative sign of our times that the 21st century has seen an increasing number of commentaries stressing the putative importance of religious beliefs for Adam Smith's social thought. See, for example, Hill (2001) and the articles in Cockfield, Firth and Laurent (eds) (2007); a relatively strange accusation to be made of someone whose best, closest friend was David Hume. Smith's student James Boswell called him an 'infidel' (1963: 337; 1977: 298).

[42]   However, the neoclassical theory of income distribution, the idea that basically people are rewarded according to their marginal productivity, I expect to remain. It is much too valuable a tool in defense of unequal distribution of incomes in capitalist societies to think that it will vanish anytime soon, as long as we have very wealthy people in need of a theoretical defense for their bountiful incomes.

subject matter of economics.[43] Institutionalist economists themselves are arguably becoming more important and numerous. This is perhaps most clearly evident in the field of development economics. There economists are rediscovering that most countries, including the US, historically developed through detailed, administrative government policies. They did not develop through 'Washington Consensus'-type policies emphasizing a limited economic role for government planning, open economies and full integration into the international economy (Chang, 2002; Reinert, 2008).

Then there are the administrative problems discussed in this study.[44] How do we control our managers so they behave responsibly and do not loot us? How do we control our governments so they govern for the people, and not for the governors and their predatory friends? Or, more generally, how do we control our private and public managers? How do we prevent taxation, regulatory and wage arbitrage from reducing taxes, especially on property income; inciting undue deregulation; and lowering wages in the advanced capitalist countries? Then there are other pressing administrative challenges not discussed in this study; for example global climate change. How do we control/manage/administer the effects of humans from deleteriously changing the world climate? And, of course, the ever present threat of nuclear war: how do we control the spread of nuclear weapons and/or eliminate the ones we already have, and prevent catastrophic wars in general?

The administrative challenges facing humans in the 21st century are too great to be ignored. Moreover, they are too great to imagine that they can be solved by simply letting some mystical invisible hand of the marketplace work its phony magic.

---

[43] For a good introduction to feminist economics, see, for example, Barker and Feiner (2004). That Xenophon may be viewed as the first economist in the western tradition, see, for example, his '*Oeconomicus*' (1994); *The Education of Cyrus* (2001); also Lowry (1987, Chapter III, 'Xenophon and the Administrative Art': 45–81).

[44] The current worldwide economic difficulties also cry out for administrative solutions.

14. Concluding thoughts for the 21st century (and the third millennium)

The issues discussed in this study, and tackled variously by Aristotle, Adam Smith and Karl Marx over the last couple thousand years or so, are still with us. How to understand, clarify, handle exchange value, money, capital, character, government and change remain challenges in the 21st century. I daresay they will remain challenges beyond this century. These issues are not now finally 'solved'; nor will they be in the foreseeable future. They are not going away; hence, in a sense, this book will not be closed. There is no one, putatively scientific solution to these issues. Here, however, is my brief summing up of where I think we are now, in light of the insights offered by Aristotle, Smith and Marx in their various theoretical systems, near the beginning of the 21st century, near the beginning of the third millennium.

Consider the cause of exchange value, the material cause, what it is that makes things commensurate so they may be exchanged with each other in definite ratios. It is not that goods are produced by labor power, by workers, as stressed by Marx when he thought he had solved this two thousand-year-old Aristotelian question. Rather, following Sraffa's work, it is that commodities themselves are produced in various proportions by other commodities. Commodities need to be exchanged in various ratios for the economy to reproduce itself through time. Thus, it is the mere fact that goods are produced as commodities with the goal (and the absolute need) to be exchanged which makes them commensurable.

As far as money is concerned, if Aristotle, Smith and Marx are correct that the exchange of commodities will necessarily generate money, a universal equivalent, then in a global economy, a world economy, a world money will be generated. The system apparently cries out for a world universal equivalent. There is evidence that since the end of the Bretton Woods system, the US dollar is in the process of becoming world money. To the extent this is true, then the US will generally have a balance of trade and/or current accounts deficits. Hence, it makes approximately no sense to try to 'correct' these deficits. Moreover, this means that the Federal Reserve Board will to some extent further lose the control of the supply of money in the US. This fact should further dampen any residual monetarist dreams that the Fed can and should target the money supply in its efforts to pursue its economic goals. This also means that to some extent US currency is equivalent to gold coins under the old international gold system. Moreover, the US debt is in some ways similar to gold, since it is a store of value which is extremely liquid, and easily convertible into US currency/ world money. To the extent this is true, it means that the US can borrow its own money extremely cheaply. It is as if the US government owned its own gold mine. Indeed, it is even better than owning a gold mine since the US government can produce its money for basically zero cost. This also suggests that changes in the value of the dollar *vis-à-vis* other currencies could change world price levels. This would happen particularly in those raw material and commodity markets that are global and deal in standardized contracts. Similar to changes in the value of gold under the old gold standard, one would think that changes in the value of the US currency will tend to cause changes in the general worldwide price level (in, of course, opposite directions).

Consider now the question of the source of surplus value, of property income, of money being able to acquire more money. It is not only the commodity labor power which is able to create more value than it costs to produce and purchase that labor power. Rather, again following Sraffa's work, it is that commodities in general are able to produce more commodities as outputs than are used up as inputs in the production process. Indeed, theoretically, there can be a fully automated society with no labor power utilized at all; there could still be property income, where the owners of the productive processes had legal access to the surplus. Thus, it is commodities in general, and how they are used, that generate the surplus value, the source of property income. Sraffa's work in a sense can be seen as a generalization of the labor theory of value. Yet, it is also a generalization of the physiocratic theory that only land can produce an economic surplus. And it is also in a sense a generalization of the neoclassical theory that physical capital, machinery and equipment, is basically the source of property income.[1] Rather, for Sraffa, *all* commodities in general are the source of surplus value and property income when they create more commodities than are used up in the production process.

As far as what is in a sense the flip or the 'supply' side of capital is concerned, saving: if Smith and particularly Marx are correct, then

---

[1] I am thinking here in terms of the so-called marginal product or marginal revenue product of capital. The neoclassical theory of profit is a slippery one, hard to pin down since, among other reasons, it generally also takes into account such issues as returns to risk, entrepreneurship, intertemporal time preference, and so on. Like a virgin wearing many chastity belts, the neoclassical core is guarded by many protective belts and is quite difficult to definitively deflower.

increases in wealth, capital and economic growth are not held back by inadequate saving in the advanced capitalist countries. That is, a lack of saving is not generally the pertinent constraint to the accumulation of capital or to economic growth. This also suggests that problems to economic growth come from what may be called the demand side: that firms cannot sell what they produce at prices covering their costs of production, including an average rate of profit on their investment. Or, as is now occurring, there may be a crisis in confidence, a freezing up of loans and/or credit sales, and so on. Nonetheless, typically the system can grow and the capitalists may accumulate wealth and surplus value; when this does not happen, it is generally not due to a lack of saving and/or investment funds.

Arguments to reduce taxes on property income and to privatize social security in the US are largely based upon this error: that it is a lack of saving which inhibits economic growth. They are also in large part based upon a sophistry created by confusing and mixing the term saving*s*, which is basically the stock of wealth, with *personal saving*, which is a flow, and which in any case is a misleadingly narrow definition of societal saving. This sophistry is used to try to shift the tax burden from the relatively wealthy to the relatively poor.[2] Moreover, the real keys to financial security for the elderly are reliable claims to future streams of income, which may then be used to purchase goods and services. These claims may indeed be more reliably secured through the political system, with a transfer of income (or claims to goods and services) from one generation to another, than through privatized personal financial investing which is subject to the vicissitudes of the financial markets.

It is true that privatization of social security could indeed give our private financial managers more opportunities to fleece the elderly. Yet, this is no doubt something which should be avoided, not encouraged. But it also points to a larger problem with our society. If Adam Smith is correct, then how do we control our lying, wasteful, fraudulent managers? People who out of habit, and their economic positions, have developed bad characters. Competition between Russia (and the old USSR) and the US seems to have been in part a question of competing managers – which set of managers can grab the most surplus value? The old communist system and the system in the West may indeed be converging, but they are converging to a domain of managerial corruptness, of managerial self-largesse.

Yet, this also leads us to an even larger problem. How do we control

---

2   Oftentimes also to starve the liberal welfare state of fiscal resources.

our managers in general – be they corporate or government managers?[3] The general problem, if Aristotle is correct, is that governments have an innate tendency to become corrupt, to become unnatural: to rule in the interests of the rulers and governors, rather than in the interests of society at large. Yet, in a sense our contemporary problem may be more severe than Aristotle imagined. For, if Marx and perhaps particularly Smith are correct, this problem is compounded in the 21st century because of the undue influence of capitalists and/or the major corporate managers in using the government to rule in their narrow, short-run economic interests. Smith complained in his day about the capitalists turning international trade, which (in a sense following Aristotle) Smith thought should be a source of friendship, to rivalry, jealousy, discord, animosity, war. In our own age, scarcely a day goes by when one cannot open the daily newspaper and read another story about how a businessperson or one of their hired 'brains' lied and misled the public for their own absurd narrow economic gain at the expense of the rest of society – and, indeed, the world at large. So, for example, today as I write this, the current fabrication discussed in the newspaper is 'On Climate Issue, Industry Ignored Its Scientists':

> For more than a decade the Global Climate Coalition, a group representing industries with profits tied to fossil fuels, led an aggressive lobbying and public relations campaign against the idea that emissions of heat-trapping gases could lead to global warming. . . . But a document filed in a federal lawsuit demonstrates that even as the coalition worked to sway opinion, its own scientific and technical experts were advising that the science backing the role of greenhouse gasses in global warming could not be refuted. (Revkin, 2009)

Merely exposing these, on the one hand quite silly, on the other hand quite dangerous, lies will not make them go away. As long as the expected (private) marginal benefits of producing and promulgating lies – either by capitalists and/or their managers or their competent hirelings – exceed the expected (private) marginal costs, we need to expect the adroit, efficient production and distribution of these lies to continue.

Moreover, Marx's point that rules and regulations on capital must be general, covering all capital, is also pertinent. In the absence of relatively common global rules and regulations on capital, capital will tend to migrate to where wages are lowest; to where taxes, especially on property

---

[3]   See, for example, Benedict (2009). The description of the character of Claire Gaudiani, former President of Connecticut College, former President of the New London Development Corporation, and front for Pfizer Inc. as that drug company pursued its perceived economic self-interests is particularly unflattering – and accurate.

income, are lowest, thus weakening the tax basis of the modern liberal welfare state; and to where regulations are fewest and/or the least capably enforced. This is what the international finance practitioners openly call wage, taxation and regulatory arbitrage. How to achieve fair and equitable global, international rules and regulations on capital throughout the entire world will be one, or perhaps, *the*, major economic challenge of the rest of the 21st century.

Since the fall of communism in Eastern Europe and the former USSR, wages for the average worker in the capitalist West have largely stagnated. There is less fear of a communist or socialist revolution by the ruling class; thus emboldening capitalists and/or their managers to become more aggressive in resisting demands for wage increases. Increased globalization, and the potential and real threat of international capital flight, also plays its part in limiting and/or preventing increased wages for the average worker in the advanced capitalist countries.

Moreover, the failure of various nominal Marxist regimes at the end of the 20th century may be interpreted to some extent as a failure of reason. Largely in consequence, protest movements of the poor have tended to change from secular, Marxist, reason-based movements to religious, supernatural, faith-based movements. This renews the startling relevance of Smith's concerns with these types of fundamentalist, enthusiastic religions; harsh, dogmatic movements which focus on cultural and social issues, and the vices associated with too much mirth and gaiety. Thus, in the 21st century, the protest movements of the poor have tended to manifest themselves not as reason-based *economic* protests, so much as religious-based *social* and *cultural* protests.

Nonetheless, in the long run, there could indeed be communism as envisioned by Marx: a post-market society characterized by free goods, and hence an absence of money, a universal equivalent. Indeed, there are signs in 21st century society that this is coming about. For example, if we do live in an information society, then it basically costs zero to reproduce information. This suggests that information, so large a part of this perhaps post-industrial, possibly post-modern society, should become (or is in the process of becoming) a free good (or resource). Moreover, most people in the advanced capitalist countries now work in the so-called service industries. They are not providing goods needed by other people's bodies. The number of people actually producing goods is, relatively speaking, not so large.

So, are we approaching a fully automated society, where human workers are not needed to produce the output? If so, this is not necessarily an unmitigated good, given current property relations. For, in a fully automated society, how would the former workers be supported? These would be people (or descendants of the people) who previously were needed in the production process, in the economic sector, but would now be completely marginalized; not needed. What rights would they have to the output? How would they manage to merely physically survive?

On the final hand, even if society is eventually headed to some kind of fully automated society, or some sort of communist society where there will be plenty, where commodities will not need to be exchanged, and where there will be no need for money, a universal equivalent, nonetheless there are still currently some pressing, nay nasty, administrative issues which need to be urgently addressed. As stressed above, there is the question of how do we control our private and public managers? Also, how can we manage, or really stop, human-induced climate change? How can we reduce the possibility of nuclear war and the problem that some nations possess nuclear weapons which other nations naturally desire to obtain? Then there are also the administrative problems associated with wage, financial and taxation arbitrage, due to the international mobility of capital, as capital seeks to minimize its private costs by avoiding regulations, taxation and high wages. Finally, there is the general problem of the undue influence of capitalists and their managers on government policies in general; people who have the short-run interests and ample resources to promote their own agendas at the expense of the rest of society. How do we control them? Hence, in general, what administrative policies can be advanced to mitigate the above problems? Economic concerns and issues, particularly when economics is viewed in the pre-modern (and possibly again post-modern) sense of the study of administration and administrative behavior, are certainly not going away anytime soon.

Studying Aristotle, Smith and Marx – their various competing theoretical systems, which in spite of various definitions, concepts, rhetoric and attitudes, talk to each other and are capable of talking to us – encourages the taking of a long-run view of our problems. This long-run view helps political economists to highlight some of the fundamental, key (even essential) issues and concerns confronting us at the beginning of the 21st century and, indeed, the beginning of the third millennium. Insights from these three great systematic thinkers can help us to focus upon and to address some of the key problems currently facing humanity. The human drama continues.

Selected bibliography

PRIMARY SOURCES

Part One

Aristotle. 1984. *The Complete Works of Aristotle.* Edited by Jonathan Barnes. Princeton: Princeton University Press.

Part Two

Smith, Adam. 1976–83. *The Glasgow Edition of the Works and Correspondence of Adam Smith*, Six Volumes, Oxford: Oxford University Press.
Vol. I: *The Theory of Moral Sentiments*, ed. A.L. Macfie and D.D. Raphael, 1976.
Vol. II: *An Inquiry into the Nature and Causes of the Wealth of Nations*, ed. R.H. Campbell and A.S. Skinner, 1976.
Vol. III: *Essays on Philosophical Subjects*, ed. W.P.D. Wightman and J.C. Bryce with Dugald Stewart's 'Account of Adam Smith', ed. I.S. Ross, 1980.
Vol. IV: *Lectures on Rhetoric and Belles Lettres* containing 'Considerations Concerning the First Formation of Languages', ed. J.C. Bryce, 1983.
Vol. V: *Lectures on Jurisprudence*, ed. R.L. Meek, D.D. Raphael and P.G. Stein, 1978.
Vol. VI: *Correspondence of Adam Smith*, ed. E.C. Mossner and I.S. Ross, 1977.

Part Three

Marx, Karl. 1963 [1862–63]. *Theories of Surplus Value Part I.* Moscow: Progress Publishers.
Marx, Karl. 1967a [1885]. *Capital: A Critique of Political Economy; Volume Two: The Process of Circulation of Capital.* Edited by Frederick Engels. New York: International Publishers.
Marx, Karl. 1967b [1894]. *Capital: A Critique of Political Economy; Volume Three: The Process of Capitalist Production as a Whole.* Edited by Frederick Engels. New York: International Publishers.

Marx, Karl. 1967c [1835–47]. *Writings of the Young Marx on Philosophy and Society*. Edited and translated by Loyd D. Easton and Kurt H. Guddat. New York: Anchor Books.

Marx, Karl. 1968 [1862–63]. *Theories of Surplus Value: Part II*. Moscow: Progress Publishers.

Marx, Karl. 1970 [1859]. A *Contribution to the Critique of Political Economy*. ed., with an Introduction by Maurice Dobb. New York: International Publishers.

Marx, Karl. 1971a. *On Revolution*. Arranged and edited, with an Introduction and new translations by Saul K. Padover. New York: McGraw-Hill.

Marx, Karl. 1971b [1862–63]. *Theories of Surplus Value: Part III*. Moscow: Progress Publishers.

Marx, Karl. 1973 [1857–58]. *Grundrisse: Foundations of the Critique of Political Economy*. Translated with a Foreword by Martin Nicolaus. New York: Random House.

Marx, Karl. 1976 [1867]. *Capital: A Critique of Political Economy; Volume One: The Process of Production of Capital*. Introduced by Ernest Mandel. Translated by Ben Fowkes. New York: Penguin Books.

Marx, Karl and Engels, Frederick. 2005 [1848]. *The Communist Manifesto*: *A Road Map to History's Most Important Political Document*, ed. by Phil Gasper. Chicago: Haymarket Books.

SECONDARY SOURCES

Albritton, Robert. 1986. *A Japanese Reconstruction of Marxist Theory*. London: Macmillan Press.

Albritton, Robert. 1991. *A Japanese Approach to Stages of Capitalist Development*. London: Macmillan.

Albritton, Robert. 2007. *Economics Transformed: Discovering the Brilliance of Marx*. London: Pluto Press.

Althusser, Louis. 1969. *For Marx*. Middlesex, England: Penguin.

Althusser, Louis and Balibar, Etienne. 1979. *Reading Capital*. London: Verso.

American Heritage Dictionary of the English Language, 3rd edition. 1992. Boston: Houghton Mifflin.

Amin, Samir. 1976. *Unequal Development*. New York: Monthly Review Press.

Amin, Samir. 2009. 'Nepal, a Promising Revolutionary Advance', *Monthly Review*, **60**(9), February: 12–17.

Andrews, Edmund. 2006. 'Interior Official Faults Agency Over Its Ethics', *New York Times*, September 14, 2006, Front Page.

Arbatov, Georgi. 1997. 'Origins and Consequences of "Shock Therapy"', in Marshall Pomer (ed.), *Rebuilding Russia: The Economic Role of Government*, Economic Transition Group, pp. 61–7.

Arendt, Hannah. 1968. 'The Concept of History: Ancient and Modern' in *Between Past and Future*. New York: Viking, pp. 41–90.

Aspromourgos, Tony. 2009. *The Science of Wealth: Adam Smith and the Framing of Political Economy*. New York: Routledge.

Backhouse, Roger E. and Medema, Steven G. 2009. 'On the Definition of Economics', *Journal of Economic Perspectives*, **23**(1): 221–33.

Baeck, Louis. 1994. *The Mediterranean Tradition in Economic Thought*. New York: Routledge.

Baird, Charles W. 1973. *Macroeconomics: An Integration of Monetary, Search and Income Theories*. Chicago: Science Research Associates.

Baran, Paul. 1957. *The Political Economy of Growth*. New York: Monthly Review Press.

Barker, Drucilla K. and Feiner, Susan F. 2004. *Liberating Economics: Feminist Perspectives on Families, Work, and Globalization*. Ann Arbor: University of Michigan Press.

Barth, Karl. 1973. *Protestant Theology in the Nineteenth Century: Its Background and History*. Valley Forge: Judson Press.

Bazerman, Charles. 1993. 'Money Talks: The Rhetorical Project of the *Wealth of Nations*' in Willie Henderson, Tony Dudley-Evans and Roger Backhouse (eds), *Economics and Language*. New York: Routledge.

Bebchuk, Lucian and Grinstein, Yaniv. 2005. 'The Growth of Executive Pay', Discussion Paper No. 510, Revised 06/2005, The Harvard John M. Olin Discussion Paper Series: http://www.law.harvard.edu/programs/olin-center/; also in *Oxford Review of Economic Policy*, 2005, **21**(2): 283–303.

Bell, Daniel. 1973. *The Coming of Post-Industrial Society*. New York: Basic Books.

Bellofiore, Riccardo and Fineschi, Roberto (eds). 2009a. *Re-reading Marx: New Perspectives after the Critical Edition*. New York: Palgrave Macmillan.

Bellofiore, Riccardo and Fineshi, Roberto. 2009b. 'Introduction', pp. 1–16 in Bellofiore and Fineschi 2009a.

Benedict, Jess. 2009. *Little Pink House: One Woman's Historic Battle Against Eminent Domain*. New York: Grand Central Publishing.

Ben-Sasson, H.H. (ed.). 1976. *A History of the Jewish People*. Cambridge, MA: Harvard University Press.

Berlin, Isaiah. 1969. *Four Essays on Liberty*. New York: Oxford University Press.

Berns, Laurence. 1994. 'Aristotle and Adam Smith: Cooperation Between Ancients and Moderns?', *Review of Metaphysics*, 48, September.

Berry, Christopher J. 1974. 'Adam Smith's Considerations on Language', *Journal of the History of Ideas*, **35**(1): 130–38.

Bivens, Josh. 2008. *Everybody Wins: Except for Most of Us*. Washington, DC: Economic Policy Institute.

Blaug, Mark. 1978. *Economic Theory in Retrospect*. 3rd ed. New York: Cambridge University Press.

Blaug, Mark (ed.). 1980. *A Methodological Appraisal of Marxian Economics*. New York: North-Holland Publishing.

Blaug, Mark (ed.). 1991. *Aristotle (384–322 BC)*. Aldershot, UK and Brookfield, USA: Edward Elgar Publishing Co.

Blaug, Mark. 1999. 'Misunderstanding Classical Economics: The Sraffian Interpretation of the Surplus Approach', *History of Political Economy*, **31**(2): 213–37.

Blaug, Mark. 2001. 'No History of Ideas, Please, We're Economists', *Journal of Economic Perspectives*, **15**(1): 145–64.

Blaug, Mark. 2003. 'The Formalist Revolution of the 1990s' in Warren Samuels, John Biddle and John Davis (eds), *A Companion to the History of Economic Thought*. Oxford: Basil Blackwell, pp. 395–410.

Blaug, Mark. 2009. 'The Trade-Off Between Rigour and Relevance: Sraffian Economics as a Case in Point', *History of Political Economy*, **41**(2): 219–47.

Boswell, James. 1963. *Boswell: The Ominous Years 1774–1776*. Charles Ryskamp and Frederick A. Pottle (eds). New York: McGraw-Hill.

Boswell, James. 1977. *Boswell: Laird of Auchinleck 1778–1782*. Joseph W. Reed and Frederick Pottle (eds). New York: McGraw-Hill.

Boulding, Kenneth. 1970. *Economics as a Science*. New York: McGraw-Hill.

Bowles, Samuel and Park, YongJin. 2005. 'Emulation, Inequality and Workers' Hours: Was Thorstein Veblen Right?', *Economic Journal*, **115** (November): F397–F412.

Boyer-Xambeu, Marie-Therese, Deleplace, Ghislain and Gillard, Lucien. 1994. *Private Money and Public Currencies: The 16th Century Challenge*. Armonk, New York: M.E. Sharpe.

Braguinsky, Serguey and Yavlinsky, Grigory, 1997. 'Crime, Corruption and the Disfigurement of the Economy', in Marshall Pomer (ed.), *Rebuilding Russia: The Economic Role of Government*. Economic Transition Group, pp. 78–88.

Braverman, Harry. 1974. *Labor and Monopoly Capital*. New York: Monthly Review Press.

Broder, John M. 2007. 'New Glimpse at Players in Task Force Led by Cheney', *New York Times*, July 19, 2007, National Report.

Brown, Vivienne. 1994. *Adam Smith's Discourse*. London: Routledge.

Bruni, Luigino. 2004a. 'The "Technology of Happiness" and the Tradition of Economic Science', *Journal of the History of Economic Thought*, **26**(1): 19–44.

Bruni, Luigino. 2004b. 'The "Happiness Transformation Problem" in the Cambridge Tradition', *The European Journal of the History of Economic Thought*, **11**(3): 433–51.

Buchan, James. 1997. *Frozen Desire: The Meaning of Money*. New York: Farrar, Straus and Giroux.

Bureau of Economic Analysis. 2007. Chapter VII: 'Contributions for Government Social Insurance' in *State Personal Income and Employment Methodology*. Washington, DC: U.S. Department of Commerce.

Bureau of Economic Analysis. 2008. *Concepts and Methods of the U.S. National Income and Product Accounts*. Washington, DC: U.S. Department of Commerce.

Burke, Edmund. 1968. *Reflections on the Revolution in France*. Penguin.

Calkins, Martin J. and Werhane, Patricia H. 1998. 'Adam Smith, Aristotle, and the Virtues of Commerce', *The Journal of Value Inquiry*, **32**: 43–60.

Carter, Susan B., Gartner, Scott Sigmund, Haines, Michael R., Olmstead, Alan L., Sutch, Richard and Wright, Gavin (eds). 2006. *Historical Statistics of the United States, Earliest Times to the Present: Millennial Edition*. New York: Cambridge University Press.

Cartledge, Paul (ed.). 1998. *Cambridge Illustrated History of Ancient Greece*. New York: Cambridge University Press.

Cassel, Elaine. 2004. *The War on Civil Liberties*. Chicago: Lawrence Hill Books.

Chang, Ha-Joon. 2002. *Kicking Away the Ladder: Development Strategy in Historical Perspective*. London: Anthem Press.

Clary, Betsy Jane. 2009. 'Smith and Living Wages', *American Journal of Economics and Sociology*, **68**(5), 1063–84.

Cockfield, Geoff, Firth, Ann and Laurent, John (eds). 2007. *New Perspectives on Adam Smith's The Theory of Moral Sentiments*. Cheltenham, UK and Northhampton, MA, USA: Edward Elgar.

Cohen, Edward E. 1992. *Athenian Economy and Society: A Banking Perspective*. Princeton, NJ: Princeton University Press.

Cohen, Sheldon M. 1996. *Aristotle on Nature and Incomplete Substance*. New York: Cambridge University Press.

Cooper, Richard N. 2006. 'Understanding Global Imbalances' in Jane Little (ed.), *Global Imbalances and the Evolving World Economy*. Boston: Federal Reserve Bank of Boston, pp. 237–61.

Cooper, Richard N. 2008. 'Global Imbalances: Globalization, Demography, and Sustainability', *Journal of Economic Perspectives*, **22**(3): 93–112.

Corrado, Carol, Hulten, Charles and Sichel, Daniel. 2006. 'Intangible Capital and Economic Growth'. Finance and Economics Discussion Series, Divisions of Research and Statistics and Monetary Affairs, Federal Reserve Board, Washington, DC, 2006–24.

Costello, Tim, Smith, Brendan and Brecher, Jeremy. 2007. 'Labor Rights in China', *Post-Autistic Economics Review*, **41**, March 5: 34–8, http://www.paecon.net/PAEReview/issue41/CostelloSmithBrecher41.htm.

Cremaschi, Sergio. 1981. 'Adam Smith, Newtonianism and Political Economy', *Manuscrito*, **5**(1): 117–34.

Cremaschi, Sergio. 1989. 'Adam Smith: Skeptical Newtonianism, Disenchanted Republicanism, and the Birth of Social Science', in Marcelo Dascal and Ora Gruengard (eds), *Knowledge and Politics: Case Studies in the Relationship Between Epistemology and Political Philosophy*. Boulder, CO: Westview Press.

Crespo, Ricardo F. 2006. 'The Ontology of "the Economic": An Aristotelian Analysis', *Cambridge Journal of Economics*, **30**: 767–81.

Crespo, Ricardo F. 2008, 'The "Economic" According to Aristotle: Ethical, Political and Epistemological Implications', *Foundations of Science*, **13**(3–4): 281–94.

Cropsey, Joseph. 1957. *Polity and Economy: An Interpretation of the Principles of Adam Smith*. Martinus Nijhoff.

Darwall, Stephen. 1998. 'Empathy, Sympathy, Care', *Philosophical Studies*, **89**: 261–82.

Darwall, Stephen. 1999. 'Sympathetic Liberalism: Recent Work on Adam Smith', *Philosophy and Public Affairs*, **28**: 139–64.

Davenport-Hines, Richard. 2002. *The Pursuit of Oblivion: A Global History of Narcotics*. New York: W.W. Norton.

Davidson, Paul. 2008. 'Reforming the World's International Money', *Real-World Economics Review*, 48, December 6: 293–305, http://www.paecon.net/PAEReview/issue48/Davidson48.pdf.

Davis, John B. 2006. 'The Turn in Economics: Neoclassical Dominance to Mainstream Pluralism?', *Journal of Institutional Economics*, **2**(1): 1–20.

Dawson, Deidre. 1991–92. 'Teaching Sensibility: Adam Smith, Rousseau, and the Formation of the Moral Spectator', *Etudes Ecossaises Colloquium Pros.* TS, Grenoble.

Dean, John W. 2004. *Worse Than Watergate*. New York: Little Brown and Company.

DeGolyer, Michael. 1992. 'The Greek Accent of the Marxian Matrix', in McCarthy (ed.) (1992), pp. 107–53.

Denis, Henri. 1968. 'Postface: V.K. Dmitriev ou les Malheurs de la Sagesse Mathematique'. In V.K. Dmitriev, *Essais Economiques*. Paris: Editions du Centre National de la Recherche Scientifique, pp. 261–9.

Diaye, Marc-Arthur and Lapidus, Andre. 2005a. 'A Humean Theory of Choice of which Rationality May Be one Consequence', *European Journal of the History of Economic Thought*, **12**(1): 89–111.

Diaye, Marc-Arthus and Lapidus, Andre. 2005b. 'Why Rationality *May* be a Consequence of Hume's Theory of Choice', *European Journal of the History of Economic Thought*, **12**(1): 119–26.

Dmitriev, V.K. 1974 [1898]. *Economic Essays on Value, Competition and Utility*. Cambridge: Cambridge University Press.

Dobb, Maurice. 1973. *Theories of Value and Distribution Since Adam Smith*. New York: Cambridge University Press.

Domhoff, G. William. 1967. *Who Rules America?* Englewood Cliffs, NJ: Prentice-Hall.

Domhoff, G. William. 1970. *The Higher Circles: The Governing Class in America*. New York: Random House.

Domhoff, G. William. 1972. *Fat Cats and Democrats*. Englewood Cliffs, NJ: Prentice-Hall.

Domhoff, G. William. 1974. *The Bohemain Grove and Other Retreats: A Study in Ruling-Class Cohesiveness*. New York: Harper and Row.

Duhs, L.A. 2008. 'Sen's Economic Philosophy: Capabilities and Human Development in the Revival of Economics as a Moral Science', *Real World Economics Review*, 47, 3 October: 173–91, http://www.paecon.net/PAEReview/issue47/Duhs47.pdf.

Dunn, John. 1972. *Modern Revolutions*. New York: Cambridge University Press.

Eagleton, Terry. 2005. 'On Telling the Truth', in Panitch and Leys (eds) (2005), pp. 269–85.

Engels, Frederick. 1967 [1893]. 'Preface' to Karl Marx, *Capital*, Vol. II (1967a: 1–19).

Engels, Frederick. 1972 [1884]. *The Origin of the Family, Private Property, and the State*. New York: Pathfinder.

Engels, Frederick. 1999 [1845]. *The Condition of the Working Class in England*. New York: Oxford University Press.

Evensky, Jerry. 2005. *Adam Smith's Moral Philosophy: A Historical and Contemporary Perspective on Markets, Law, Ethics, and Culture*. New York: Cambridge University Press.

Fayazmanesh, Sasan. 2001. 'Barter, Money, and Commercial Arithmetic', *Journal of the History of Economic Thought*, **23**(1): 77–98.

Fayazmanesh, Sasan. 2003. 'Aristotle's "Money" and "Exchange"'. Presentation to the History of Economics Society, Duke University, Durham, NC.

Fayazmanesh, Sasan. 2006. *Money and Exchange: Folktales and Reality*. New York: Routledge.

Feldstein, Martin. 2008. 'Resolving the Global Imbalance: The Dollar and the U.S. Saving Rate', *Journal of Economic Perspectives*, **22**(3): 113–25.

Ferrarin, Alfredo. 2001. *Hegel and Aristotle*. Cambridge: Cambridge University Press.

Ferreira, Rodolphe Dos Santos. 2002. 'Aristotle's Analysis of Bilateral Exchange: An Early Formal Approach to the Bargaining Problem', *European Journal of the History of Economic Thought*, **9**(4): 568–90.

Fineschi, Roberto. 2009. 'Dialectic of the Commodity and Its Exposition: The German Debate in the 1970s – A Personal Survey', in Bellofiore and Fineschi (eds) (2009a), pp. 50–70.

Finley, M.I. 1970, 'Aristotle and Economic Analysis', *Past and Present*, **47**, May: 3–25; in Blaug (ed.) (1991), pp. 150–72.

Finley, M.I. 1977 [1963]. *The Ancient Greeks*. New York: Penguin Press.

Finley, M.I. 1999 [1973]. *The Ancient Economy*, Updated with a new foreword by Ian Morris. Berkeley: University of California Press.

Fleetwood, Steve. 1997. 'Aristotle in the 21st Century', *Cambridge Journal of Economics*, **21**: 729–44.

Fleischacker, Samuel. 1999. *A Third Concept of Liberty: Judgment and Freedom in Kant and Adam Smith*. Princeton, NJ: Princeton University Press.

Fleischacker, Samuel. 2004. *On Adam Smith's* Wealth of Nations: *A Philosophical Companion*. Princeton, NJ: Princeton University Press.

Force, Pierre. 2003. *Self-Interest Before Adam Smith*. New York: Cambridge University Press.

Frank, Andre Gunder. 1967. *Capitalism and Underdevelopment in Latin America*. New York: Monthly Review Press.

Frank, Jill. 2005. *A Democracy of Distinction: Aristotle and the Work of Politics*. Chicago: University of Chicago Press.

Frank, Thomas. 2004. *What's the Matter with Kansas? How Conservatives Won the Heart of America*. New York: Metropolitan Books, Henry Holt and Company.

Freeman, Alan, Kliman, Andrew and Wells, Julian (eds). 2004. *The New Value Controversy and the Foundations of Economics*. Cheltenham, UK and Northampton, MA, USA: Edward Elgar.

Fuller, Errol. 2002. *Dodo: A Brief History*. New York: Universe Publishing.

Galbraith, James K. 2008. *The Predator State*. New York: Free Press.

Galbraith, John Kenneth. 1967. *The New Industrial State*. Boston: Houghton Mifflin Co.

Galbraith, John Kenneth. 1970. *Who Needs the Democrats and What it Takes to be Needed*. New York: Signet Classics.

Galbraith, John Kenneth. 1987. *Economics in Perspective: A Critical History*. Boston: Houghton Mifflin Co.

Galbraith, John Kenneth. 1992. *The Culture of Contentment.* Boston: Houghton Mifflin Co.

Galbraith, John Kenneth. 2004. *The Economics of Innocent Fraud: Truth for Our Time.* Boston: Houghton Mifflin Co.

Galbraith, John Kenneth and Menshikov, Stanislav. 1988. *Capitalism, Communism and Coexistence.* Boston: Houghton Mifflin Co.

Glater, Jonathan D. 2005. 'Big Bucks May Stop Here', *New York Times*, Business Section, August 10, 2005.

Glinkina, Svetlana P., Grigoriev, Andrei and Yakobidze, Vakhtang. 2001. 'Crime and Corruption', in Lawrence R. Klein and Marshall Pomer (eds), *The New Russia: Transition Gone Awry.* Stanford, CA: Stanford University Press, pp. 233–50.

Godfrey, David. 1986. 'Foreword' to Harold A. Innis, *Empire and Communications.* Victoria, BC: Press Porcepic Limited, pp. vii–xiv.

Gordon, Barry. 1975. *Economic Analysis Before Adam Smith: Hesiod to Lessius.* New York: The Macmillan Press.

Grant, Michael. 1995. *Greek and Roman Historians: Information and Misinformation.* New York: Routledge.

Gray, Alexander. 1931. *The Development of Economic Doctrine.* New York: John Wiley and Sons Inc.

Griswold, Charles L. Jr. 1991. 'Rhetoric and Ethics: Adam Smith on Theorizing about the Moral Sentiments', *Philosophy and Rhetoric*, **24**: 213–37.

Griswold, Charles L. Jr. 1999. *Adam Smith and the Virtues of Enlightenment.* New York: Cambridge University Press.

Groenewegen, Peter D. 1982. 'History and Political Economy: Smith, Marx, and Marshall', *Australian Economic Papers*, **21**(38): 1–17.

Haakonssen, Knud. 1981. *The Science of a Legislator: The Natural Jurisprudence of David Hume and Adam Smith.* New York: Cambridge University Press.

Haakonssen, Knud. 1996. *Natural Law and Moral Philosophy: From Grotius to the Scottish Enlightenment.* New York: Cambridge University Press.

Hamlyn, D.W. 1993. *Aristotle De Anima Books II and III (With Passages from Book I).* Oxford: Clarendon Press.

Hammond, N.G.L. 1986. *A History of Greece to 322 B.C.* (Third Edition). New York: Oxford University Press.

Hamowy, Ronald. 1987. *The Scottish Enlightenment and the Theory of Spontaneous Order.* Carbondale: Southern Illinois Press.

Hanley, Ryan Patrick. 2006. 'Adam Smith, Aristotle and Virtue Ethics', in Schliesser and Montes (2006), pp. 17–39.

Hawkins, David. 1948. 'Some Conditions of Macroeconomic Stability'. *Econometrica*, **16**, October: 309–22.

Hawkins, David. 1964. *The Language of Nature: An Essay on the Philosophy of Science*. San Francisco: W.H. Freeman and Co.

Hawkins, David and Simon, Herbert. 1949. 'Note: Some Conditions of Macroeconomic Stability', *Econometrica*, **17**, July–October: 245–48.

Hayek, Friedrich, A. 1944. *The Road to Serfdom*. Chicago: University of Chicago Press.

Hayek, Friedrich A. 1967. 'Dr. Bernard Mandeville', Proceedings of the British Academy, Vol. LII, London, in Hayek 1984, pp. 176–94.

Hayek, Friedrich, A. 1984. *The Essence of Hayek*, ed. Chiaki Nishiyama and Kurt R. Leube. Stanford: Hoover Institution Press.

Hecker, Rolf. 2009. 'New Perspectives Opened by the Publication of Marx's Manuscripts of *Capital*, Vol. II', in Bellofiore and Fineschi (eds) (2009a), pp. 17–26.

Hegel, Friedrich. 1952. *Hegel's Philosophy of Right*. Translated with Notes by T.M. Knox. New York: Oxford University Press.

Hegel, Friedrich. 1995. *Lectures on the History of Philosophy: Plato and the Platonists. In Three Volumes; Volume 2*. Translated by E.S. Haldane and Frances H. Simson. Lincoln: University of Nebraska Press.

Heilbroner, Robert L. 1975. 'The Paradox of Progress: Decline and Decay in *The Wealth of Nations*', in Andrew Skinner and Thomas Wilson (eds), *Essays on Adam Smith*. Oxford: Clarendon Press, pp. 524–39.

Heinrich, Michael. 2009. 'Reconstruction or Deconstruction? Methodological Controversies about Value and Capital, and New Insights from the Critical Edition', in Bellofiore and Fineschi (eds) (2009a), pp. 71–98.

Held, Dirk t. D. 2005. 'Review of Lorraine Smith Pangle, *Aristotle and the Philosophy of Friendship*', *Ancient Philosophy*, **25**: 193–7.

Henderson, James P. and Davis, John B. 1991. 'Adam Smith's Influence on Hegel's Philosophical Writings', *Journal of the History of Economic Thought*, **13**(2): 184–204.

Henriques, Diana B. 2009. 'Madoff Will Plead Guilty; Faces Life for Vast Swindle', *New York Times*, March 11, Front Page.

Henry, John. 2008. 'The Theory of the State: The Position of Marx and Engels', *Forum for Social Economics*, **37**(1): 13–25.

Hicks, John. 1939. *Value and Capital: An Inquiry into Some Fundamental Principles of Economics Theory*. Oxford: Clarendon Press.

Hicks, John. 1969. *A Theory of Economic History*. Oxford: Clarendon Press.

Hicks, John. 1989. *A Market Theory of Money*. Oxford: Clarendon Press.

Hill, Lisa. 2001. 'The Hidden Theology of Adam Smith', *European Journal of the History of Economic Thought*, **8**(1), Spring: 1–29.

Hirschman, Albert O. 1977. *The Passions and the Interests: Political*

Argument for Capitalism before Its Triumph. Princeton, NJ: Princeton University Press.

Hoch, Paul. 1972. *Rip Off the Big Game: The Exploitation of Sports by the Power Elite*. Garden City, New York: Doubleday and Company.

Hollander, Samuel. 1987. *Classical Economics*. New York: Basil Blackwell.

Hollander, Samuel. 2008. *The Economics of Karl Marx: Analysis and Application*. New York: Cambridge.

Holt, Jim. 2005. 'Of Two Minds: Are We Sure We Really Want to Know How the Brain Functions?', *New York Times Magazine*, May 8: 11–13.

Hosseini, Hamid. 1998. 'Seeking the Roots of Adam Smith's Division of Labor in Medieval Persia', *History of Political Economy*, **30**(4).

Howard, M.C. and King, J.E. 1989. *A History of Marxian Economics: Volume I, 1883–1929*. Princeton, NJ: Princeton University Press.

Howard, M.C. and King, J.E. 1992. *A History of Marxian Economics: Volume II, 1929–1990*. Princeton, NJ: Princeton University Press.

Howes, Candace and Singh, Ajit (eds). 2000. *Competitiveness Matters: Industry and Economic Performance in the U.S.* Ann Arbor, MI: University of Michigan Press.

Hubbard, R. Glenn and O'Brien, Anthony P. 2008. *Macroeconomics*. 2nd ed. Prentice Hall.

Hueckel, Glenn Russell. 2000a. 'The Labor "Embodied" in Smith's Labor-Commanded Measure: A "Rationally Reconstructed" Legend', *Journal of the History of Economic Thought*, **22**: 461–85.

Hueckel, Glenn Russell. 2000b. 'On the "Insurmountable Difficulties, Obscurity, and Embarrassment" of Smith's Fifth Chapter', *History of Political Economy*, **32**: 317–45.

Hume, David. 1955 [1748]. 'Of Miracles', in *An Inquiry Concerning Human Understanding*, Bobbs-Merrill Company.

Innis, Harold. 1951. *The Bias of Communication*. Toronto: University of Toronto Press.

Innis, Harold. 1972 [1950]. *Empire and Communications*. Revised by Mary Q. Innis. Foreword by Marshall McLuhan. Toronto: University of Toronto Press.

Johansen, T.K. 1998. *Aristotle on the Sense-Organs*. Cambridge: Cambridge University Press.

Jouvenal, Bertrand de. 1962. *On Power: Its Nature and the History of its Growth*. Boston: Beacon Press.

Jowett, B. 1885. *The Politics of Aristotle*. Oxford: Clarendon Press.

Justman, Stewart. 1993. *The Autonomous Male of Adam Smith*. Norman, OK: University of Oklahoma Press.

Kant, Immanuel. 1983 [1784–95]. *Perpetual Peace and other Essays on*

Politics, History and Morals. Translated, with Introduction, by Ted Humphrey. Indianapolis: Hackett.

Kay, Carol. 1986. 'Canon, Ideology and Gender: Mary Wollstonecraft's Critique of Adam Smith', *New Political Science*, 15: 63–76.

Kennedy, Gavin. 2009. 'The Hidden Adam Smith in his Alleged Religiosity', Paper, History of Economics Society Conference, Denver.

Keynes, John Maynard. 1964 [1936]. *The General Theory of Employment, Interest, and Money*. New York: Harcourt Brace Jovanovich.

Kierkegaard, Soren. 1968. *Soren Kierkegaard's Papier, Vol. V* [The Papers of Soren Kierkegaard], 2nd ed. Copenhagen: Gyldendal.

Kim, Kwangsu. 2009. 'Adam Smith's Theory of Economic History and Economic Development', *European Journal of the History of Economic Thought*, **16**(1): 41–64.

Kliman, Andrew. 2007. *Reclaiming Marx's Capital: A Refutation of the Myth of Inconsistency*. New York: Lexington Books.

Kozel, Philip. 2006. *Market Sense: Toward a New Economics of Markets and Society*. New York: Routledge.

Krasne, Dave. 2009. 'Money for Nothing', *New York Times*, January 27, Op-Ed page.

Kuiper, Edith. 2006. 'Adam Smith and his Feminist Contemporaries', in Schliesser and Montes (eds) (2006), pp. 40–60.

Langholm, Odd. 1983. *Wealth and Money in the Aristotelian Tradition*. Universitetsforlaget.

Langholm, Odd. 1984. *The Aristotelian Analysis of Usury*. Universitetsforlaget.

Langholm, Odd. 1998. *The Legacy of Scholasticism in Economic Thought: Antecedents of Choice and Power.* Cambridge: Cambridge University Press.

Lapidus, Andre. 1986. *Le Detour de Valeur*. Paris: Economica.

Lawson-Tancred, Hugh. 1986. *Aristotle: De Anima (On the Soul).* New York: Penguin Books.

Lennox, James G. 2001. *Aristotle's Philosophy of Biology: Studies in the Origins of Life Science.* Cambridge: Cambridge University Press.

Lewis, William Arthur. 1954. 'Economic Development With Unlimited Supplies of Labour', *Manchester School of Economic and Social Studies*, 22 (May), 139–91.

Linz, Susan J. and Krueger, Gary. 1996. 'Russia's Managers in Transition: Pilferers or Paladins?', *Post-Soviet Geography and Economics*, **37**(7): 397–425.

Lippi, Marco. 1979. *Value and Naturalism in Marx*. London: New Left Books.

240 Aristotle, Adam Smith and Karl Marx

Lloyd, G.E.R. 1968. *Aristotle: The Growth and Structure of His Thought.* Cambridge: Cambridge University Press.

Lloyd, G.E.R. 1996. *Aristotelian Explorations.* Cambridge: Cambridge University Press.

Lowry, S. Todd. 1965. 'The Classical Greek Theory of Natural Resource Economics', *Land Economics*, **XLI**(3): 203–8.

Lowry, S. Todd. 1969. 'Aristotle's Mathematical Analysis of Exchange', *History of Political Economy*, **1**: 57–63.

Lowry, S. Todd. 1974. 'Aristotle's "Natural Limit" and the Economics of Price Regulation', *Greek, Roman and Byzantine Studies*, **15**: 57–63.

Lowry, S. Todd. 1979. 'Recent Literature on Ancient Greek Economic Thought', *Journal of Economic Literature*, **17**(1), March: 65–86, in Blaug (1991), pp. 195–221.

Lowry, S. Todd. 1987. *The Archaeology of Economic Ideas: The Classical Greek Tradition.* Durham, NC: Duke University Press.

Lowry, S. Todd. 1991. 'Understanding Ethical Individualism and the Administrative Tradition in Pre-Eighteenth Century Political Economy', in William J. Barber (ed.), *Perspectives on the History of Economic Thought V.* Aldershot, UK and Brookfield, US: Edward Elgar, pp. 39–46.

Lowry, S. Todd. 1995. 'The Ancient Greek Administrative Tradition and Human Capital', *Archives of Economic History*, **VI**(1): 7–18.

Macpherson, C.B. (ed.). 1978. *Property: Mainstream and Critical Positions.* Toronto: University of Toronto Press.

Mandel, Ernest. 1975. *Late Capitalism.* London: New Left Books.

Mandeville, Bernard. 1924 [1729]. *The Fable of the Bees, or Private Vices, Publick Benefits*, Volume II, with a commentary, critical, historical and explanatory by F.B. Kaye. New York: Oxford University Press.

Mankiw, Gregory. 2005. 'Social Security Reform: National Saving and Macroeconomic Performance in the Global Economy', Address to the Council on Foreign Relations, January 18.

Mannheim, Karl. 1936. *Ideology and Utopia: An Introduction to the Sociology of Knowledge.* New York: Harcourt, Brace and World.

Marcuse, Herbert. 1960 [1941]. *Reason and Revolution: Hegel and the Rise of Social Theory.* Boston: Beacon Press.

Marcuse, Herbert. 1961. *Soviet Marxism.* New York: Vintage Books.

Marcuse, Herbert. 1964. *One-Dimensional Man.* Boston: Beacon Press.

Marcuzzo, Maria Cristina. 2005. 'Piero Sraffa at the University of Cambridge', *European Journal of the History of Economic Thought*, **12**(3): 425–52.

Maslow, Abraham. 1954. *Motivation and Personality.* New York: Harper and Brothers.

Mauss, Marcel. 1990 [1950]. *The Gift*. Translated by W.D. Halls, Foreword by Mary Douglas. London: Routledge.

McCarthy, George E. 1990. *Marx and the Ancients: Classical Ethics, Social Justice, and Nineteenth-Century Political Economy*. Savage, MD: Rowman and Littlefield.

McCarthy, George E. (ed.). 1992. *Marx and Aristotle: Nineteenth-century German Social Theory and Classical Antiquity*. Savage, MD: Rowman and Littlefield.

McCarthy, George E. 2003. *Classical Horizons: The Origins of Sociology in Ancient Greece*. Albany: State University of New York.

McChesney, Robert W., Foster, John Bellamy, Stole, Inger L. and Holleman, Hannah. 2009. 'The Sales Effort and Monopoly Capital', *Monthly Review*, **60**(11), April: 1–23.

McKenna, Edward and Zannoni, Diane. 1990. 'The Relation between the Rate of Interest and Investment in Post-Keynesian and Neo-Ricardian Analysis', *Eastern Economic Journal*, **16**(2): 133–43.

McLuhan, Marshall. 1964. *Understanding Media*. New York: McGraw-Hill.

McLuhan, Marshall. 1969. *The Gutenberg Galaxy*. New York: The New American Library.

McNally, David. 1988. *Political Economy and the Rise of Capitalism: A Reinterpretation.* Berkeley: University of California Press.

Meek, Ronald. 1961. 'Mr. Sraffa's Rehabilitation of Classical Economics', *Science and Society* (Spring).

Meek, Ronald. 1976. *Social Science and the Ignoble Savage.* New York: Cambridge University Press.

Meek, Ronald. 1977. *Smith, Marx, and After*. New York: John Wiley and Sons.

Meikle, Scott. 1985. *Essentialism in the Thought of Karl Marx.* La Salle, IL: Open Court Publishing.

Meikle, Scott. 1995. *Aristotle's Economic Thought.* Oxford: Clarendon Press.

Meikle, Scott. 2001. 'Quality and Quantity in Economics: The Metaphysical Construction of the Economic Realm', in Uskali Maki (ed.), *The Economic World View: Studies in the Ontology of Economics*. Cambridge: Cambridge University Press, pp. 32–54.

Menshikov, Stanislav M. 1969. *Millionaires and Managers*. Moscow: Progress Publishers.

Menshikov, Stanislav M. 2007. *The Anatomy of Russian Capitalism*. Washington, DC: EIR News Service.

Meulendyke, Ann-Marie. 1998. *U.S. Monetary Policy and Financial Markets*. New York: Federal Reserve Bank of New York.

Miliband, Ralph. 1969. *The State in Capitalist Society*. New York: Basic Books.

Millar, John. 1771. *Observations Concerning the Distinction of Ranks in Society*. Dublin: T. Ewing, in Capel-Street.

Miller, Richard. 1992. 'Marx and Aristotle: A Kind of Consequentialism', in McCarthy (ed.) (1992), pp. 275–302.

Minsky, Human P. 1986. *Stabilizing an Unstable Economy*. New Haven: Yale University Press.

Mongiovi, Gary. 2002. 'Vulgar Economy in Marxian Garb: A Critique of Temporal Single System Marxism', *Review of Radical Political Economics*, **34**: 393–416.

Montes, Leonidas. 2004. *Adam Smith in Context: A Critical Reassessment of Some Central Components of his Thought*. New York: Palgrave Macmillan.

Montesquieu. 1989 [1748]. *The Spirit of the Laws*. Anne Cohler, Basia Miller and Harold Stone (eds). New York: Cambridge University Press.

Moore, Basil. 1988. *Horizontalists and Verticalists: The Macroeconomics of Credit Money*. New York: Cambridge University Press.

Morrow, Glenn. 1928. 'Adam Smith: Moralist and Philosopher', in John Maurice Clark et al. (eds), *Adam Smith, 1776–1926: Lectures to Commemorate the Sesquicentennial of the Publication of the 'Wealth of Nations'*, Chicago: University of Chicago Press.

Moseley, Fred (ed.). 2005. *Marx's Theory of Money: Modern Appraisals*. New York: Palgrave Macmillan.

Muller, Jerry Z. 1995. *Adam Smith: In His Time and Ours*. Princeton, NJ: Princeton University Press.

Murphy, James Bernard. 1993. *The Moral Economy of Labor: Aristotelian Themes in Economic Theory*. New Haven: Yale University Press.

Murray, Patrick (ed.). 1997. *Reflections on Commercial Life: An Anthology from Plato to the Present*. New York: Routledge.

New York Times. 2005. 'Morgan Payoff for Short Stint is 32 Million', July 12, Front Page.

Nicolaus, Martin. 1973. 'Foreword', in Marx, *Grundrisse*, 1973, pp. 7–63.

Nietzsche, Friedrich. 1994 [1887]. *On the Genealogy of Morality*. New York: Cambridge University Press.

Nussbaum, Martha C. 1989. 'Nature, Function, and Capability: Aristotle on Political Distribution', *Political Theory*, **17**(2): 152–186.

Nussbaum, Martha C. 1990. 'Aristotelian Social Democracy', in R. Bruce Douglas (ed.), *Liberalism and the Good*. New York: Routledge, pp. 203–52.

Nussbaum, Martha C. 2001. *The Fragility of Goodness: Luck and Ethics in Greek Tragedy and Philosophy*, rev. ed. Cambridge: Cambridge University Press.

Nuti, D.M. 1974a. 'V.K. Dmitriev: A Biographical Note', in V.K. Dmitriev, *Economic Essays on Value, Competition and Utility.* Cambridge: Cambridge University Press, pp. 29–32.

Nuti, D.M. 1974b. 'Introduction' to V.K. Dmitriev, *Economic Essays on Value, Competition and Utility.* Cambridge: Cambridge University Press, pp. 7–28.

Nyland, Chris. 1993. 'Adam Smith, Stage Theory, and the Status of Women', *History of Political Economy*, **25**(4): 617–40.

O'Donnell, Rory. 1990. *Adam Smith's Theory of Value and Distribution: A Reappraisal.* New York: St. Martin's Press.

Orwell, George. 1946. *Animal Farm.* New York: Harcourt, Brace and Company.

Orwell, George. 1949. *Nineteen Eighty-Four, A Novel.* New York: Harcourt, Brace and Company

Orwell, George. 1968 [1946]. 'Politics and the English Language', in *The Collected Essays, Journalism and Letters of George Orwell, Volume IV In Front of Your Nose 1945–1950*, ed. by Sonia Orwell and Ian Angus. London: Martin Secker and Warburg, pp. 127–40.

Ostwald, Martin, 1962. *Aristotle: Nicomachean Ethics.* Translated, with Introduction and Notes by Martin Ostwald. New York: The Bobbs-Merrill Company, Inc.

Pack, Spencer J. 1985a. 'Aristotle and the Problem of Insatiable Desires', *History of Political Economy*, **17**: 391–4, in Blaug (ed.) (1991), pp. 271–74.

Pack, Spencer J. 1985b. *Reconstructing Marxian Economics: Marx Based upon a Sraffian Commodity Theory of Value.* New York: Praeger Press.

Pack, Spencer J. 1987. 'Schumpeter Plus Optimism Equals Gilder (Ceteris Paribus)', *History of Political Economy*, **19**(3): 469–80.

Pack, Spencer J. 1991. *Capitalism as a Moral System: Adam Smith's Critique of the Free Market Economy*, Aldershot, UK and Brookfield, US: Edward Elgar.

Pack, Spencer J. 1993. 'Adam Smith on the Limits to Human Reason', in Robert F. Hebert (ed.), *Perspectives on the History of Economic Thought: Selected Papers from the History of Economic Thought Conference 1991*, Volume IX, pp. 53–62.

Pack, Spencer J. 1995a. 'Adam Smith's Unnaturally Natural (Yet Naturally Unnatural) Use of the World "Natural"', in Ingrid H. Rima (ed.), *The Classical Tradition in Economic Thought: Perspectives on the History of Economic Thought*, Volume XI, pp. 31–42.

Pack, Spencer J. 1995b. 'Theological (and Hence Economic) Implications of Adam Smith's "Principles Which Lead and Direct Philosophic Enquiries"', *History of Political Economy*, **27**(2): 289–307.

Pack, Spencer J. 1996a. 'Adam Smith's Invisible/Visible Hand/Chain/ Chaos', in Laurence S. Moss (ed.), *Joseph Schumpeter, Historian of Economics: Perspectives on the History of Economic Thought: Selected Papers from the History of Economics Society Conference, 1994*. New York: Routledge, pp. 181–95.

Pack, Spencer J. 1996b. 'Slavery, Adam Smith's Economic Vision and the Invisible Hand' with an appendix: 'Adam Smith and the Late Resolution of the Quakers of Pennsylvania: A Response to a False Report' by Robert W. Dimand, *History of Economic Ideas*, **IV**(1–2): 253–69.

Pack, Spencer J. 1997. 'Adam Smith on the Virtues: A Partial Resolution of the Adam Smith Problem', *Journal of the History of Economic Thought*, **19**, Spring: 127–40.

Pack, Spencer J. 1998. 'Murray Rothbard's Adam Smith', *The Quarterly Journal of Austrian Economics*, **1**: 73–9.

Pack, Spencer J. 2000. 'The Rousseau–Smith Connection: Towards An Understanding of Professor West's "Splenetic Smith"', *History of Economic Ideas*, **VIII**(2): 35–62.

Pack, Spencer J. 2001a. 'S. Todd Lowry and Ancient Greek Economic Thought: an Interpretation', in Stephen Medema and Warren Samuels (eds), *Historians of Economics and Economic Thought: The Construction of Disciplinary Memory,* New York: Routledge, pp. 166–84.

Pack, Spencer J. 2001b. 'Unpacking "Adam Smith: Critical Theorist?"', *Research in the History of Economic Thought and Methodology*. 19-A: 33–46.

Pack, Spencer J. 2008a. 'Aristotle's Difficult Relationship with Modern Economic Theory', *Foundations of Science*, **13** (3–4): 265–80.

Pack, Spencer J. 2008b. *Hush Slimbaugh and the Economics of Darkness: A Parable for Our Times*. Economics Faculty Publications Paper 1: http://digitalcommons.conncoll.edu/econfacpub/1.

Pack, Spencer J. 2009. 'John Kenneth Galbraith's New Industrial State 40 Years Later: A Radical Perspective', in Frederic Lee and Jon Bekken (eds), *Radical Economics and Labour*. New York: Routledge.

Pack, Spencer J. and Schliesser, Eric. 2006. 'Smith's Humean Criticism of Hume's Account of the Origin of Justice', *Journal of the History of Philosophy*, **44**(1): 47–63.

Paganelli, Maria Pia. 2008. 'Approbation and the Desire to Better One's Condition in Smith', History of Economics Society Annual Meeting, Toronto 27–30 June.

Pangle, Lorraine Smith. 2003. *Aristotle and the Philosophy of Friendship.* Cambridge: Cambridge University Press.

Panitch, Leo and Leys, Colin (eds). 2005. *Socialist Register 2006: Telling the Truth*. New York: Monthly Review Press.

Park, YongJin. Forthcoming. 'The Second Paycheck to Keep Up With the Joneses: Relative Income Concerns and Labour Market Decisions of Married Women', *Eastern Economic Journal*.

Partnoy, Frank. 1997. *F.I.A.S.C.O.: Blood in the Water on Wall Street*. New York: W.W. Norton and Company.

Pasinetti, Luigi L. 2005. 'The Sraffa-enigma: Introduction', *European Journal of the History of Economic Thought*, **12**(3): 373–8.

Peach, Terry. 2009a. 'Measuring "The Happiness of Nations": The Conundrum of Adam Smith's "Real Measure of Exchangeable Value"', Paper presented to the 2009 History of Economics Society Conference, Denver, 26–29 June.

Peach, Terry. 2009b. 'Adam Smith and the Labor Theory of (Real) Value: A Reconsideration', *History of Political Economy*, **41**(2): 383–406.

Peart, Sandra. 2008. 'We're all "Persons" Now: Classical Economists and their Opponents on Marriage, the Franchise, and Socialism', Presidential Address, 35th Annual Meeting of the History of Economics Society, 27–30 June.

Perelman, Michael. 1989. 'Adam Smith and Dependent Social Relations', *History of Political Economy*, **21**(3): 503–20.

Perrotta, Cosimo. 2003. 'The Legacy of the Past: Ancient Economic Thought on Wealth and Development', *European Journal of the History of Economic Thought*, **10**(2): 177–229.

Pieper, Josef. 1998. *Leisure, The Basis of Culture*. South Bend, Indiana: St. Augustine's Press.

Polanyi, Karl. 1968 [1957]. 'Aristotle Discovers the Economy', in G. Dalton (ed.), *Primitive, Archaic and Modern Economies*. Garden City, New York: Anchor Books.

Popper, Karl. 1945. *Open Society and Its Enemies: Volume 2 Hegel and Marx*. London: Routledge and Kegan Paul.

Popper, Karl. 1957. *The Poverty of Historicism*. Boston: Beacon Press.

Popper, Karl. 1962. *Open Society and Its Enemies: Volume 1 The Spell of Plato*, 4th ed. London: Routledge and Kegan Paul.

Popper, Karl. 1976. *Unended Quest: An Intellectual Autobiography*. La Salle, IL: Open Court.

Porter, Richard D. and Judson, Ruth A. 1966. 'The Location of U.S. Currency: How Much is Abroad?', *Federal Reserve Bulletin*, October: 883–903.

Poulanztas, Nicos. 1973. *Political Power and Social Classes*. London: NLB; Sheed and Ward.

Puro, Edward. 1992. 'Uses of the Term "Natural" in Adam Smith's

Wealth of Nations', *Research in the History of Economic Thought and Methodology*, **9**: 73–86.

Rae, John. 1965 [1895]. *Life of Adam Smith*. New York: Augustus M. Kelley.

Randall, John Herman Jr. 1960. *Aristotle*. Columbia University Press.

Rashid, Salim. 1998. *The Myth of Adam Smith*. Cheltenham, UK and Lyme, USA: Edward Elgar.

Rasmussen, Dennis C. 2008. *The Problems and Promise of Commercial Society: Adam Smith's Response to Rousseau*. University Park, PA: Pennsylvania State University Press.

Reinert, Erik S. 2008. *How Rich Countries Got Rich . . . and Why Poor Countries Stay Poor*. New York: Public Affairs.

Reitz, Charles and Spartan, Stephen. 2005. 'Workforce Remuneration and Wealth: Observations on the Origins and Outcomes of Inequality', Workforce Diversity Discussion Document, Kansas City, Kansas: Intercultural Center, Kansas City Kansas Community College.

Resnick, Stephen A. and Wolff, Richard E. 1987. *Knowledge and Class: A Marxian Critique of Political Economy*. Chicago: University of Chicago Press.

Reuten, Geert. 2003. 'Karl Marx: His Work and the Major Changes in its Interpretation', in Warren J. Samuels, Jeff E. Biddle and John B. Davis (eds) *A Companion to the History of Economic Thought*. Malden, MA: Blackwell, pp. 148–66.

Reuten, Geert. 2005. 'Money as Constituent of Value: The Ideal Introversive Substance and the Ideal Extroversive Form of Value in Marx's *Capital*', in Fred Moseley (ed.), *Marx's Theory of Money: Modern Appraisals*. New York: Palgrave-Macmillan, pp. 78–92.

Reuten, Geert. 2009. 'Marx's General Rate of Profit Transformation: Methodological and Theoretical Obstacles – an Appraisal based on the 1864–65 Manuscripts of *Das Kapital III*', in Bellofiore and Fineschi (eds) (2009a), pp. 211–230.

Reuten, Geert and Williams, Michael. 1989. *Value Form and the State*. New York: Routledge.

Revkin, Andrew C. 2009. 'On Climate Issue, Industry Ignored Its Scientists', *New York Times*, Front Page, April 24.

Ricardo, David. 1951. *On the Principles of Political Economy and Taxation. Vol. 1 of The Works and Correspondence of David Ricardo*, edited by P. Sraffa. Cambridge: Cambridge University Press.

Roberts, William Clare. 2006. 'The Origin of Political Economy and the Descent of Marx', in Warren S. Goldstein, *Marx, Critical Theory, and Religion*, Boston, MA: Brill, pp. 31–58.

Robinson, Timothy A. 1995. *Aristotle in Outline*. Indianapolis: Hackett.

Roosevelt, Frank. 1975. 'Cambridge Economics as Commodity Fetishism', *Review of Radical Political Economics*, **7**(4), reprinted in Jesse Schwartz (ed.), *The Subtle Anatomy of Capitalism*, Santa Monica, CA: Goodyear Publishing Co., 1977, pp. 412–57.

Rosenberg, Nathan. 1979. 'Adam Smith and Laissez-Faire Revisited', in Gerald O'Driscoll (ed.), *Adam Smith and Modern Political Economy*. Ames, IA: Iowa State University Press.

Rosenberg, Nathan. 1990. 'Adam Smith and the Stock of Moral Capital', *History of Political Economy*, **22**(1), Spring: 1–17.

Ross, G.R.T. 1973. *Aristotle: De Sensu and De Memoria*. Text and Translation With Introduction and Commentary. Arno Press.

Ross, Ian Simpson. 1995. *The Life of Adam Smith*. Oxford: Clarendon Press.

Roth, Regina. 2009. 'Karl Marx's Original Manuscripts in the Marx-Engels-Gesamtausgabe (MEGA): Another View of *Capital*', in Bellofiore and Fineschi (eds) (2009a), pp. 27–49.

Rothbard, Murray. 1995. *Economic Thought Before Adam Smith: An Austrian Perspective on the History of Economic Thought, Volume I.* Aldershot, UK and Brookfield, US: Edward Elgar.

Rothschild, Emma. 2001. *Economic Sentiments: Adam Smith, Condorcet, and the Enlightenment*. Cambridge, MA: Harvard University Press.

Rousseau, Jean-Jacques. 1992 [1755]. *Discourse on the Origin of Inequality*, Translated by Donald A. Cress. Indianapolis, IN: Hackett.

Samuels, Warren. 1989. 'Diverse Approaches to the Economic Role of Government: An Interpretive Essay', in Warren J. Samuels (ed.), *Fundamentals of the Economic Role of Government*. New York: Greenwood Press, pp. 213–49.

Samuels, Warren. 1992. *Essays on the Economic Role of Government: Volume I: Fundamentals*. New York: New York University Press.

Samuels, Warren. 1995. 'Society is a Process of Mutual Coercion and Governance, Selectively Perceived: Rejoinder to Higgs', *Critical Review*, **9**(3) (Summer): 437–43.

Samuels, Warren and Medema, Steven G. 2005. 'Freeing Smith from the "Free Market": On the Misperception of Adam Smith on the Economic Role of Government', *History of Political Economy*, **37**(2): 219–26.

Sanbonmatsu, John. 2005. 'Postmodernism and the Corruption of the Academic Intelligentsia', in Panitch and Leys (eds) (2005), pp. 196–227.

Saunders, Trevor J. 1995. *Aristotle: Politics Books I and II.* Oxford: Clarendon Press.

Scheidel, Walter and von Reden, Sitta (eds) (2002). *The Ancient Economy*, New York: Routledge.

Schliesser, Eric. 2003. 'The Obituary of a Vain Philosopher: Adam Smith's Reflections on Hume's Life', *Hume Studies*, **29**(2): 327–62.

Schliesser, Eric. 2005a. 'Some Principles of Adam Smith's Newtonian Methods in the *Wealth of Nations*', *Research in History of Economic Thought and Methodology*, 23: 35–77.

Schliesser, Eric. 2005b. 'Wonder in the Face of Scientific Revolutions: Adam Smith on Newton's "Proof" of Copernicanism', *British Journal for the History of Philosophy*, **13**(4): 697–732.

Schliesser, Eric. 2006a. 'Articulating Practices as Reasons: Adam Smith on the Conditions of Possibility of Property', *Adam Smith Review*, **2**: 69–97.

Schliesser, Eric. 2006b. 'Adam Smith's Benevolent and Self-Interested Conception of Philosophy', in Schliesser and Montes (eds) (2006), pp. 328–57.

Schliesser, Eric. Forthcoming. *Adam Smith*. New York: Routledge.

Schliesser, Eric and Montes, Leonidas (eds). 2006. *New Voices on Adam Smith*. New York: Routledge.

Schumpeter, Joseph A. 1950. *Capitalism, Socialism and Democracy*, 3rd ed. New York: Harper and Row.

Schumpeter, Joseph A. 1954. *A History of Economic Analysis*. New York: Oxford University Press.

Schweber, Silvan S. 1977. 'The Origin of the *Origin* Revisited', *Journal of the History of Biology*, **10**(2): 229–316.

Schweber, Silvan S. 1994. 'Darwin and the Agronomists: An Influence of Political Economy on Scientific Thought', in I.B. Cohen (ed.), *The Natural Sciences and the Social Sciences*, Netherlands: Kluwer Academic Publishers, pp. 305–16.

Scott, William Robert. 1965 [1937]. *Adam Smith as Student and Professor*. New York: Augustus M. Kelley.

Seaford, Richard. 2004. *Money and the Early Greek Mind: Homer, Philosophy, Tragedy*. New York: Cambridge University Press.

Sekine, Thomas. 1984. *The Dialectic of Capital: A Study of the Inner Logic of Capitalism*, Vol. I. Tokyo: Yushindo Press.

Sekine, Thomas. 1986. *The Dialectic of Capital: A Study of the Inner Logic of Capitalism*, Vol. II. Tokyo: Toshindo Press.

Setser, Brad W. 2008. *Sovereign Wealth and Sovereign Power: The Strategic Consequences of American Indebtedness*. New York: Council on Foreign Relations, Center for Geoeconomic Studies.

Shadlen, Kenneth C. 2009. 'Resources, Rules and International Political Economy: The Politics of Development in the WTO', GDAE Working Paper 09-01, January.

Simmel, Georg. 1950. *The Sociology of Georg Simmel*, edited by Kurt Wolff. New York: The Free Press.

Smith, Roy C. and Walter, Ingo. 1990. *Global Financial Services: Strategies for Building Competitive Strengths in International Commercial and Investment Banking*. New York: Harper Business.

Smith, Roy C. and Walter, Ingo. 1997. *Global Banking*. New York: Oxford University Press.

Smith, Steven. 1997. *Spinoza, Liberalism, and the Question of Jewish Identity*. New Haven: Yale University Press.

Soudek, Josef. 1952. 'Aristotle's Theory of Exchange: An Enquiry into the Origins of Economic Analysis', *Proceedings of the American Philosophical Society*, **96**(1): 45–75, in Blaug (ed.) (1991): 11–41.

Spellman, Lynne. 1995. *Substance and Separation in Aristotle*. New York: Cambridge University Press.

Spiegel, Henry William. 1991. *The Growth of Economic Thought*, 3rd ed. Durham: Duke University Press.

Sraffa, Piero. 1951. 'Introduction', *On the Principles of Political Economy and Taxation*, Vol. 1 of *The Works and Correspondence of David Ricardo*. Cambridge: Cambridge University Press.

Sraffa, Piero. 1960. *Production of Commodities by Means of Commodities: Prelude to a Critique of Economic Theory*. New York: Cambridge University Press.

Staveren, Irene van. 2001. *The Values of Economics: an Aristotelian Perspective*, New York: Routledge.

Steedman, Ian. 1977. *Marx After Sraffa*. London: New Left Books.

Stein, Ben. 2005. 'We Were Soldiers Once, and Broke'. *New York Times Inside the News*, July 17, 2005.

Stewart, Dugald. 1793. 'Account of the Life and Writings of Adam Smith, LL.D.' in Adam Smith (1980).

Stigler, George. 1988. 'The Adam Smith Lecture: The Effect of Government on Economic Efficiency', *Business Economics*, **XXIII**(1): 7–13.

Stone, Peter H. 2006. *Heist*. New York: Farrar, Straus and Giroux.

Straub, James. 2006. 'What Was the Matter with Ohio? Unions and Evangelicals in the Rust Belt', *Monthly Review*. **57**(8), January: 35–50.

Strickland, H.E. and Melville, A.G. 1848. *The Dodo and its Kindred*. London: Reeve, Benham and Reeve.

Struik, Dirk J. 1987. *A Concise History of Mathematics*. Fourth Revised Edition. New York: Dover Publications.

Sutch, Richard, 2006. 'Saving, Capital, and Wealth' in Carter, Gartner, Haines, Olmstead, Sutch, and Wright (eds) (2006), Chapter Ce.

Sweezy, Paul. 1942. *The Theory of Capitalist Development*. New York: Monthly Review Press.

Temple-Smith, Richard. 2007. 'Adam Smith's Treatment of the Greeks in *The Theory of Moral Sentiments*: the Case of Aristotle', in Cockfield,

Firth and Laurent (eds), *New Perspectives on Adam Smith's The Theory of Moral Sentiments*, pp. 29–46.

Theocarakis, Nicholas J. 2006. 'Nicomachean Ethics in Political Economy: The Trajectory of the Problem of Value', *History of Economic Ideas*, **XIV**(1): 9–53.

Thompson, E.P. 1963. *The Making of the English Working Class*. New York: Pantheon.

Tucker, Robert C. 1969. *The Marxian Revolutionary Idea*. New York: Norton.

Tucker, Robert C. 1972. *Philosophy and Myth in Karl Marx*, 2nd ed. New York: Cambridge.

Turner, Frank M. 1981. *The Greek Heritage in Victorian Britain*. New Haven, CT: Yale University Press.

Uno, Kozo. 1980. *Principles of Political Economy: Theory of a Purely Capitalist Society*. Sussex: Harvester.

Urquhart, Robert. 2008. '"The Value-Forming Substance": Marx as Left-Aristotelian', Presentation, History of Economics Society Meeting, Toronto, 27–30 June.

US Department of Commerce. 2009. *Statistical Abstract of the United States*. Washington, DC: Department of Commerce.

US Department of the Treasury. 2006. *The Use and Counterfeiting of United States Currency Abroad, Part 3. The Final Report to the Congress by the Secretary of the Treasury, in Consultation with the Advanced Counterfeit Deterrence Steering Committee, pursuant to Section 807 of PL 104-32*. Washington, DC: Department of the Treasury.

US Department of the Treasury. 2008. 'Treasury Bulletin', December. Washington, DC: Department of the Treasury.

Uyl, Douglas J. and Griswold, Charles L. 1996. 'Adam Smith on Friendship and Love', *Review of Metaphysics*, **49**: 609–37.

Veblen, Thorstein. 1948. *The Portable Veblen*, edited and with an introduction by Max Lerner, New York: Viking Press.

Veblen, Thorstein. 1975 [1904]. *The Theory of Business Enterprise*. Clifton, NJ: A.M. Kelley.

Viner, Jacob. 1928. 'Adam Smith and Laissez Faire', in John Maurice Clark et al., *Adam Smith 1776–1926*. Chicago: University of Chicago Press, pp. 116–55.

Vivenza, Gloria. 2001. *Adam Smith and the Classics: The Classical Heritage in Adam Smith's Thought*. Oxford: Oxford University Press.

von Reden, Sitta. 2003 [1995]. *Exchange in Ancient Greece*. Paperback edition. London: Duckworth.

Vyse, Stuart. 2008. *Going Broke: Why Americans Can't Hold on to Their Money*. New York: Oxford University Press.

Weber, Max. 1992 [1904–05]. *The Protestant Ethic and the Spirit of Capitalism*. New York: Routledge.

Weinstein, James. 1968. *The Corporate Ideal in the Liberal State: 1900–1918*. Boston, MA: Beacon Press.

White, Ben. 2009. 'What Red Ink? Wall St. Paid Hefty Bonuses', *New York Times*, January 29, Front Page.

Wight, Johnathan B. 2009. 'Adam Smith on Instincts, Affection, and Informal Learning: Proximate Mechanisms in Multilevel Selection', *Review of Social Economy*, **LXVII**(1): 95–113.

Williams, William A. 1961. *The Contours of American History*. New York: The World Publishing Company.

Witztum, Amos. 1997. 'Distributive Considerations in Smith's Conception of Economic Justice', *Economics and Philosophy*, **13**: 241–59.

Wolff, Edward N. 2004. 'Recent Trends in Living Standards in the United States', in Wolff (ed.), *What Has Happened to the Quality of Life in the Advanced Industrialized Nations?*, Cheltenham, UK and Northampton, MA, USA: Edward Elgar, pp. 3–26.

Wolff, Edward N. 2007. 'Recent Trends in Household Wealth in the United States: Rising Debt and the Middle-Class Squeeze', Working Paper No. 502. The Levy Economics Institute of Bard College.

Wood, Diana. 2002. *Medieval Economic Thought*. New York: Cambridge University Press.

Wray, L. Randall. 2008. 'The Commodities Market Bubble: Money Manager Capitalism and the Financialization of Commodities', Levy Economics Institute Public Policy Brief No. 96.

Xenophon. 1925. 'Ways and Means', in *Scripta Minora*. Translated by E.C. Marchant and G.W. Bowersock, Loeb Classical Library, Cambridge, MA: Harvard University Press, pp. 191–231.

Xenophon. 1994. *Oeconomicus: A Social and Historical Commentary*. Edited by Sarah Pomeroy. New York: Oxford University Press.

Xenophon. 2001. *The Education of Cyrus*. Translated and annotated by Wayne Ambler. Ithaca: Cornell University Press.

Young, Jeffrey T. 1997. *Economics as a Moral Science*. Aldershot, UK and Brookfield, US: Edward Elgar.

Index